Fine Art Portrait Photography

Commercial Techniques and Images in Black and White

Oscar Lozoya

Amherst Media, Inc. ■ Buffalo, NY

Published by:
Amherst Media, Inc.
P.O. Box 586
Buffalo, N.Y. 14226
Fax: 716-874-4508

Publisher: Craig Alesse
Senior Editor/Project Manager: Richard Lynch
Associate Editor: Michelle Perkins
Image Technician: John Gryta

ISBN: 0-936262-71-0
Library of Congress Card Catalog Number: 98-71932

Printed in the United States of America.
10 9 8 7 6 5 4 3 2 1

Acknowledgements:
Palabras para mi Mamá y Papá: Gracias por el Cariño, Inspiración, Apoyo y Disciplina.
Words to my Mother and Father: Thank you for the Love, Inspiration, Support and Discipline.

To my children, Oscar II, Zoya and Joseph: You are my strength, I love you.

I would like to thank:
José Almanza, Carol Andrews, Frank and Beth Archibeque, Jim Baker, Willie Barela, Tom Benusa, Ernest Brooks Jr., Camera and Darkroom of New Mexico, Armando Chacón, Dr. Enrique Cortazar, Frank Cricchio, Keith Drosin, Frank Eposito, Art Esquibel, Mario Fernández, José and Luz Esther Galindo, Antonia Grijalva, José Alfredo Jiménez, James Johnson, Felissa Kelly, Michele Lovato, Arturo and Maria Lozoya, Jennie Lozoya, Vicky Lozoya, Yolanda Abbud Lozoya, David Marrujo, Amarante Martinez, Frank McDaniels, Lucila Medina, Tony and Sylvia Nava, Jack Newsom, Daniel and Yolanda Parga, Michelle Perkins, Photoflex Company, Portercase Company, PPA, PPA Minority Network, PPANM, Steven Michael Quezada, Martín and Bernadette Rodríguez, Duke Salinas, Andrew Smith Gallery – Santa Fe, Yamel Soto, South Broadway Cultural Center, Speedotron Company, SWPA, John Tanguma, David and Susan Tompkins, Patricio Tláelel Trujillo, Youth Development Inc., Yvonne Ulibarri

The publisher wishes to thank Frank McDaniels for his role in the inception of this book.

Table of Contents

Interview with Oscar Lozoya

Oscar Lozoya is a professional photographer from Albuquerque, NM, whose dramatic, unorthodox, fine art and commercial photography has won international acclaim. His honors include nine photographs in the national loan collection of the Professional Photographers of America (PPA), photographer of the year of the Professional Photographers of New Mexico and inclusion in *Kodak Gallery Award Collection Album.*

What got you interested in photography?

I've liked photography since I was a kid. It was always in the back of my mind, but I didn't really know anyone who did it. Years later, a friend of mine got into the field and introduced me to it as well. His advice (especially on equipment) saved me a lot of money and work!

What kind of training have you had? How has this affected your work?

In my teens and twenties, I was a professional musician. Later I studied design and worked as a designer. Photography appeals to me because it captures both the artistic and the technical aspects of these fields.

I learned photography though books, and I started out by learning the theory. This meant that when I started shooting film, I knew how to predict the effects of what I was doing technically, and how to analyze the outcome. I think that this attention to learning why things work like they do has been integral to my ability to advance quickly as a photographer.

How long have you been working professionally?

I started about fifteen years ago working out of my home. I set up a studio in the living room. It was inconvenient, but my desire to do this work was so strong, I did it anyway.

I opened my studio in 1988. I do all kinds of work at the studio, including portraiture, glamour and fashion shoots (mostly model portfolios), and a lot of commercial work. The studio also offers weddings, but these are covered by other photographers.

You also do a lot of public speaking. What do you enjoy about this?

Before I joined the PPA, I had never really thought of myself as a public speaker. I'm basically shy, I have a slight speech impairment, and just thought I'd feel self conscious. Still, I needed public speaking merits to complete my credits for the PPA's Master of Photography, so I did it.

It's turned out to be a great experience. It has certainly helped (and continues to help) my national and international exposure. From a financial standpoint, I usually sell work at my speaking engagements. Additionally, travelling and speaking have allowed me to pick up on photographic trends across the country, and I think this makes me a better photographer.

What do people ask you?

People are always curious about the imagery, and even the models – especially where I find them. Lighting is a topic of great interest among people at my speaking engagements, and recently printing is something I am frequently asked about.

You make it a point to be involved with your community. Why is this important to you?

When it was time to set up my studio, I could have put it anywhere in Albuquerque. I chose to locate it in the neighborhood where I grew up, even though it's not known as one of the best neighborhoods in town. I feel close to this neighborhood and draw a lot of inspiration from it.

Several photographs in this book are the result of work with a local youth program. Working with young people is especially close to my heart. Growing up on the streets, I know how easy it can be to get detoured. Providing a positive example, and showing what you have accomplished can have a big impact.

Why do you choose to shoot in B&W? Do you do other work in color?

I do a lot of color work for commercial purposes, and for portraiture. I try to keep up on all styles of photography.

My personal work tends to be in B&W because I've always seen B&W, properly executed, as an art. I love the tonalities, and the timeless quality. I also like the fact that I can develop it myself. This means I can have complete control of a project, from beginning to end.

Why do you choose to work in low key?

When I was getting started as a photographer, I was very resistant to having a "style." I worked in a lot of styles – and this gave me great experience, especially with lighting. Later, I started to see that having a recognizable style was important. I decided that if I had to settle on one style, it would be one that was going to continue to challenge me. Low key is one of the most technical styles of photography, since even small errors in lighting result in loss of detail. Starting with a dark canvas also means that I can apply more light (and do more with it) before detail is lost.

Images from Hispanic culture occur throughout your work. Could you talk about the influence of this material on your photography?

My work has been strongly impacted by going to art galleries and looking at the work of other photographers. It has particularly influenced my style and my choice of B&W. Additionally, I noticed that fine art photographers tended to work in themes or a series.

At first I was a bit lost for what my own theme would be. As it turned out, it was right under my nose all the time: my culture. Hispanic culture has proved to be an endless source of inspiration.

Additionally, I think that people like to learn about other cultures (like I do). Even if they misinterpret the imagery of my photographs at first, I think these images cause people to ask questions and to learn from the answers. I think that's good for people of all cultures.

What do you see yourself doing in the future?

I would really like to get into doing some digital imaging, but that is still a long way down the road since my studio keeps me so busy.

I'd also like to do more color work. When I was doing a lot of color work earlier in my career, I was too busy trying to make a living to take the time to shoot the artistic work I wanted to do. Now I'd like to go back and work on some of that.

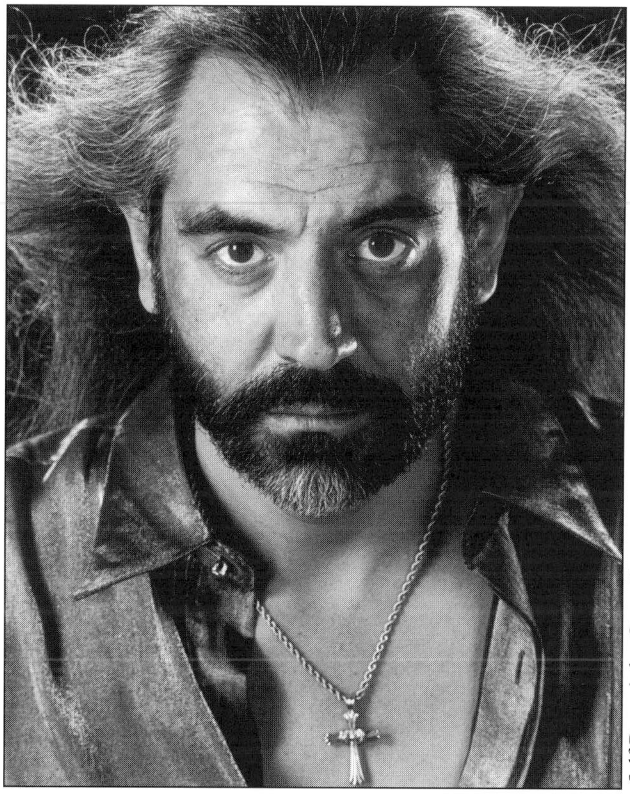

Self Portrait by Oscar Lozoya

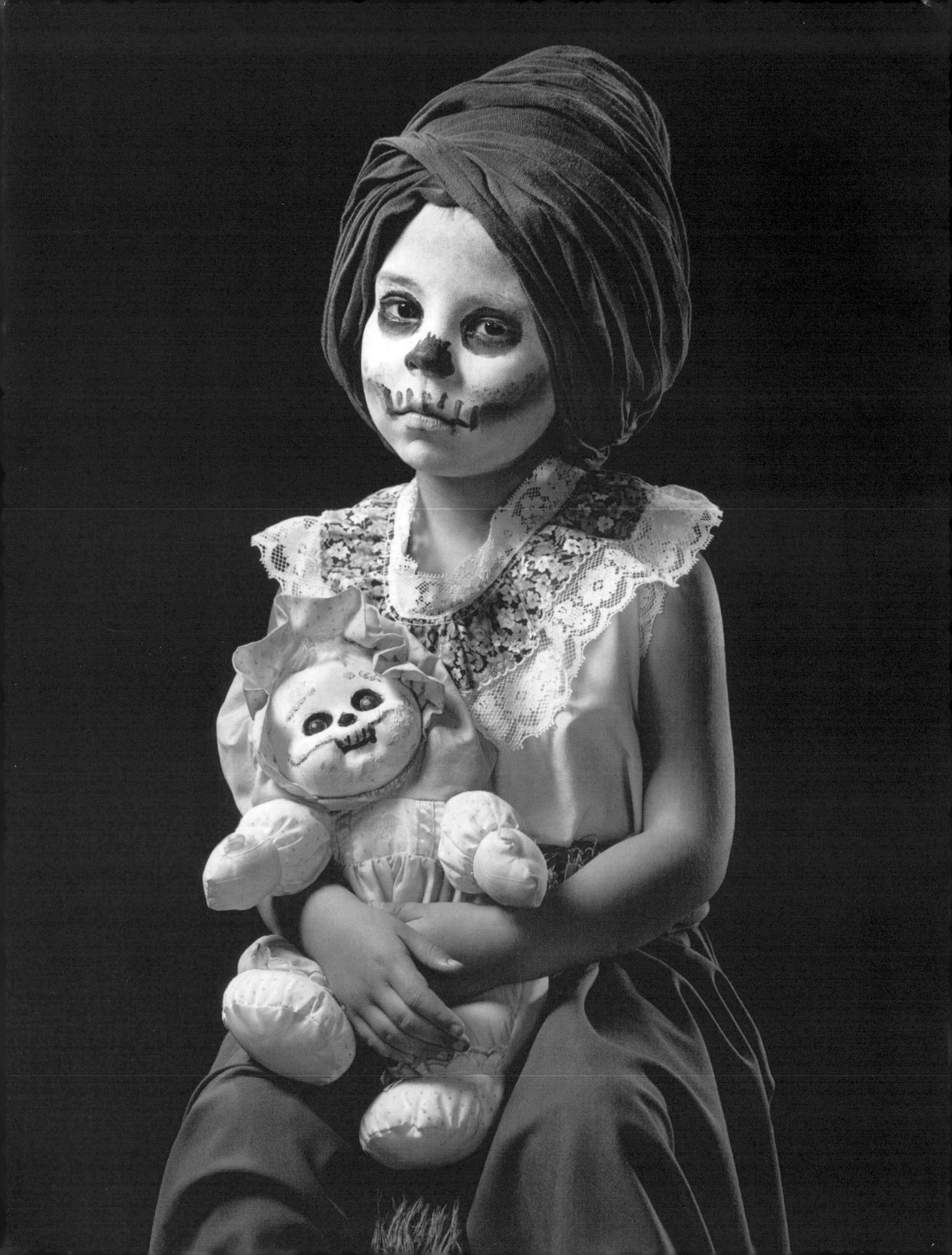

Dia de los Muertos

The images in this section reflect the Day of the Dead (Dia de los Muertos), an important and festive Mexican holiday celebrated (in various forms) since the time of the Aztecs. The festival, celebrated on All Saints Day, honors the dead, but also mocks death and has fun with it, all the while aware that death in folklore is not the same as death in reality. The use of these images also has political meaning; artist José Posada popularized the skeleton imagery in the 1800's as a poke at the government during the Mexican Revolution.

Having grown up around this imagery, I decided to use the skeleton imagery popularized by Posada, with my own characters. Rather than depict a complete skeleton, I chose to paint only the face of my subjects. This preserves the human element and helps suggest that this folklorish imagery is not meant to be frightening.

Lighting

This photograph of my daughter was taken using a five light system. Two skimmers were placed as accent lights on either side of the subject, a hair light illuminates the scarf on her head, a fill light was placed next to the camera lens and a main light was positioned to place light on the side of the model's face that is away from the camera (short loop lighting).

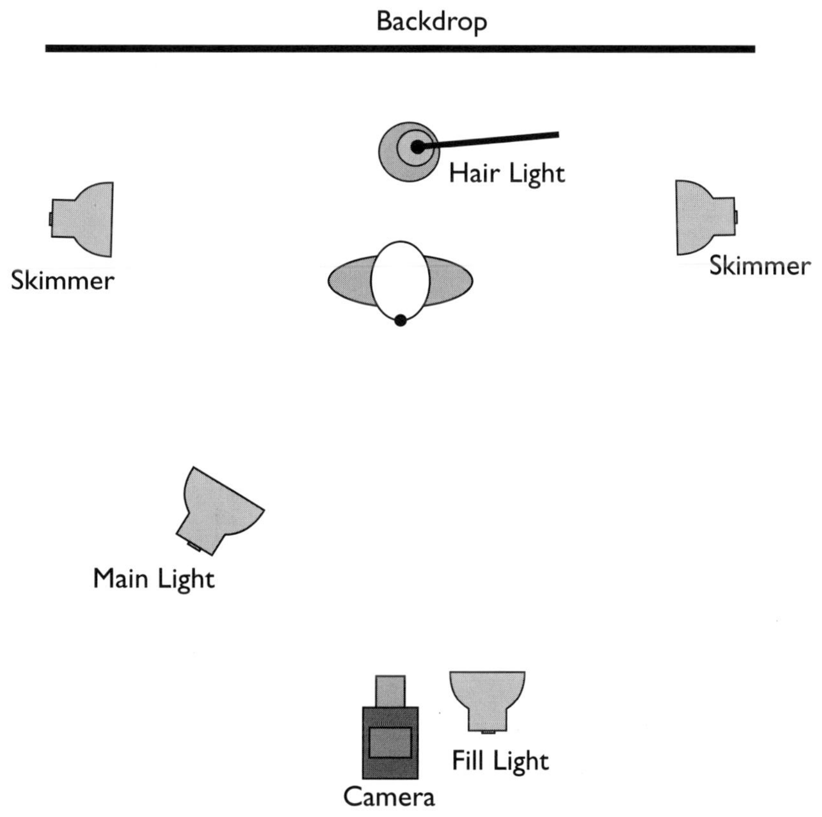

Props and Costumes

This photograph draws on the political imagery of the Day of the Dead, depicting soldiers of the Revolution having fun during a free moment. While I tend to minimize props (since I'm more interested in lighting), here the props (such as the cards, and bandolier) as well as the period clothing add to the sense of narrative in the image. Fortunately, my subjects for this photograph, a group of Mexican dancers from the Expressiones Academy of Arts, had all the costumes on hand. The cemetery backdrop was also provided by the same academy.

Make-up

The skull make-up for the images in this series is created with regular theatrical products. When shooting images with stage performers, I have had the benefit of professional make-up work, but at other times the make-up has been applied by my assistant, myself, and even my babysitter! In the end, it's not important to me that the make-up be consistent from image to image. After all, as individuals we all look different in life, so the dead probably all look different too.

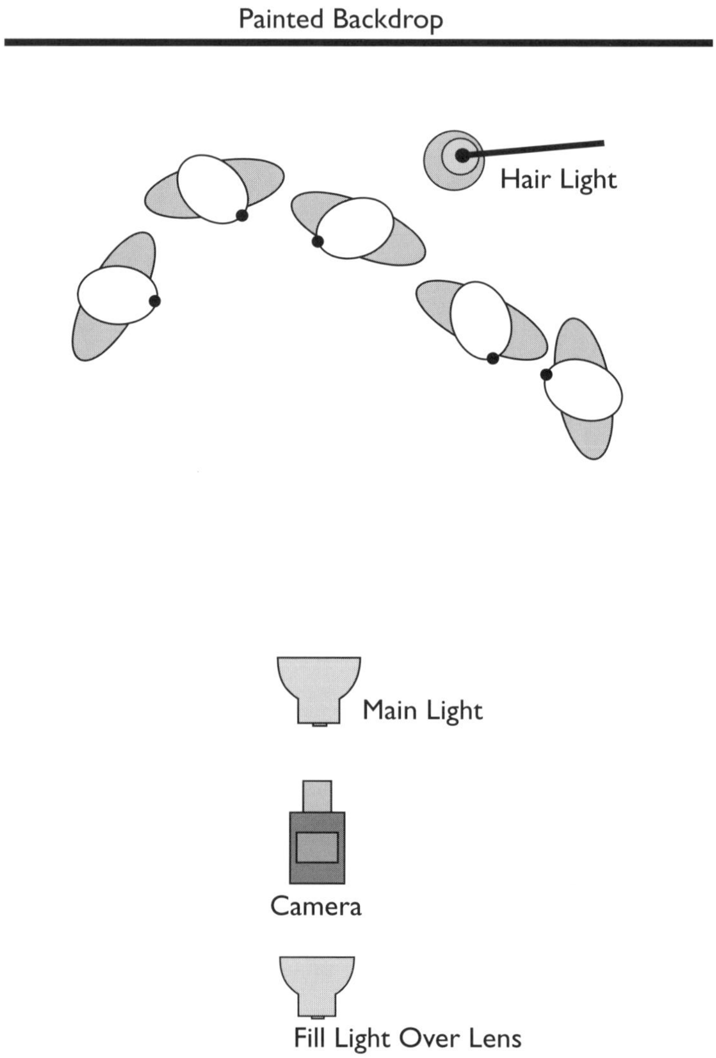

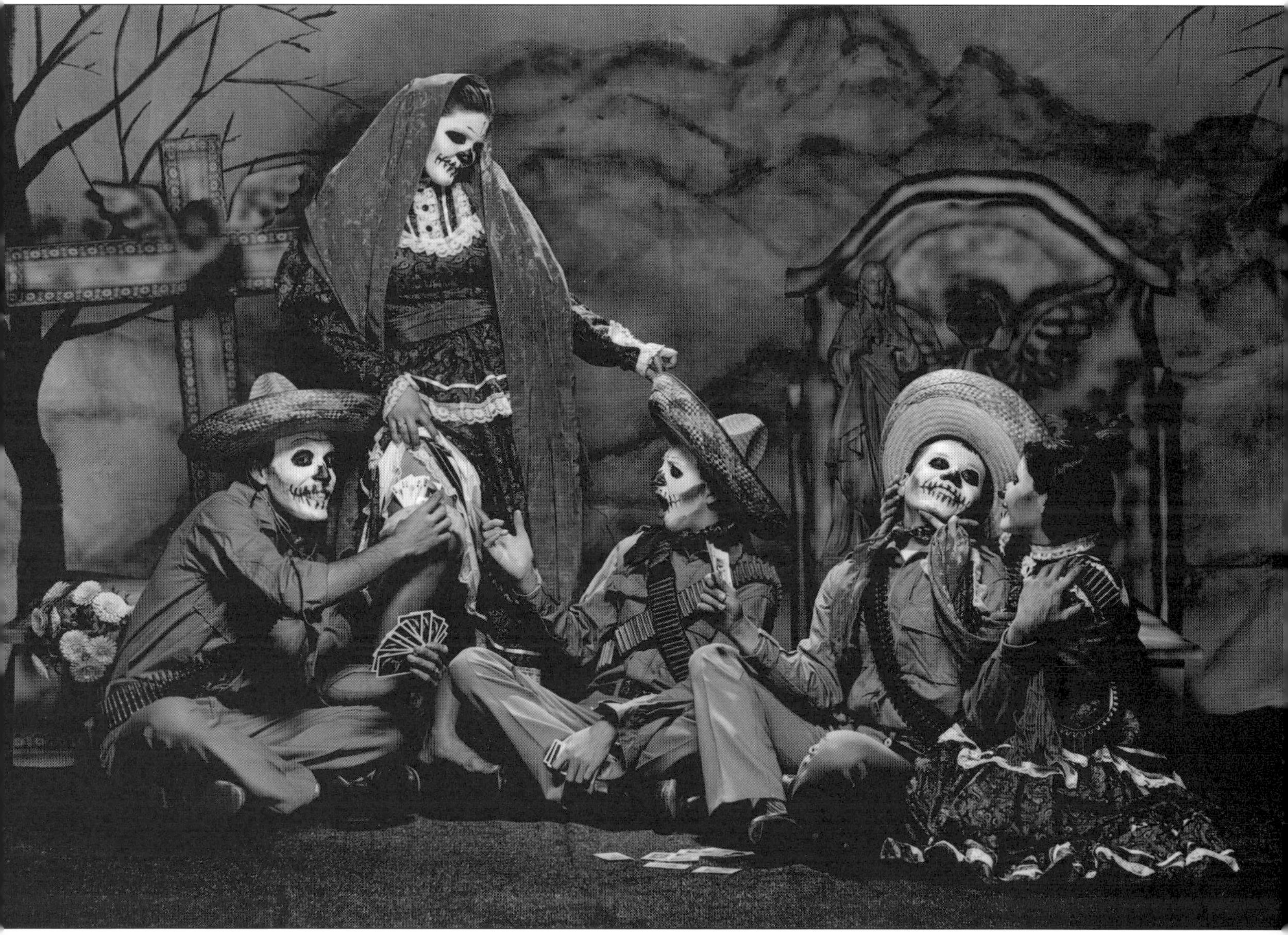

Camera and Accessories

I work with a Mamiya RB67 (medium format) camera. Features I like about this camera include the revolving back which allows me to switch from a vertical to a horizontal setup without moving the camera. Also, the 6"x7" negative is the standard print proportion. I always try to use as much of the negative as possible.

I also use a tripod when shooting. On occasion (when shooting extremely long exposures) I may also use a cable release.

Film

I have experimented with many kinds of film, but now shoot with Kodak TriX which consistently provides the contrast and grain I'm looking for.

Lighting

I use Speedotron lighting and Photoflex lighting accessories. The lighting set-up for this image consists of two skimmers (placed to either side of the subject), a hair light, and a fill light close to the camera. The main light was positioned for front lighting (lighting coming primarily from directly in front of the subject).

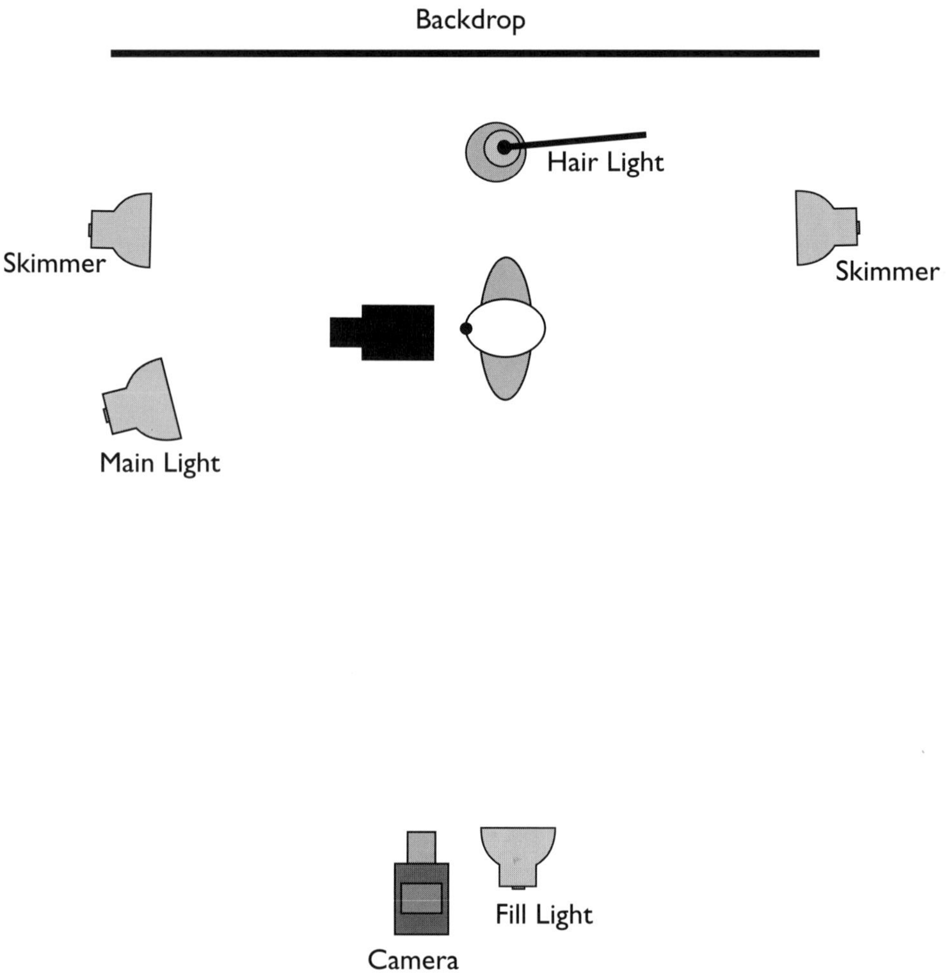

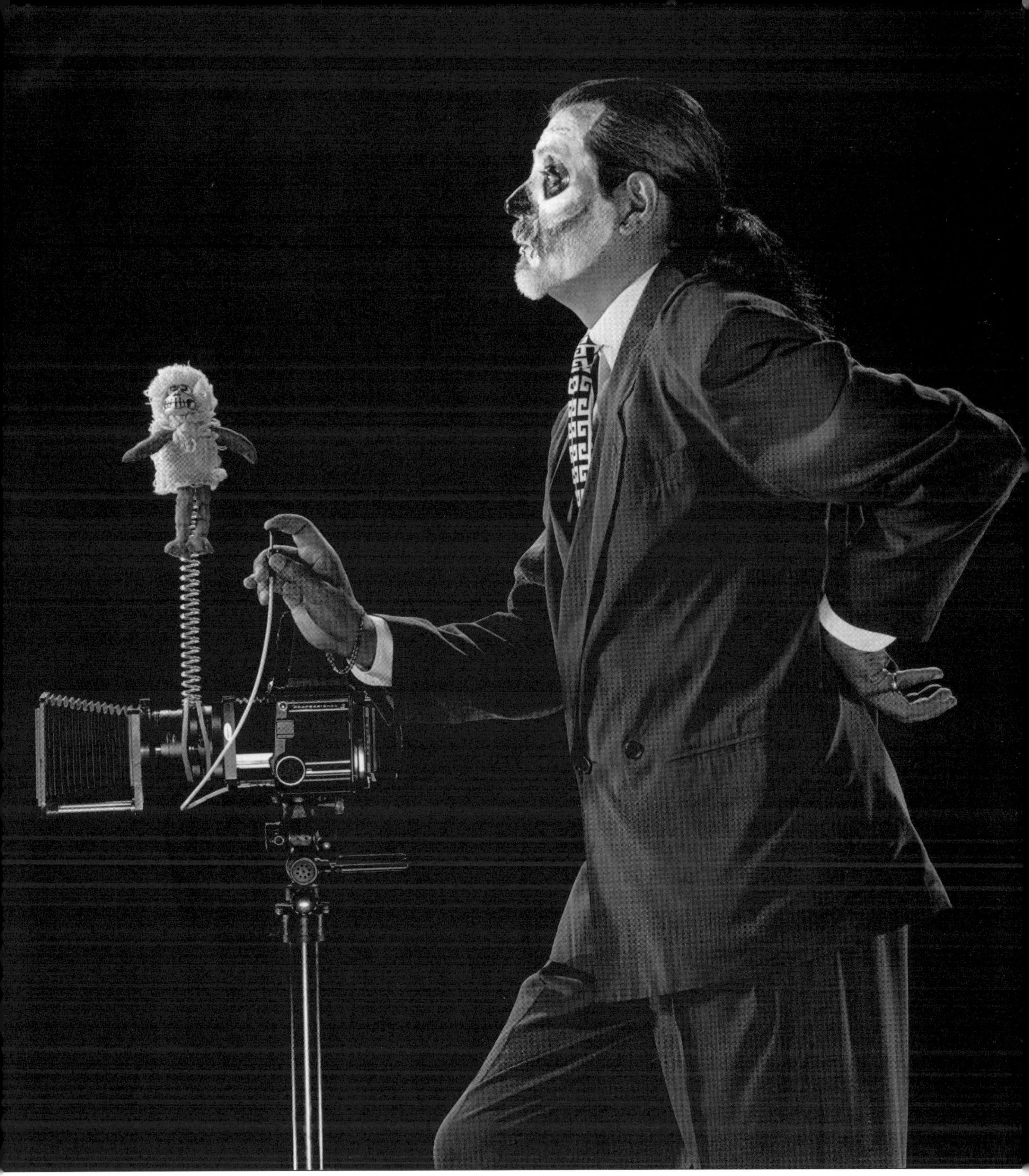

Costuming

For this image of my son I chose an outfit to reflect the way that a lot of kids dress today in super baggy clothes. This Muerte figure is a young, teenage, 90's sort of guy. Additionally, his shirt features the Aztec calendar, a reference back to the origins of the festival which emphasizes the tying-together of traditional themes with contemporary imagery.

Lighting

Skimmers were placed to either side of the subject and a main light illuminates him from 45° to the camera's left. A hair light was positioned above the subject, and a fill light was used close to the camera.

History of the Series

The Muerte series began several years ago when I was called by a local cultural center which was seeking material for an exhibition on the Day of the Dead. The deadline for submission was in two days, so I worked fast and contacted local performing academies to arrange for models and costumes and props. The very first shoot was a success, and since then the series has continued to grow. Now, even when I'm working on commercial shoots, if a particular model inspires an idea (or seems appropriate for an image I've preconceived), I ask them to do it. If they consent, we go ahead and shoot!

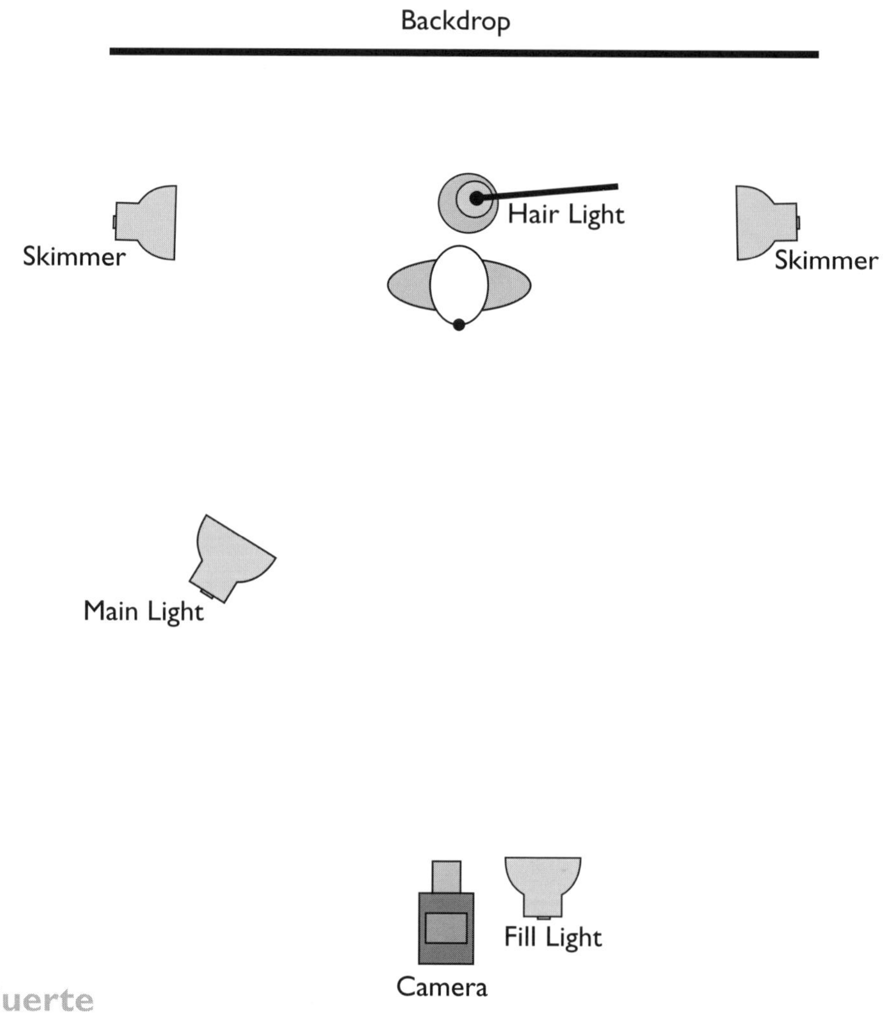

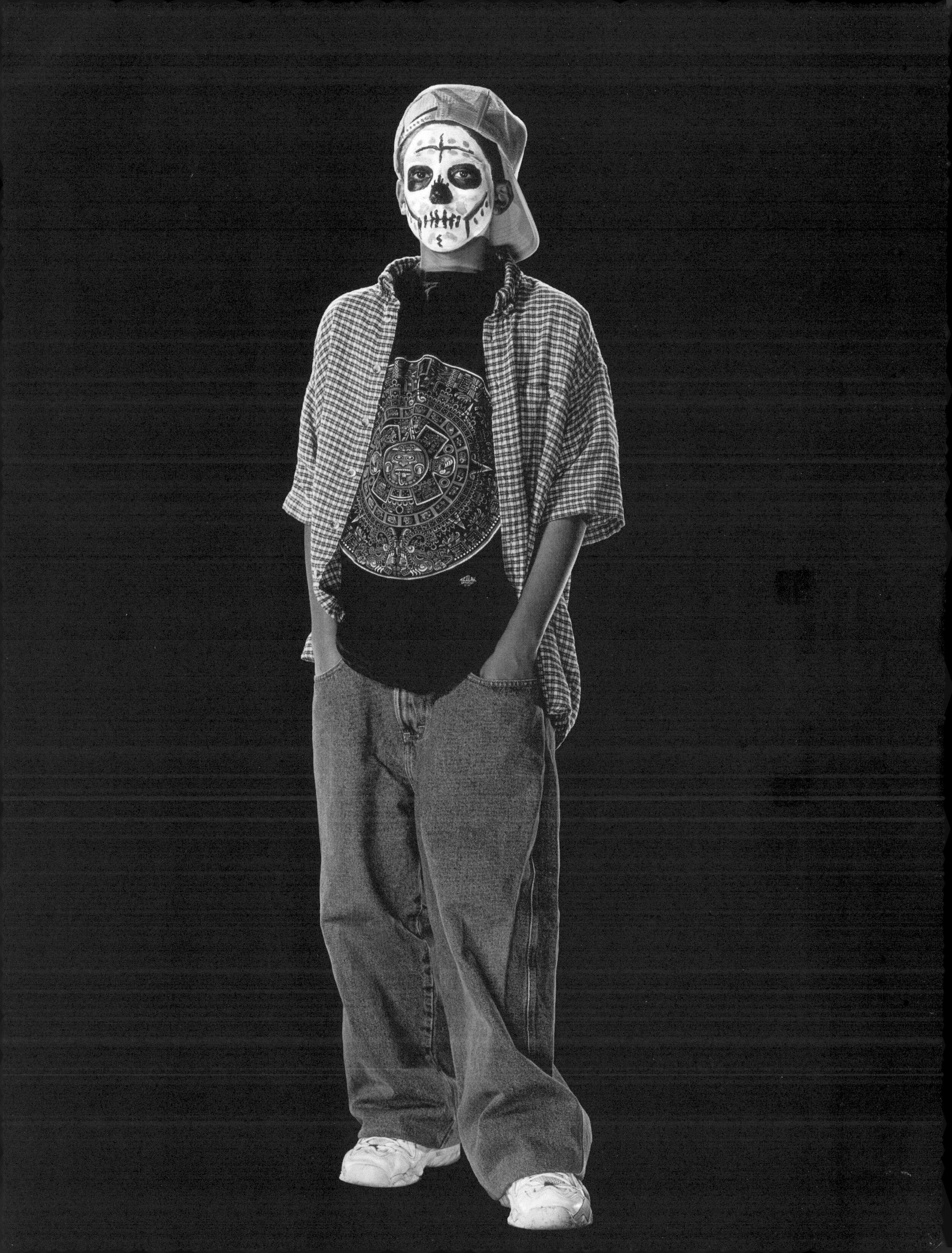

Title

Like many other images in the series, the title is a play on words where "muerte" (meaning "death") is substituted for part of another word. Here, I imagine the little girl whispering, "Isn't she lovely!" ("Se ve magnifica!"), but the *magnifica* has been changed to *muernifica* to reflect the content of the picture.

Subject

From my experience as a commercial photographer, I've had lots of experience shooting weddings, and this is a spoof of the "typical" wedding portrait. After all, if death is a parallel existence to life, it seems reasonable to assume they do what we do. Thus, a wedding from the "other" side!

La Muerte Series

Although the series began as a fine art collection, it has been well accepted in the professional world. Images from the series have won Kodak Gallery Awards. They have also scored very well in PPA (Professional Photographers of America) competition, and have earned a place in the National Loan Collection.

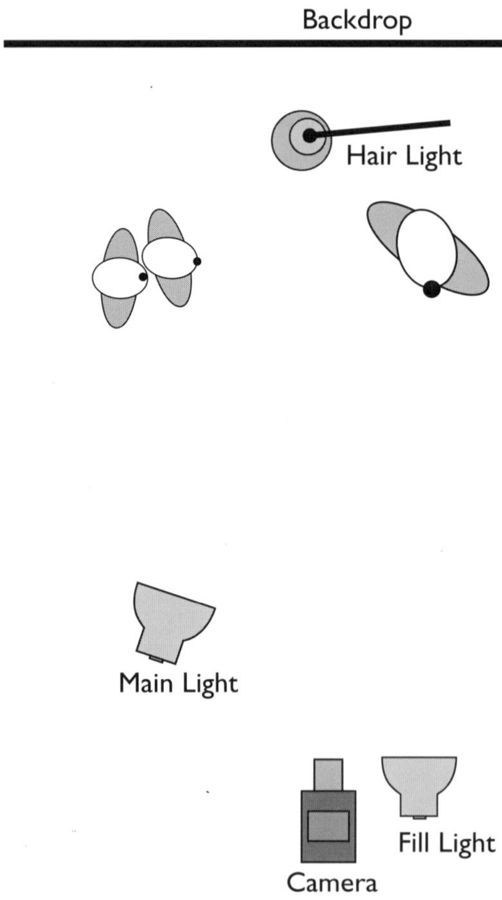

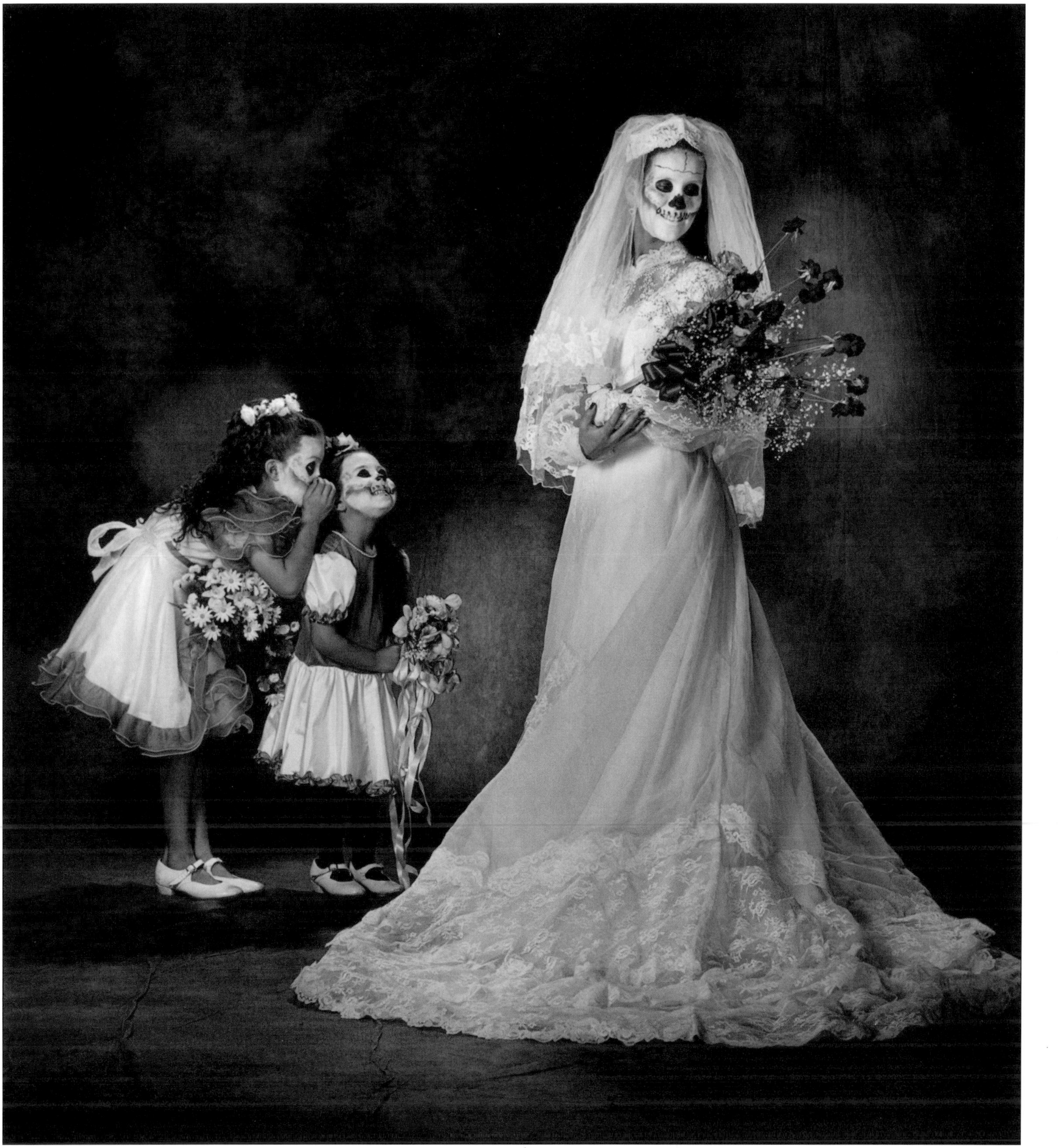

Planning

The idea behind this photo was to show that death is lurking everywhere. I had in mind about six images I wanted to shoot during this session. Thus, when preparing with my models, we were able to approach the shoot from a commercial session standpoint. Preparations included things like having this dresser on hand for shooting the image you see here.

A lot of times I do make plans for shoots like this, and it is a very efficient way to create preconceived images. Still, there are also plenty of times when I have no idea in advance for what I want to shoot. With a great model (or group of models), this can pose little problem – we just play around, then adjust the lights, and shoot!

Exposure

A double exposure was used to create the effect of death in the mirror. The figure of death was backlit and her reflection photographed with the right side of the camera covered. Then the image of the young woman brushing her hair was shot with the left side of the camera covered.

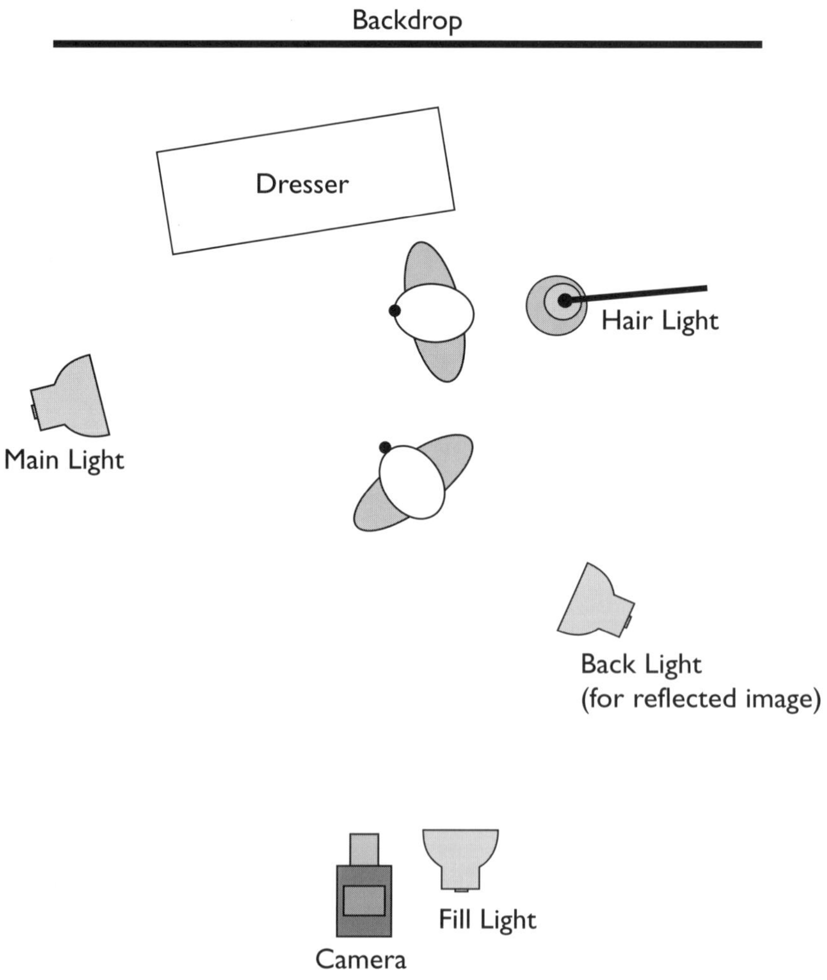

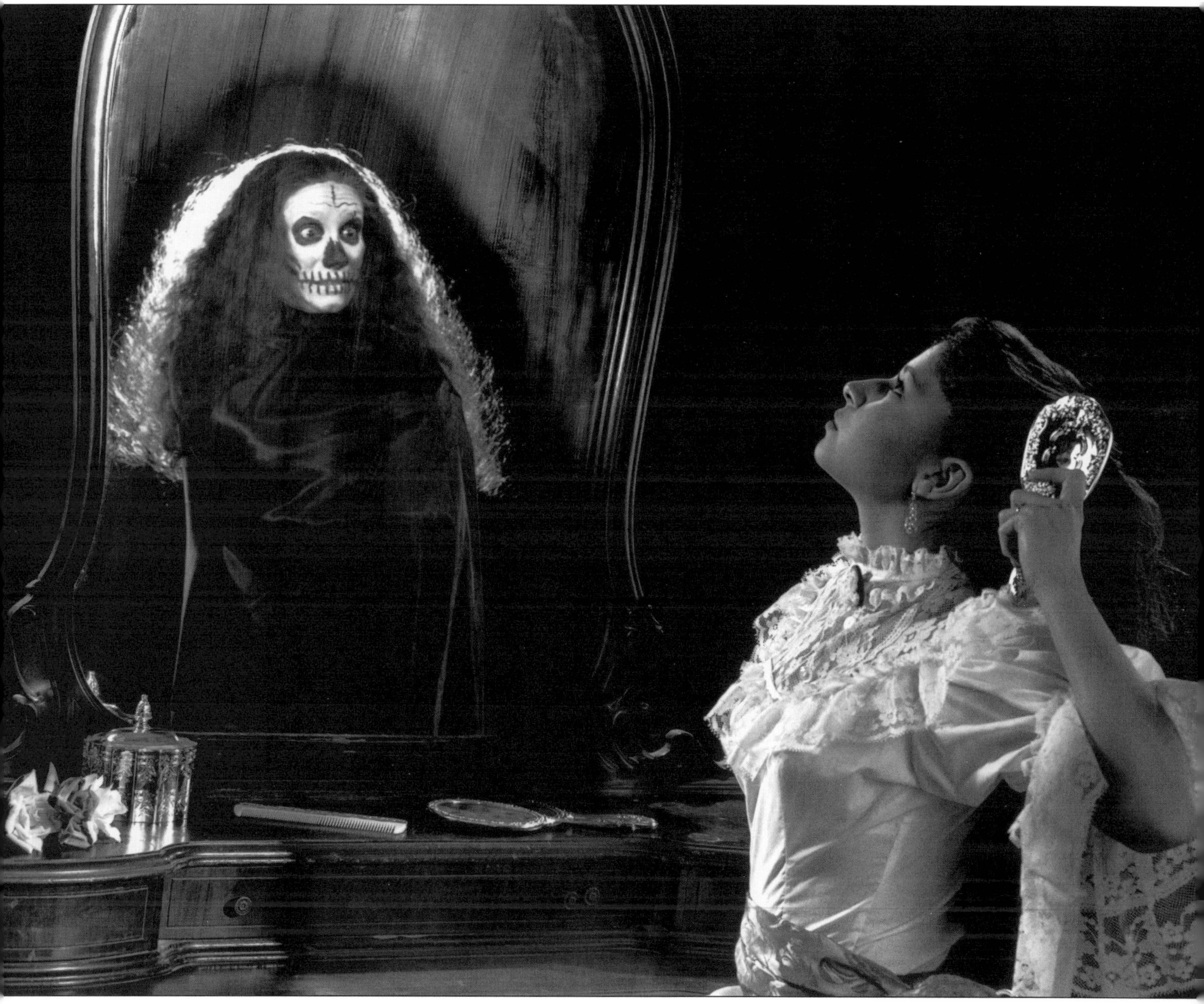

Characters

This image, a publicity shot to promote a Day of the Dead event, was strongly impacted by the fact that the models came in with established characters going back to the artwork of José Posada. The characters included, to the far right, a female general (of which there were unofficially several during the Mexican Revolution) and, to the far left, Doña Catrina, a high society lady. Doña Catrina's escort, spying the fun being had at the bar, looks back over his shoulder as if to say, "Give me a second to dump this priss, and I'll be right back!" Take a peek at the bottle being poured by the bartender and how well it fits in with the theme.

Lighting

The lighting set-up for this image included six lights. Two skimmers were placed to either side of the subjects, and a fill light was used next to the camera lens. A broad strip light was used as the main to illuminate the large group of figures, and two hair lights add specular highlights to the models' hair and faces.

Clothing

In B&W you have to be careful of certain tones. For low key images this is especially true, since light-colored clothing will tend to steal all the attention. In this picture, Doña Catrina's dress was too light, so to cut down on its brightness I wrapped a black lace scarf around the skirt.

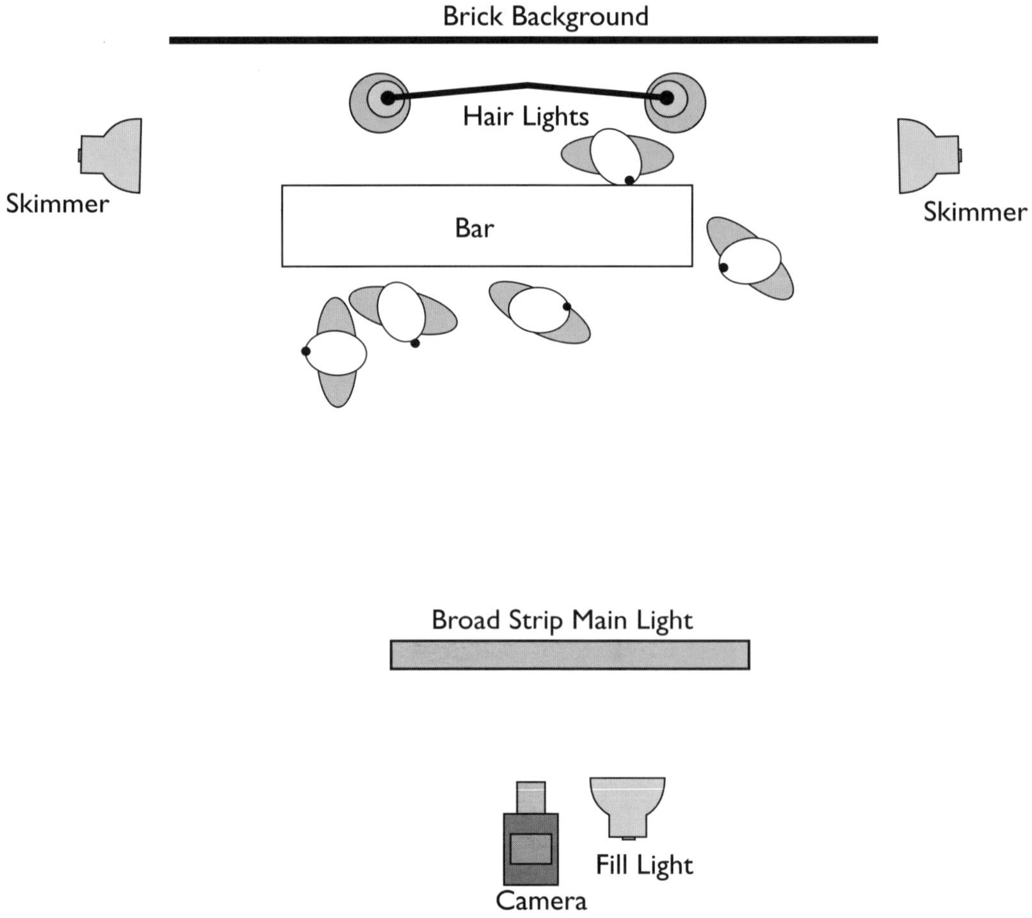

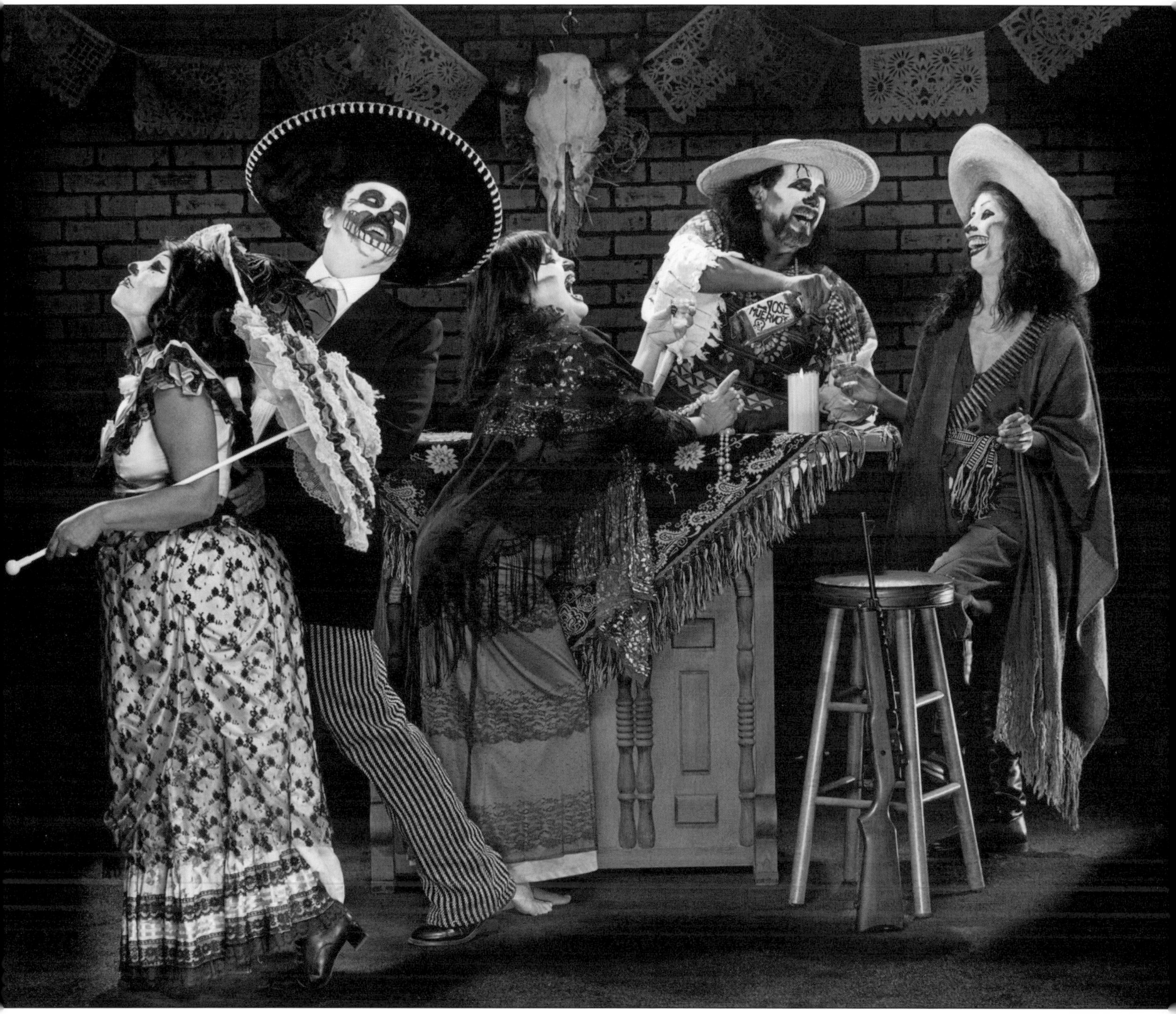
YOSE
MUERVO

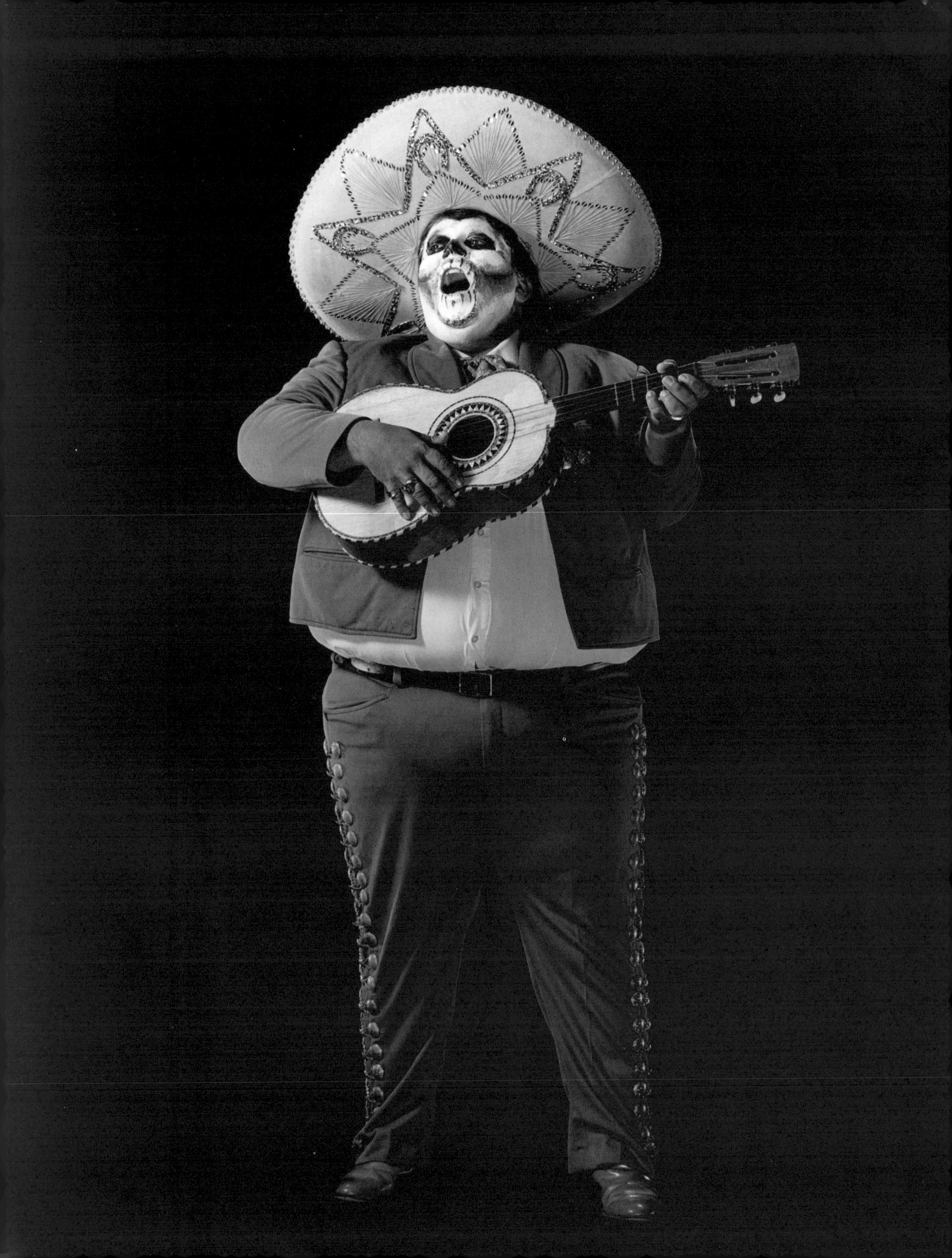

Composition

This image pokes fun (in its content and its title) at stereotypes of the mariachi. When shooting this model, a talented musician and composer, I had him bring to the studio a selection of his guitars. From these, I chose the smallest one, in order to emphasize his size. The composition of the image is very simple because sometimes "simple" is exactly what catches a viewer's eye.

Low Key Images

Early in my career I experimented with all kinds of styles in an effort to learn it all, but as I gained more experience, I began to recognize the benefits of having a recognizable "style" in your work.

Several factors determined my choice of a low key style. With high key photography I found there was only so much I could do in terms of lighting, and with middle key, even bad lighting will usually produce acceptable results because of the tonalities involved. The most challenging style, I felt, was low key, the quality of which is extremely dependent on lighting. In low key photography, if the lighting is a little off, it will translate immediately into lack of detail in the image. Of course, it also didn't hurt that black is my favorite color!

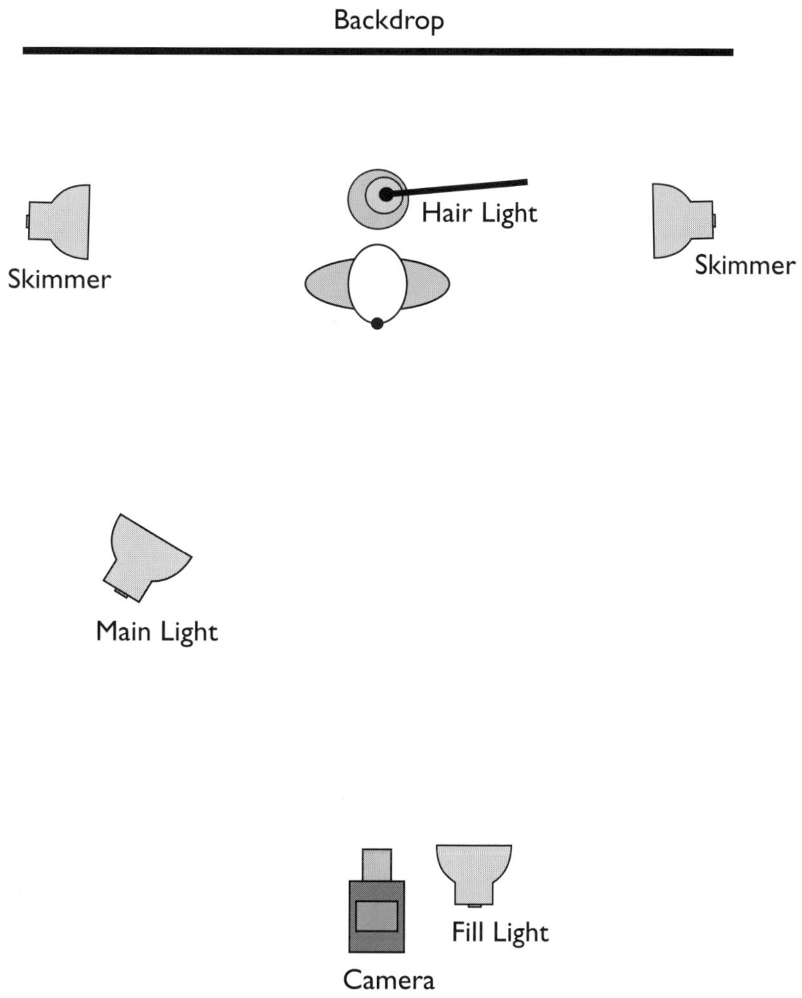

Inspiration

The idea of the devil is strong in Mexican culture, and it was with that in mind I planned the images in this section. For this photograph and the two that follow, I chose three models to portray three characters: the devil, a priest, and a young woman. While shooting the scenarios I had planned between the actors, I also took this portrait of my good friend and actor Steven Michael Quezada as the devil alone.

Makeup

After Halloween I always keep my eyes open for specials on theatrical make-up, masks, unusual props, and anything else that might someday be useful in the studio. In this case, the subject was photographed wearing horns cut off a Halloween mask and applied with theatrical adhesive.

Lighting

The bottom lighting shown here is appropriate to the subject and makes him look unnatural. The effect is also amplified by the fact that he is wearing contact lenses, which give his eyes the unusual tonality seen in this image.

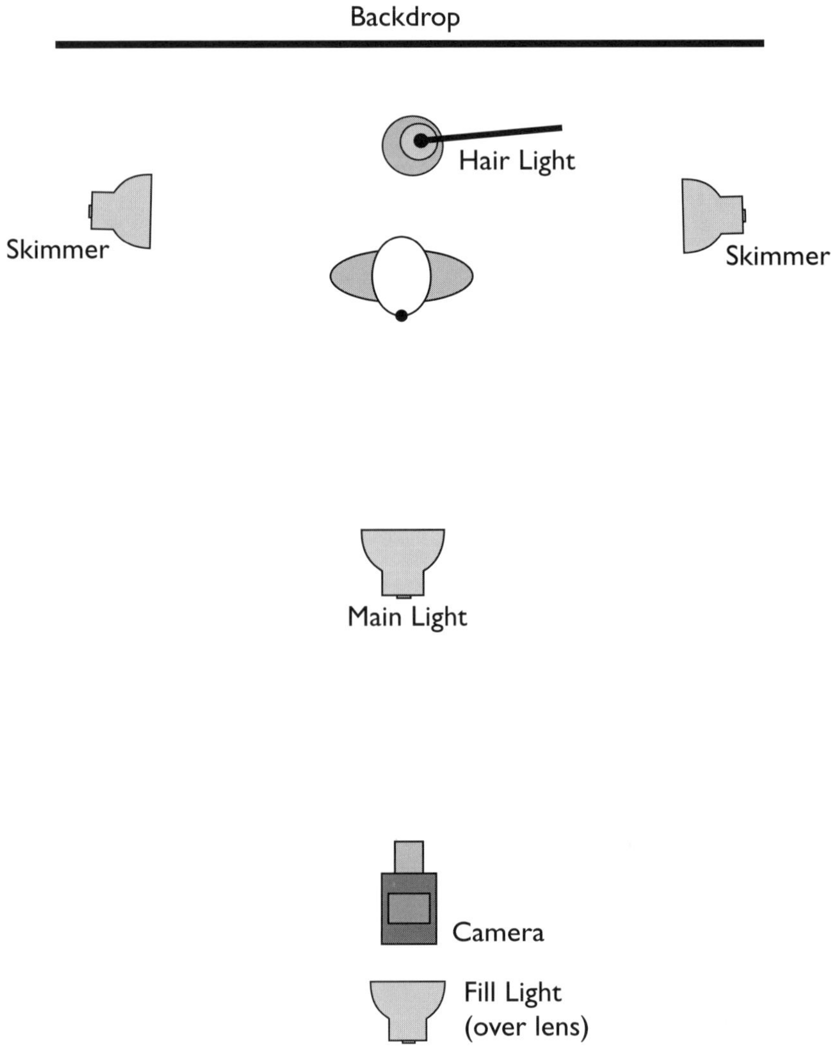

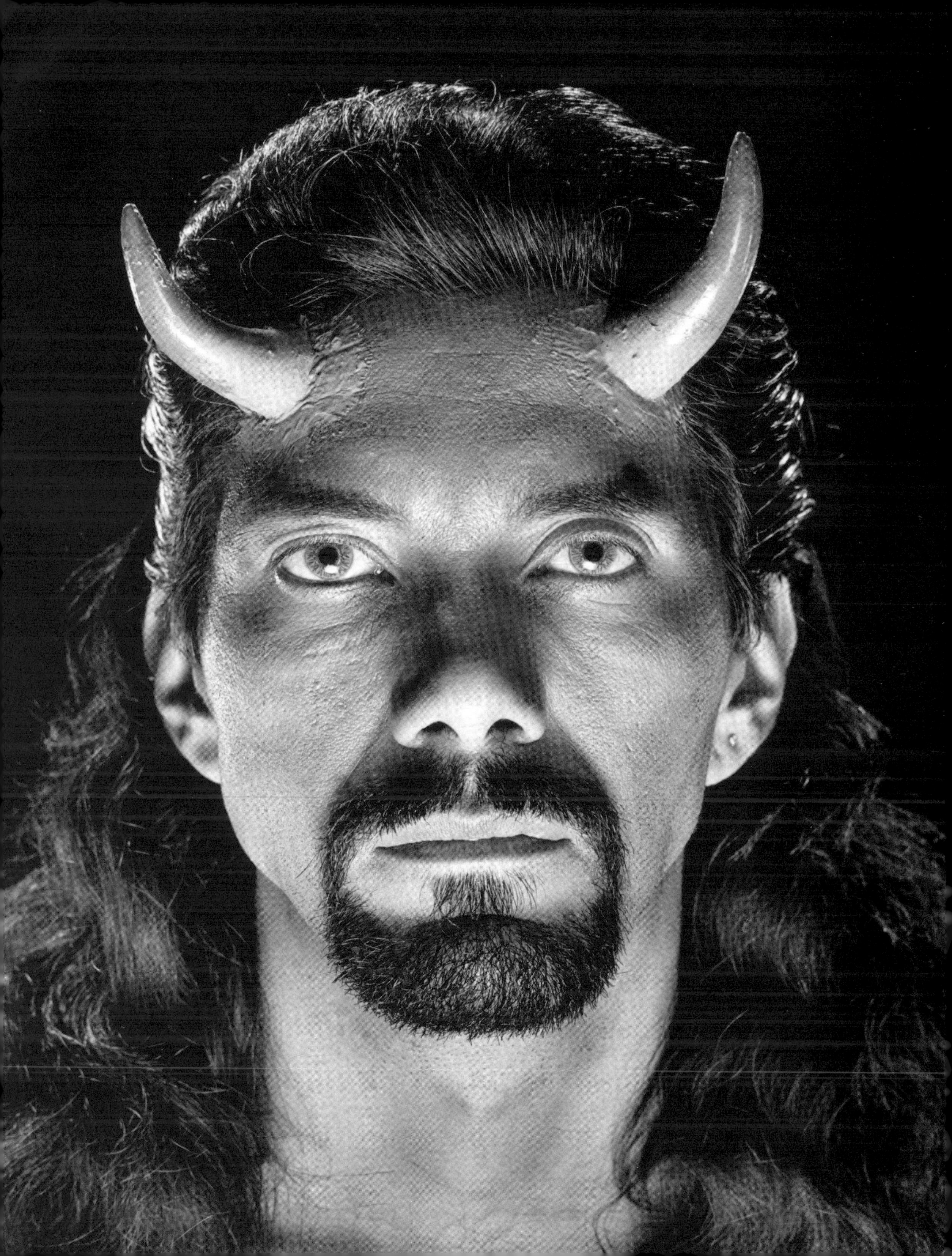

Lighting

This image was one that I pre-planned for the session. The positioning of their bodies and faces created a great potential for dramatic illumination, and the spreading of the devil's fingers allowed interesting light patterns to be created on his hand (emphasized by the dramatic fake nails).

The faces of both the devil and the girl are lit by the same main light. However, because of the posing of the shot, the lighting effect is different for each character. The devil's face shows a Rembrandt lighting pattern (a drop shadow falls from the subject's nose, onto his cheek and merges with the shadows on the unlit side of the face). The girl's face displays a loop pattern (the shadow from the nose falls just above the corner of the subject's mouth).

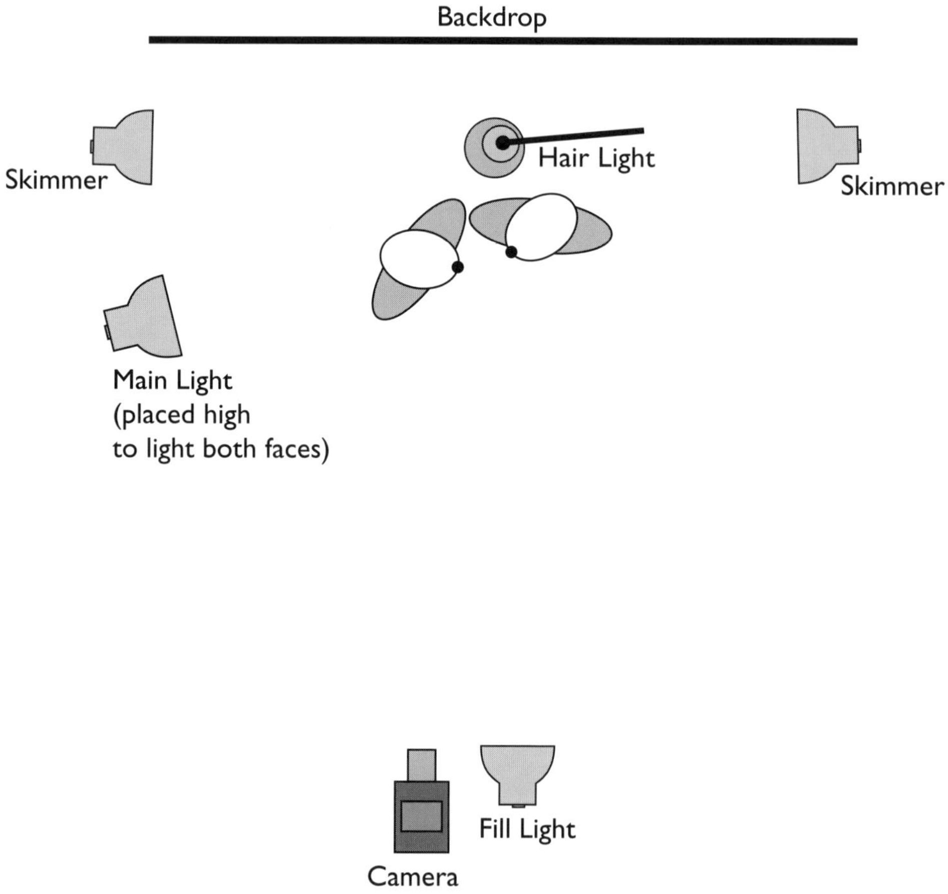

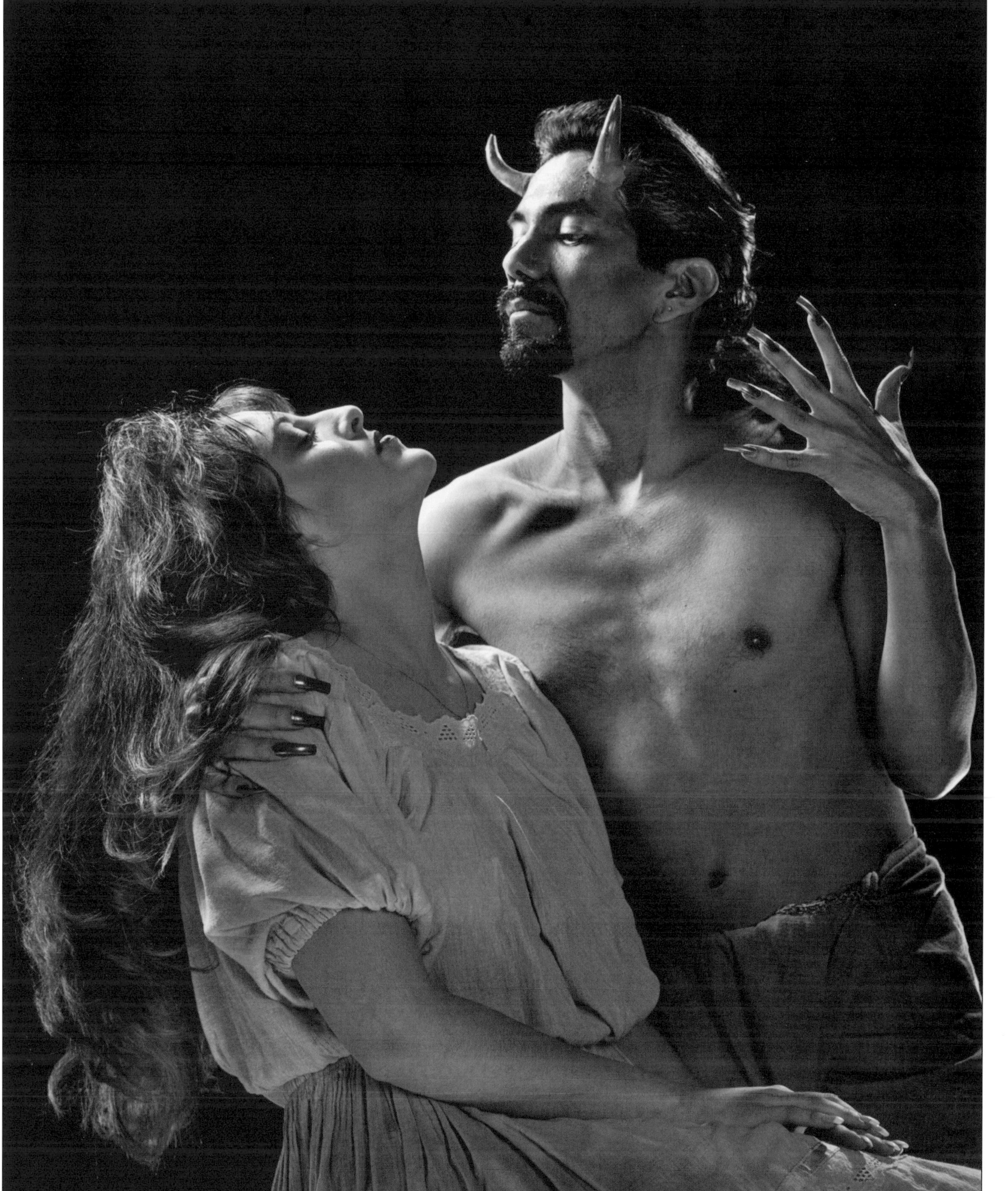

Lighting

In my take on the classic battle between good and evil, lighting was supplied from seven sources. Illumination was metered from the main light and the other lights were geared in ratio to this.

The first light used is a spotlight, which was turned to illuminate the girl's face. Two skimmers were placed on either side of the models. Two main lights were also used: one, placed behind the devil, illuminates his back and the face of the priest; the other, placed behind the priest, illuminates his back and the the face of the devil. Finally, a top light was used to highlight the hair of the models, and a fill light was used near the camera lens.

Printing

I am a printer by necessity only. Although I would love to have more time to experiment in the darkroom, when I'm in there, I'm effectively losing money. Fortunately, shooting chrome really teaches you how to expose film, so my strategy is to use my shooting skills to cut the time I need to spend in the darkroom fighting with poor negatives.

Doing my own printing also assures me of getting across my artistic vision in the final prints (something I have had problems achieving with other printers). When necessary, I sometimes will expose my prints, stick them in a black bag and have my assistant run them through the chemicals.

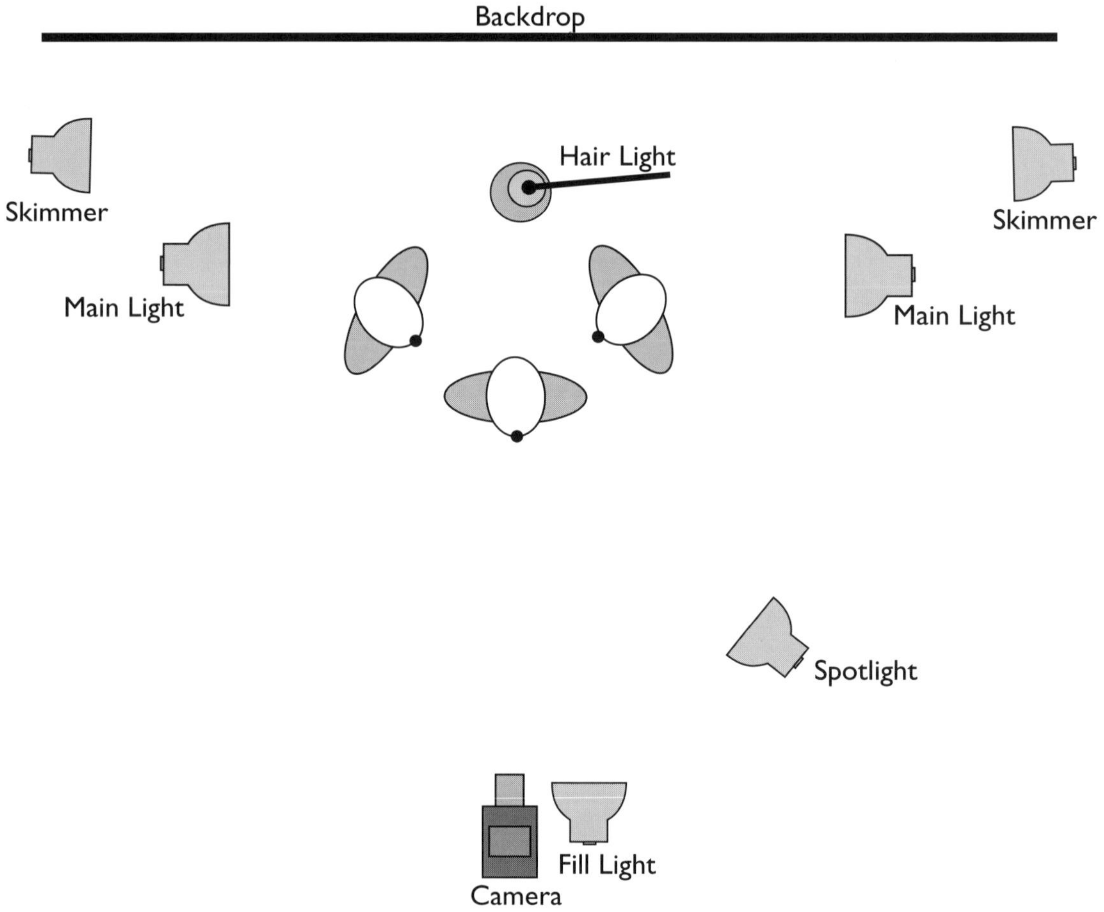

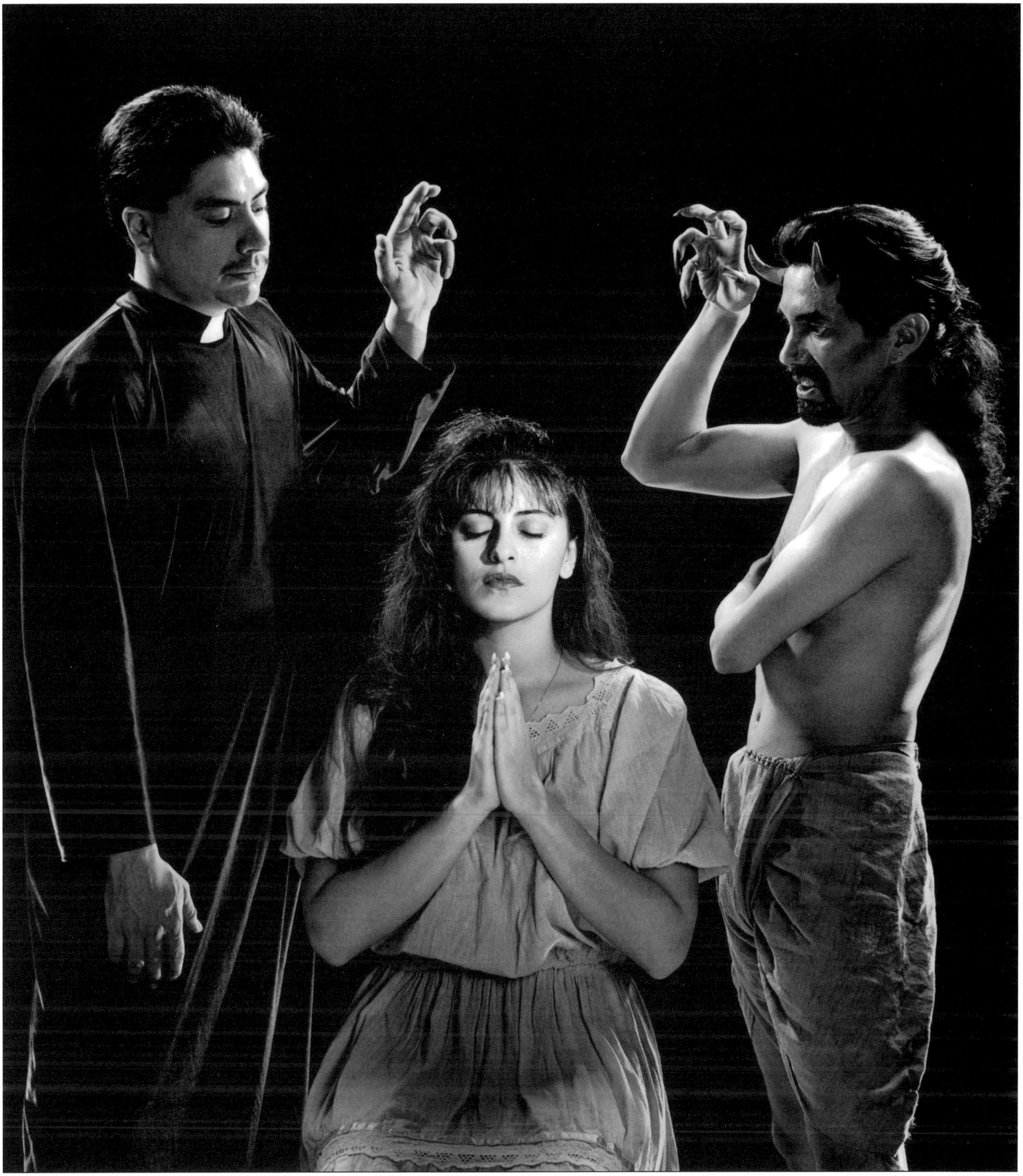

Models

I often do work for a local youth development program. This generally involves taking promotional photographs for young performers, such as these actors in a play (and their director, shown here as the devil). At this shoot, I took several images for them to use for publicity. Since they were willing, I also shot this image for my own purposes.

Although in the play, the director played a good guy, here he is posed as the devil in an image that warns against believing everything you hear. It was a happy coincidence that the smoke from his cigarette happened to form horns above his head!

Lighting

The models who surround the devil were all seated on two benches. Two main lights (placed on either side of the set) light the group. Fill light was added close to the camera lens, and a hair light placed above the scene catches all of the models.

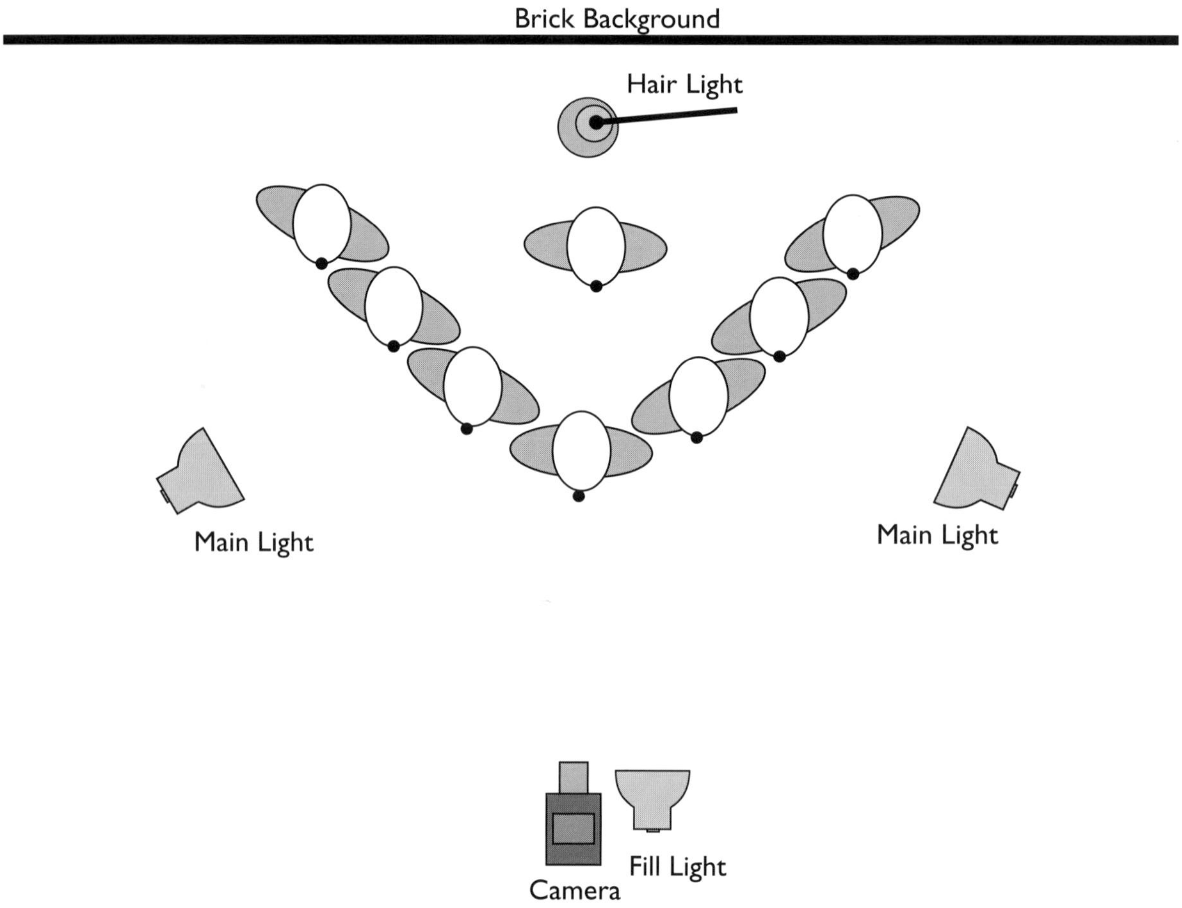

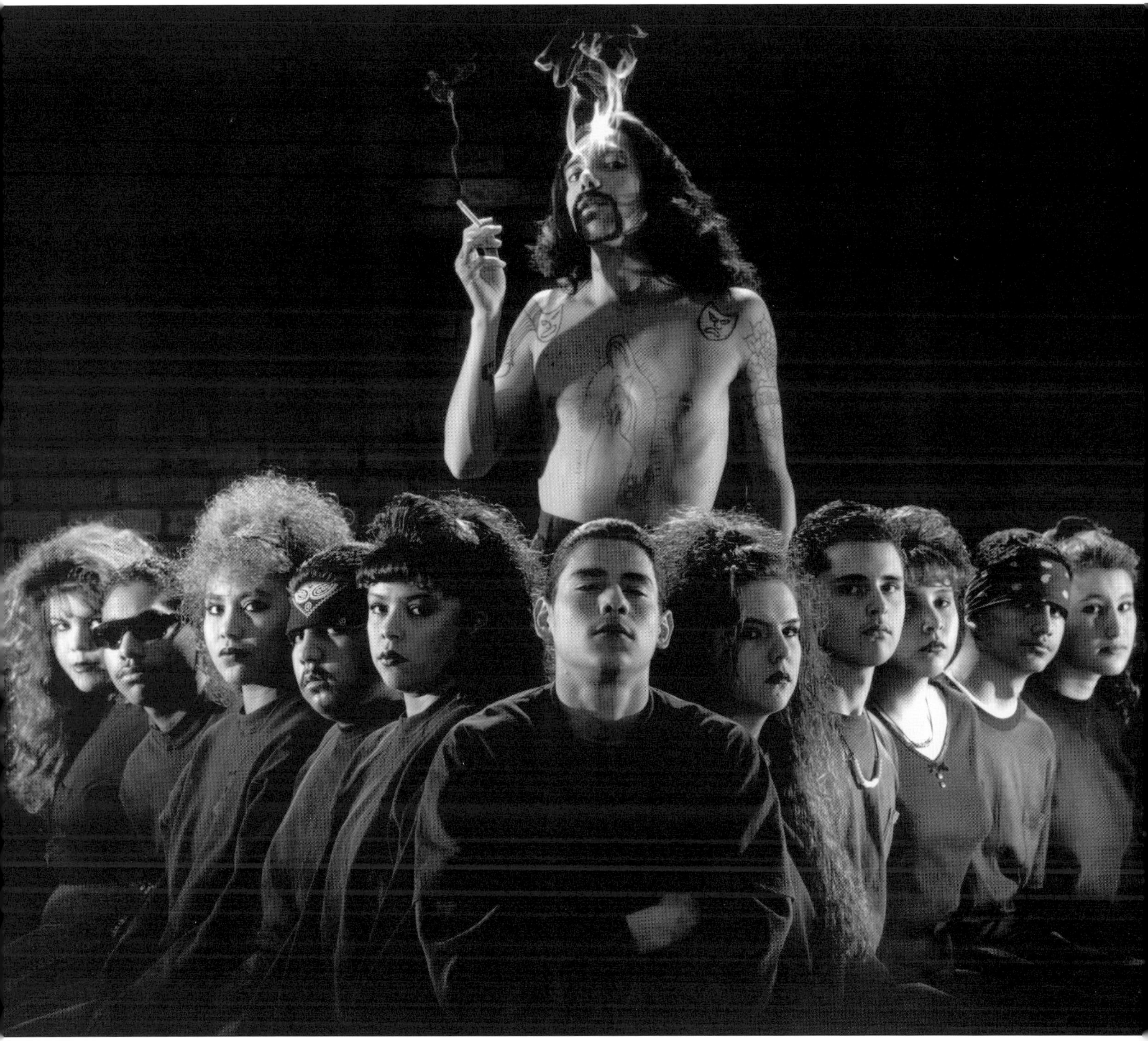

Models

In an effort to find unique subjects to photograph, I've advised all my friends to send my way any interesting people they happen to know or meet. That's how I met this model, an artist who actually calls himself Goat Boy, and whose photograph has caused much controversy in PPA competition.

Shooting

Since I didn't know what he looked like, it wasn't really possible to preconceive the kind of images I would want to create with him. So, when he arrived at the studio wearing these devil's horns, I simply set about to shooting a variety of angles, working with his features and trying to capture him in a very dramatic way. I have since used him as a model in other sessions.

Lighting

The bottom lighting in this image adds to the dramatic effect I was attempting to convey. Combined with the very symmetrical composition, this helps to accentuate his piercings and tatoos. A slight edge light also helps to define the figure.

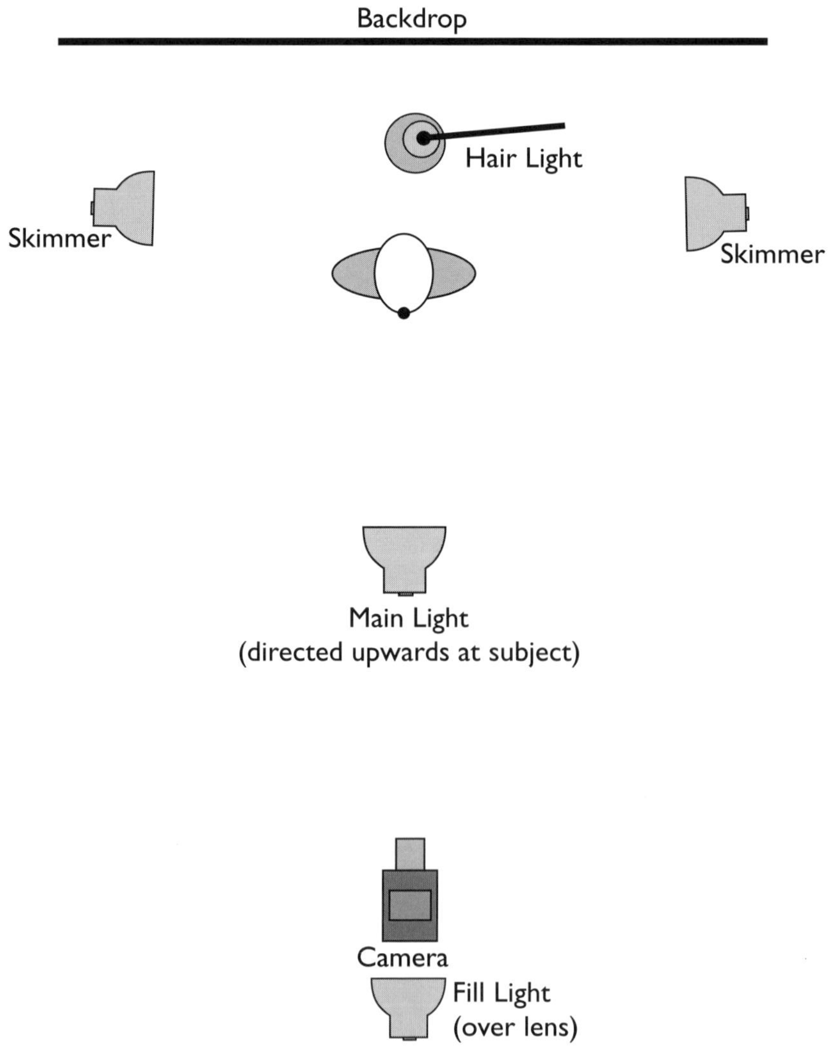

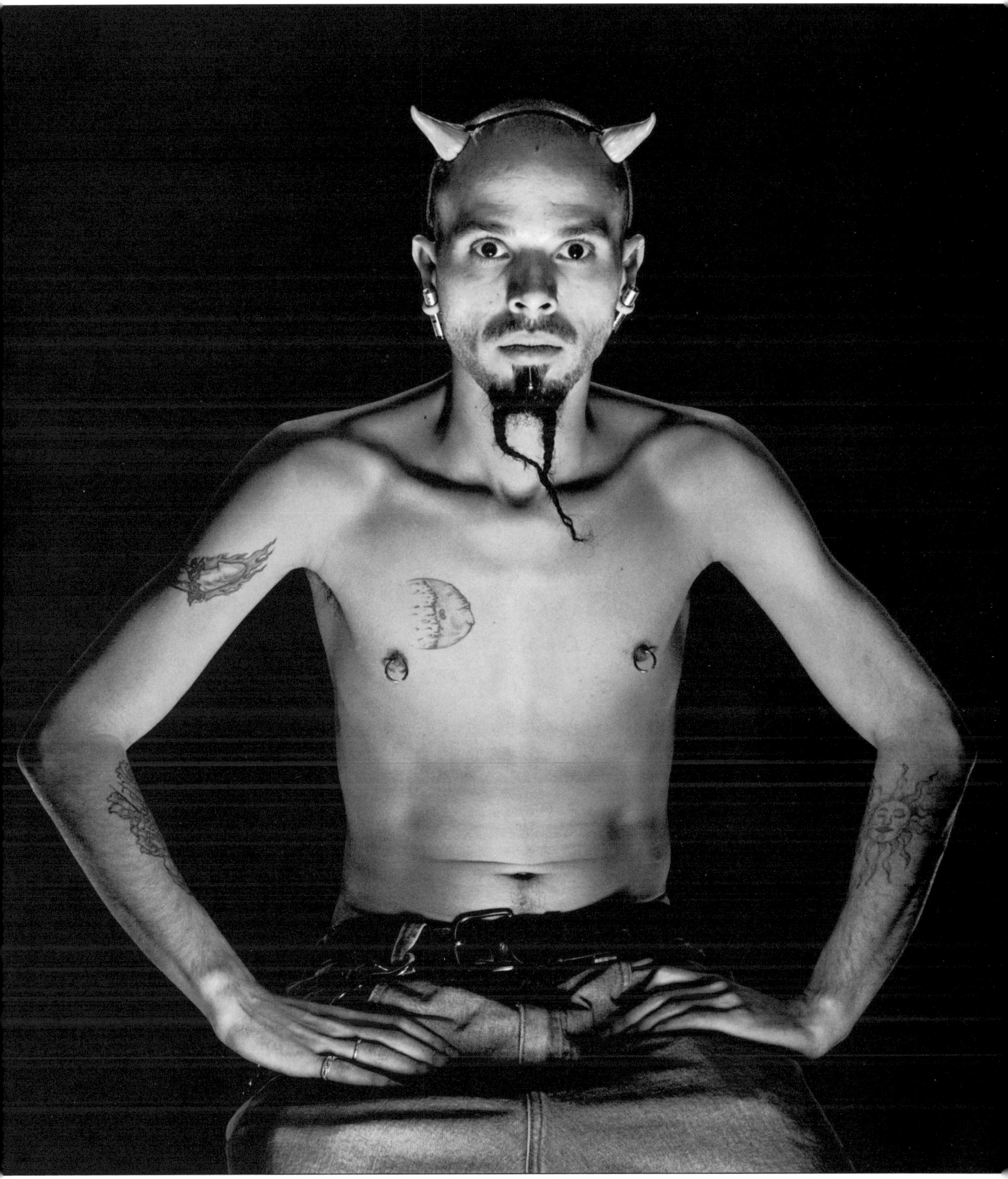

La Llorona (The Weeping Woman)

Folklore

La Llorona is a character from Mexican folklore who drowned her own children. After death she was denied entry into heaven and was condemned to walk the earth in search of her lost offspring. She is often used as a discipline tool ("Be good or La Llorona will get you!"). Here, she is depicted at the window of a house, looking in on a mother and child.

Images like this have consistently sold well for me through museums and exhibitions, but also through PPA seminars.

Lighting

Lighting was provided by two main lights, one directed at the old woman from her right and slightly behind her, one directed at the mother and child in the background. Two skimmers relatively close to the camera help light the side of the old woman's face. A hair light and a fill light complete the set-up.

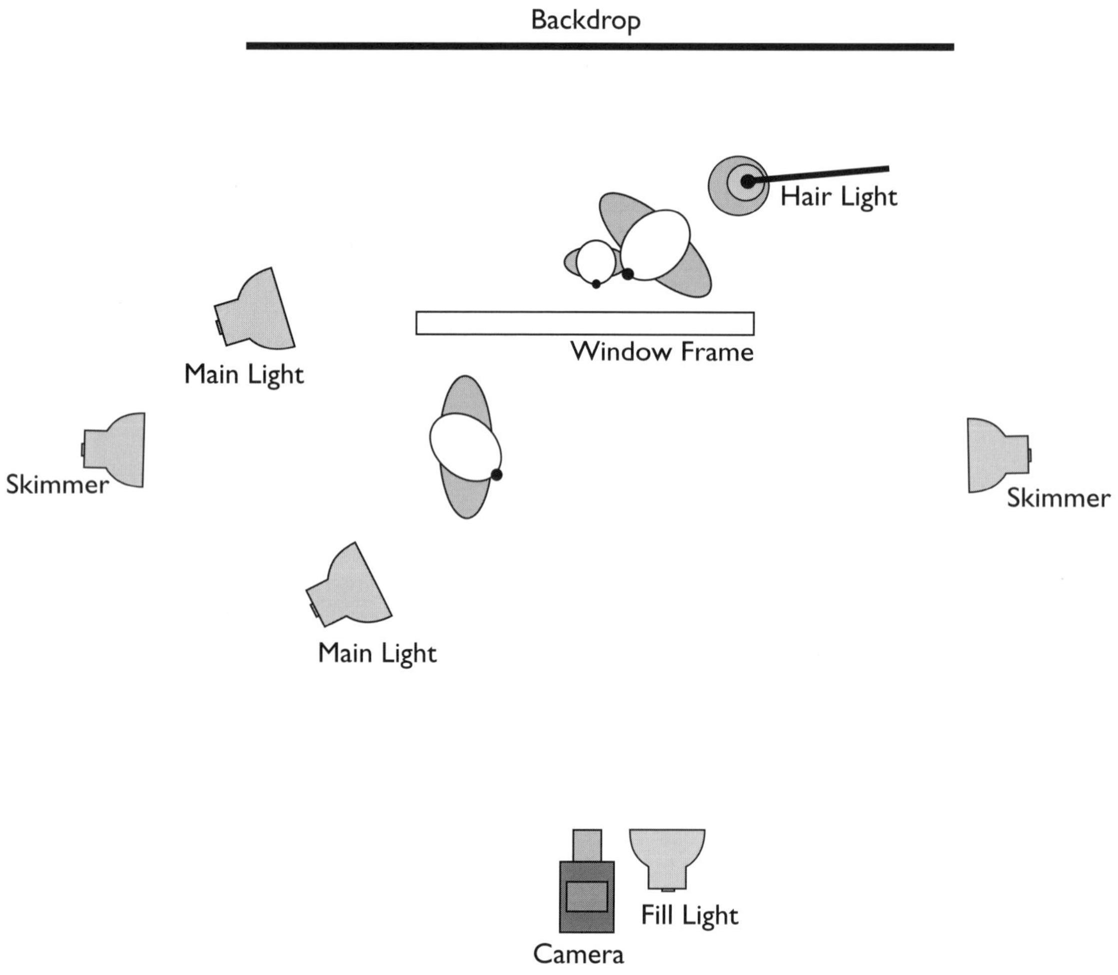

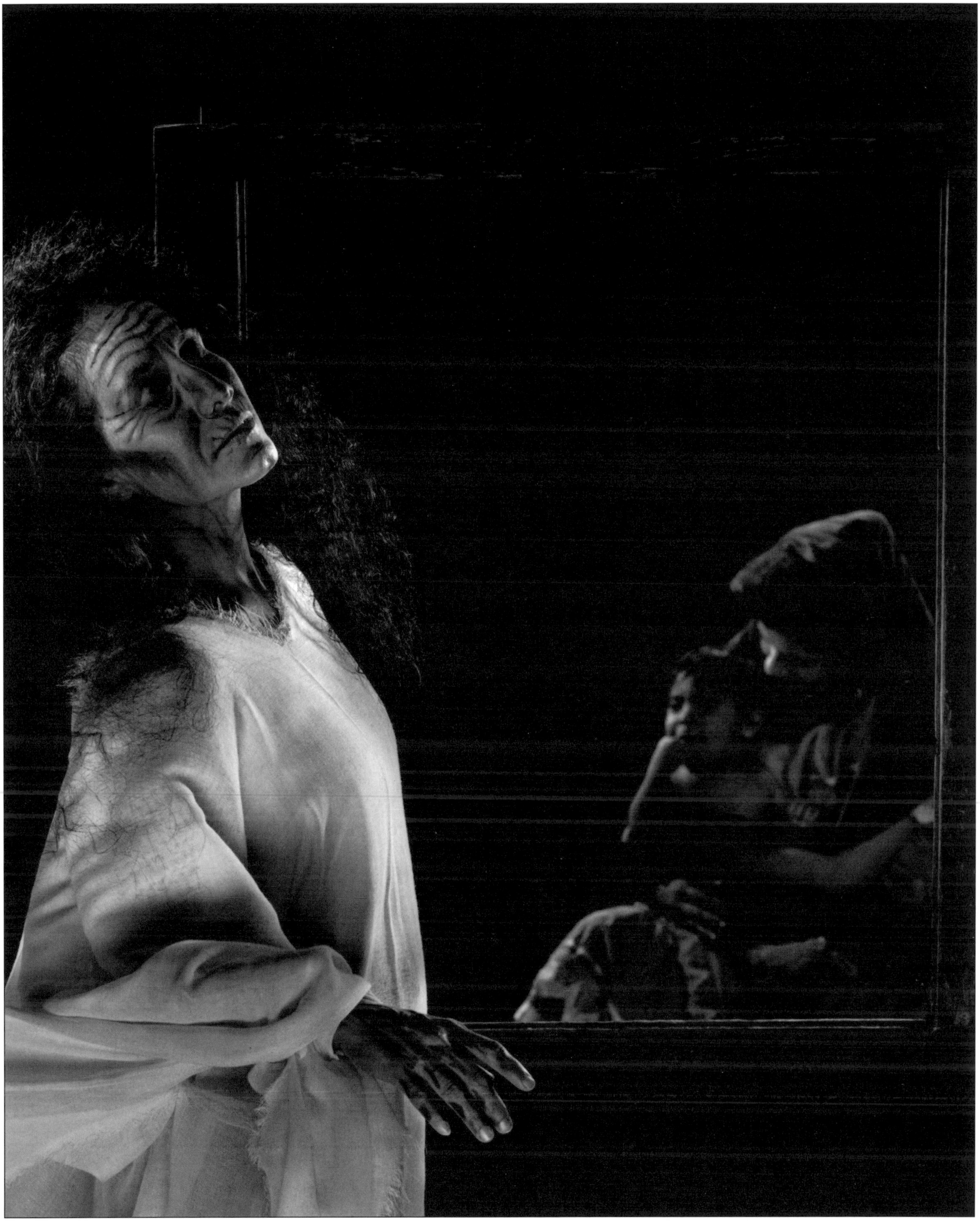

Model

La Curandera is a practitioner of folk medicine who uses herbal remedies in her healing. The image was shot for a calendar which featured Hispanic artists of all media. This woman is definitely an artist, and one closely tied to Hispanic culture.

On Location

Since it obviously wouldn't have been practical to move all of her supplies to the studio, I shot La Curandera on location in front of her shelves of herbs. Shooting on location is something I don't get to do as much as I would like to. I particularly enjoy catching people in their own element, as well as the challenge of dealing with unknown conditions and having to think on my feet to create the right pose and lighting.

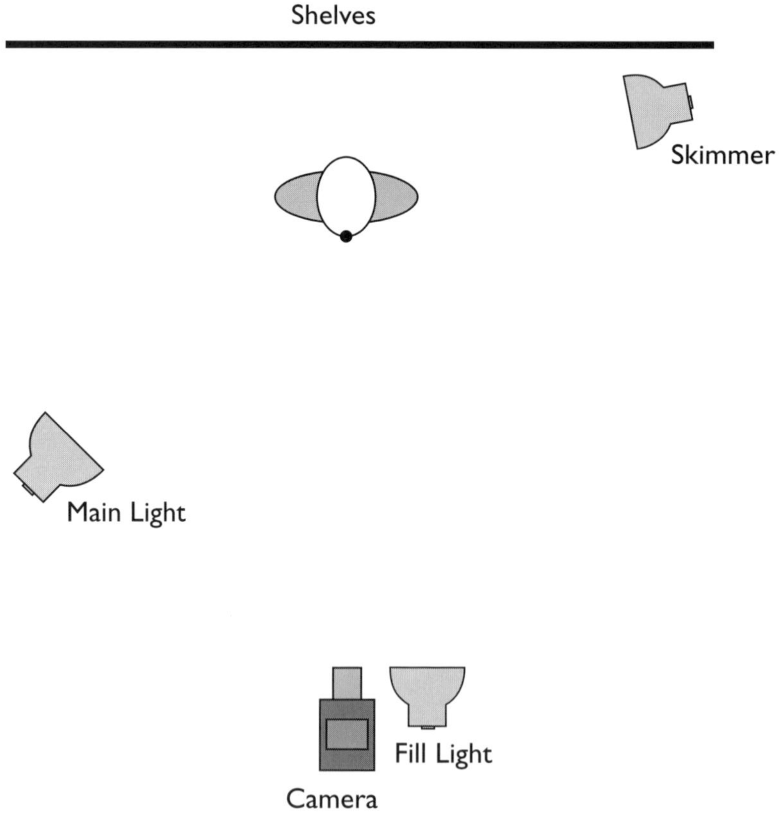

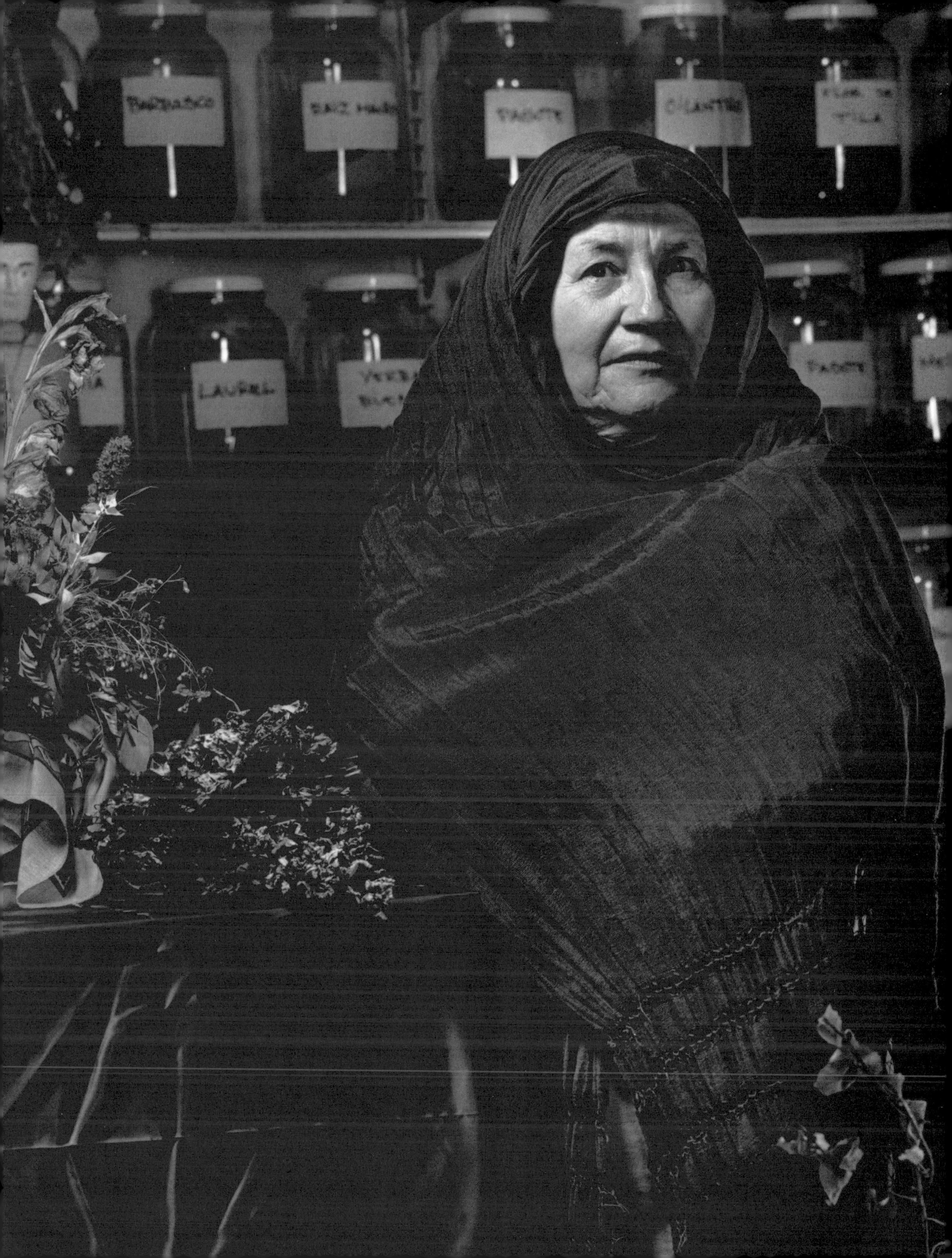
LAUREL

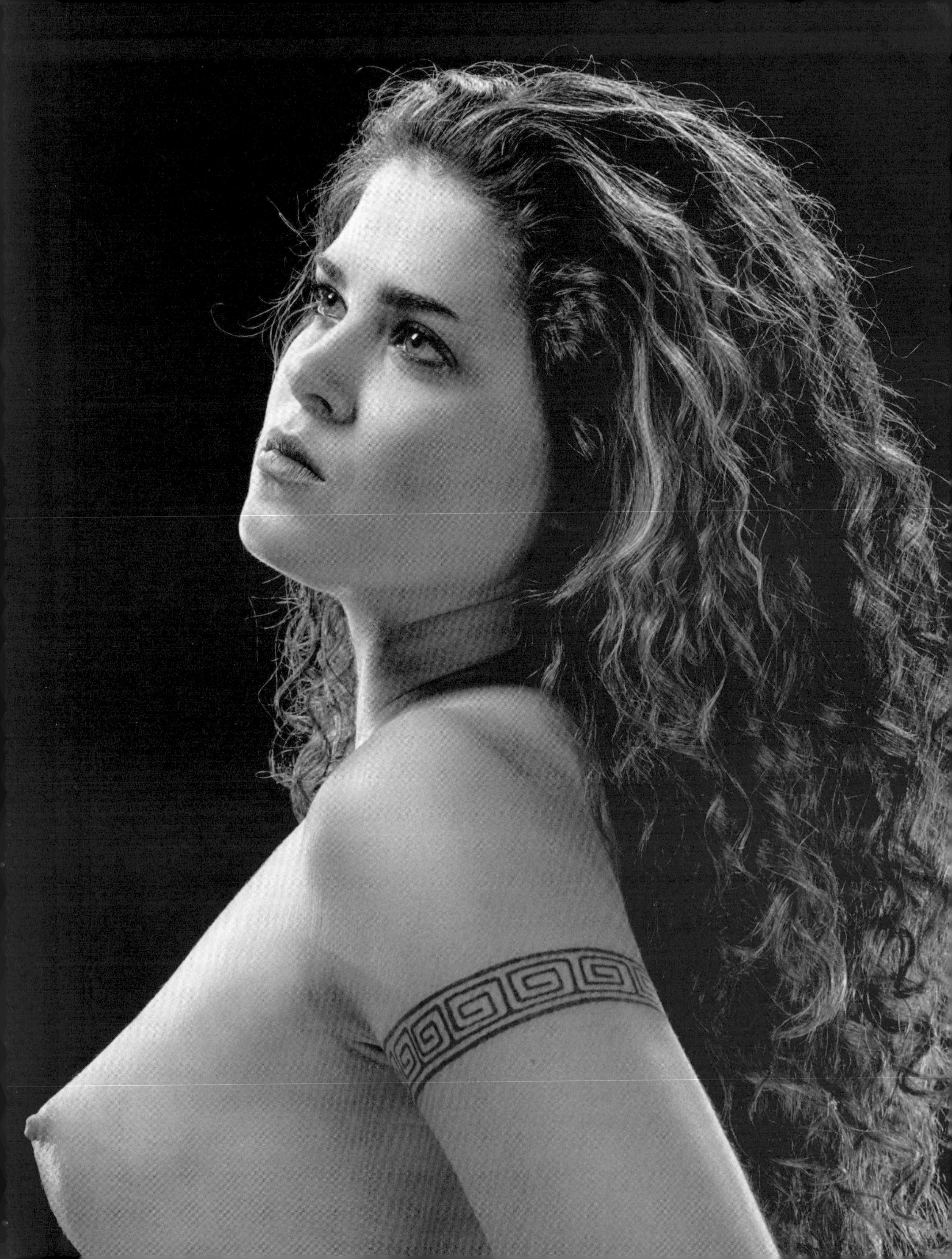

Model

This quarter figure nude image came out of a test shoot for a portfolio session. When I decided to embark upon a series of art nudes, I spoke to photographer friends and got model recommendations. When I get a recommendation, I set up an appointment and if the test shoot turns out well, trade photography for model releases.

Lighting

This image is lit as a formal portrait. The main light is positioned to the camera left, creating short loop lighting (the shadow from the model's nose falls just below her nose). Skimmers were placed on either side of the model. The left skimmer accentuates her breast and provides edge lighting. The right skimmer lights her hair and arm. Fill light was also used next to the lens, and a hair light was placed above the model.

Hair

I always try to select a model who is appropriate to the composition I have in mind. When shooting in black and white, certain tones of hair, and certain textures really make an image pop. For instance, curly or wavy hair tends to have more texture and richer tonalities than straight hair.

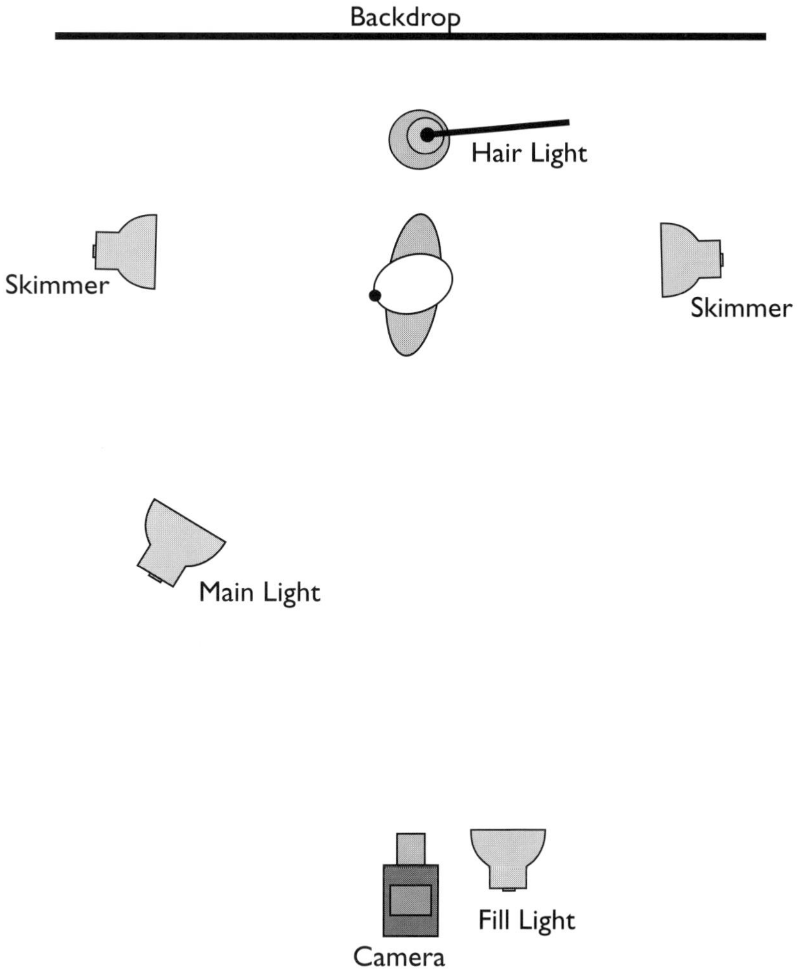

Nude Spotlight

Model

This image had its birth on a commercial assignment, when this model was a secondary subject on the shoot. I later used her as a model for some "Golden Era" images, and then as a nude model.

Lighting

Strobe lighting was used to illuminate the model. A main light hits her face directly. A fill light was used close to the camera. Skimmers were placed to either side of the model and a top light illuminates her from above. The background of black muslin was lit with a continuous theatrical light.

Printing

The shadowing that outlines the model's body was burned in in the darkroom to create a contradictory light effect.

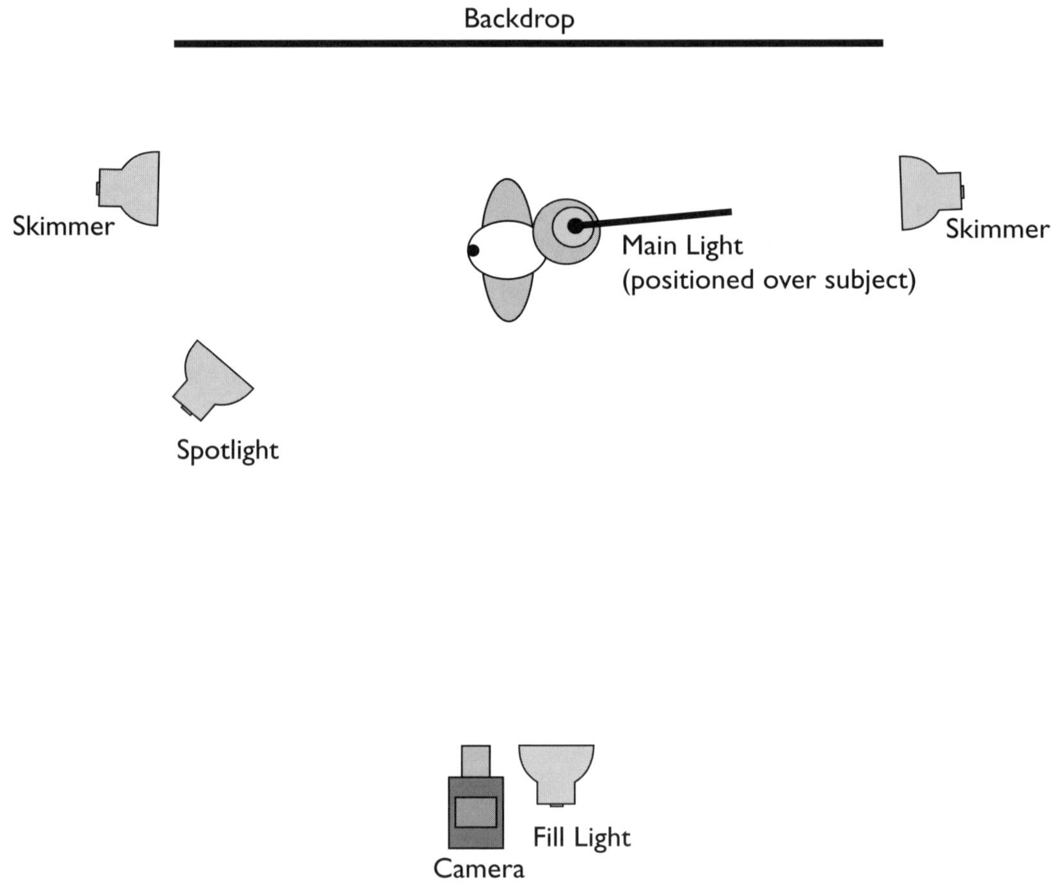

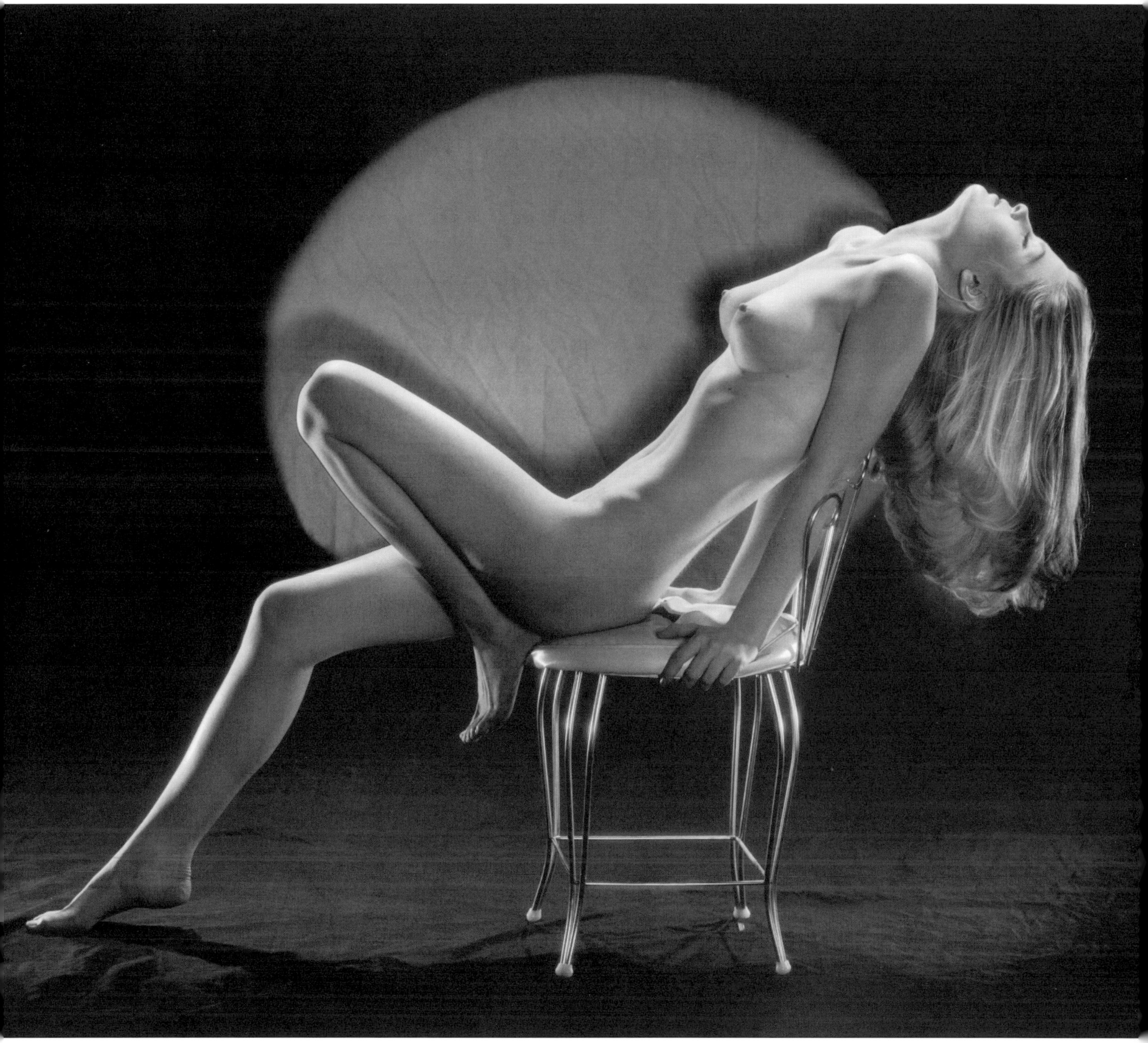

Lighting

Six sources of lighting were used in this image. A hair light illuminates the model from above. The main light also hits her from above and is positioned perpendicular to her face. Skimmers were placed on either side of the model, and a fill light was used close to the camera.

Since real pumpkins turned out to be impossible to find in June, I had to look around for a substitute. Finally, I found this trick-or-treat basket, and placed a real stem on top of the fake pumpkin.

The pumpkin was also illuminated from within, using a Morris Mini Slave, a small battery powered flash with a photo sensor that trips it along with the other flashes. The lighting for the whole image had to be balanced to compensate for shooting into this light source while still retaining light on the model.

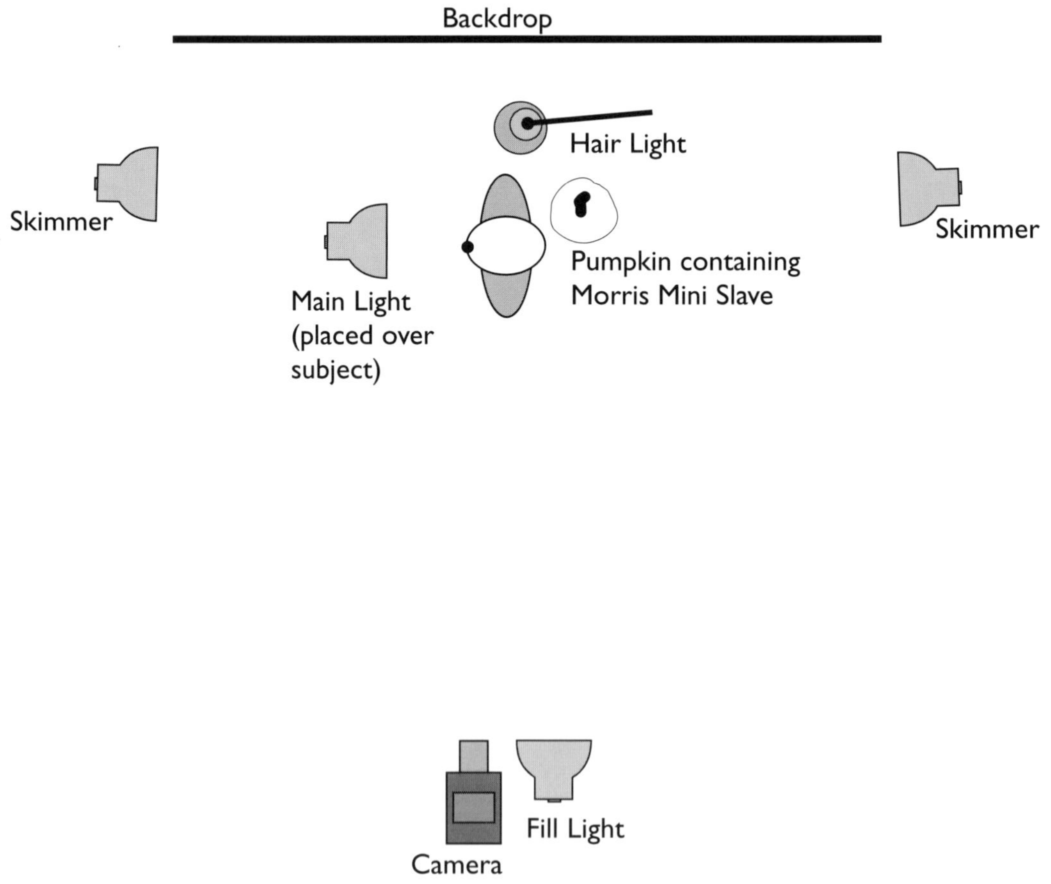

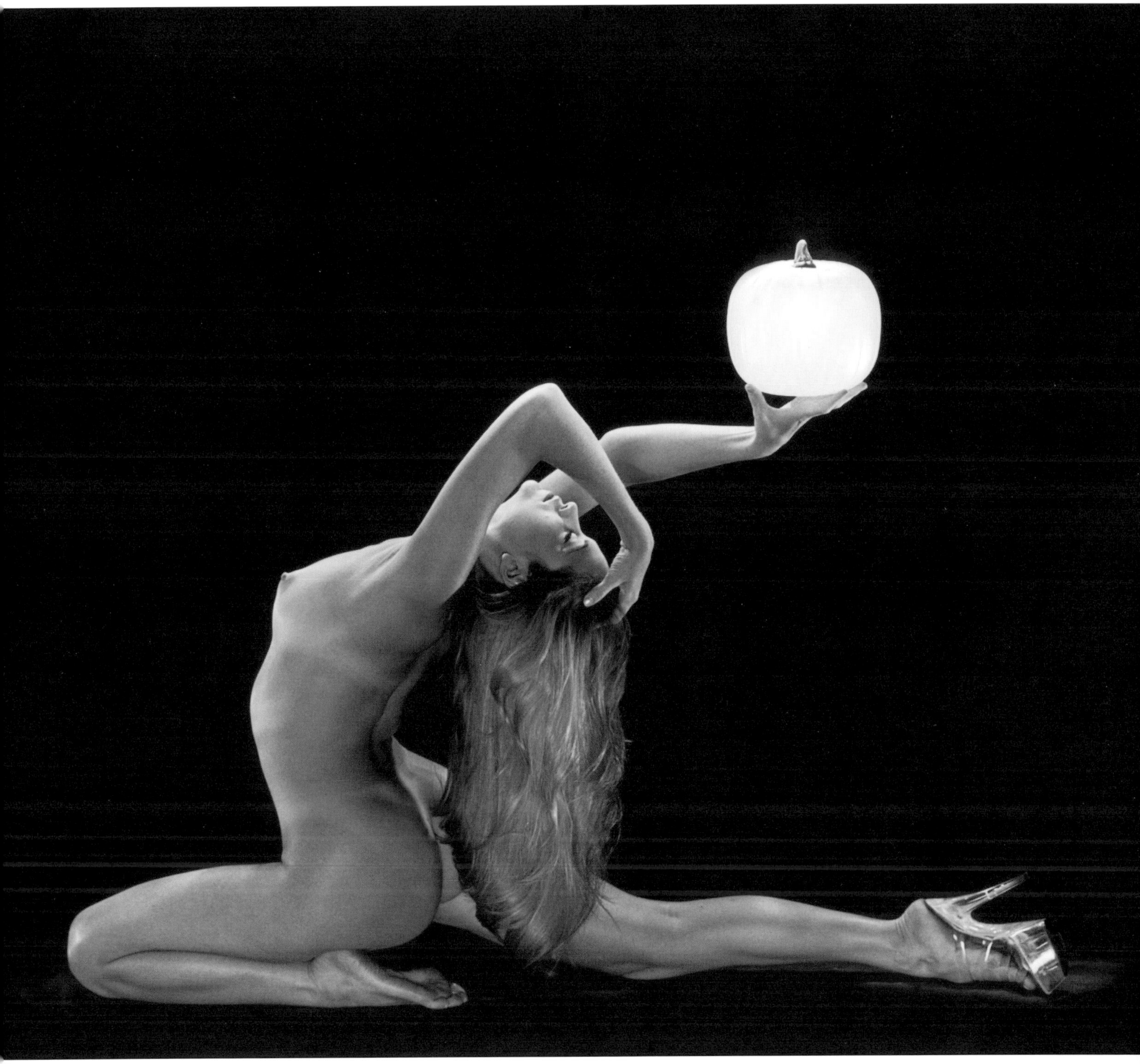

Lighting

The lighting set-up for this image is almost identical to the one used in the previous image (Cinderella at Midnight), except that the main light is moved above the model. Two additional lights were added to illuminate the drapes around the model. These were placed on the camera side of the drapes at a 45° angle to the camera, and help provide texture and shadow on the cloth.

The two spheres which the model holds were, like the pumpkin in the previous photo, illuminated from within using Morris Mini Slaves.

Idea File

The idea for this image came to me while talking to a friend shortly after finishing a figure session. I was looking at his face, and for some reason the idea just hit me. I find a lot of ideas for photographs come to me this way, almost like daydreams. I'm always careful to write them down so I can act on them later. It's great to have a file of ideas on hand for when the proper occasion arises.

Awards

Although images like this are a little out of the ordinary, this photograph has scored extremely well in Southwest regional PPA competition, taking Best of Show, Best Illustrative, Highest Print Score, Fuji Masterpiece Award, Past President's Award, and going into the National Loan Collection.

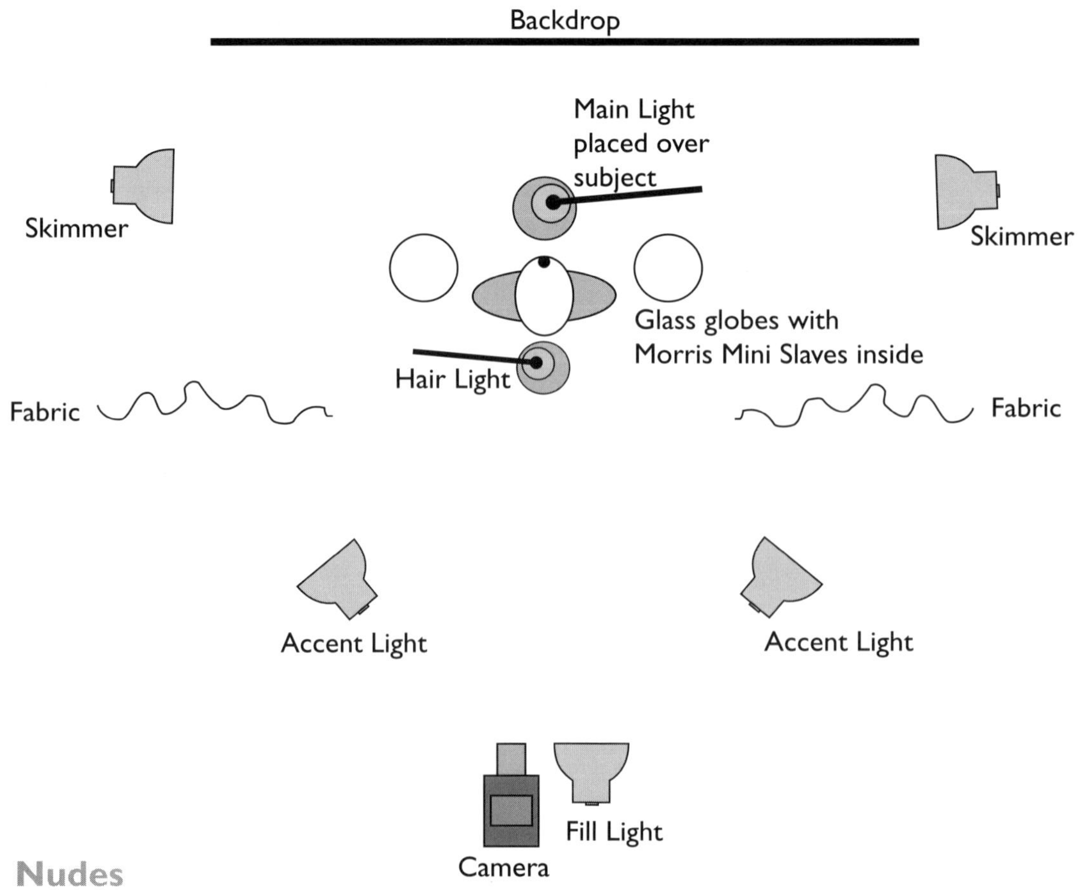

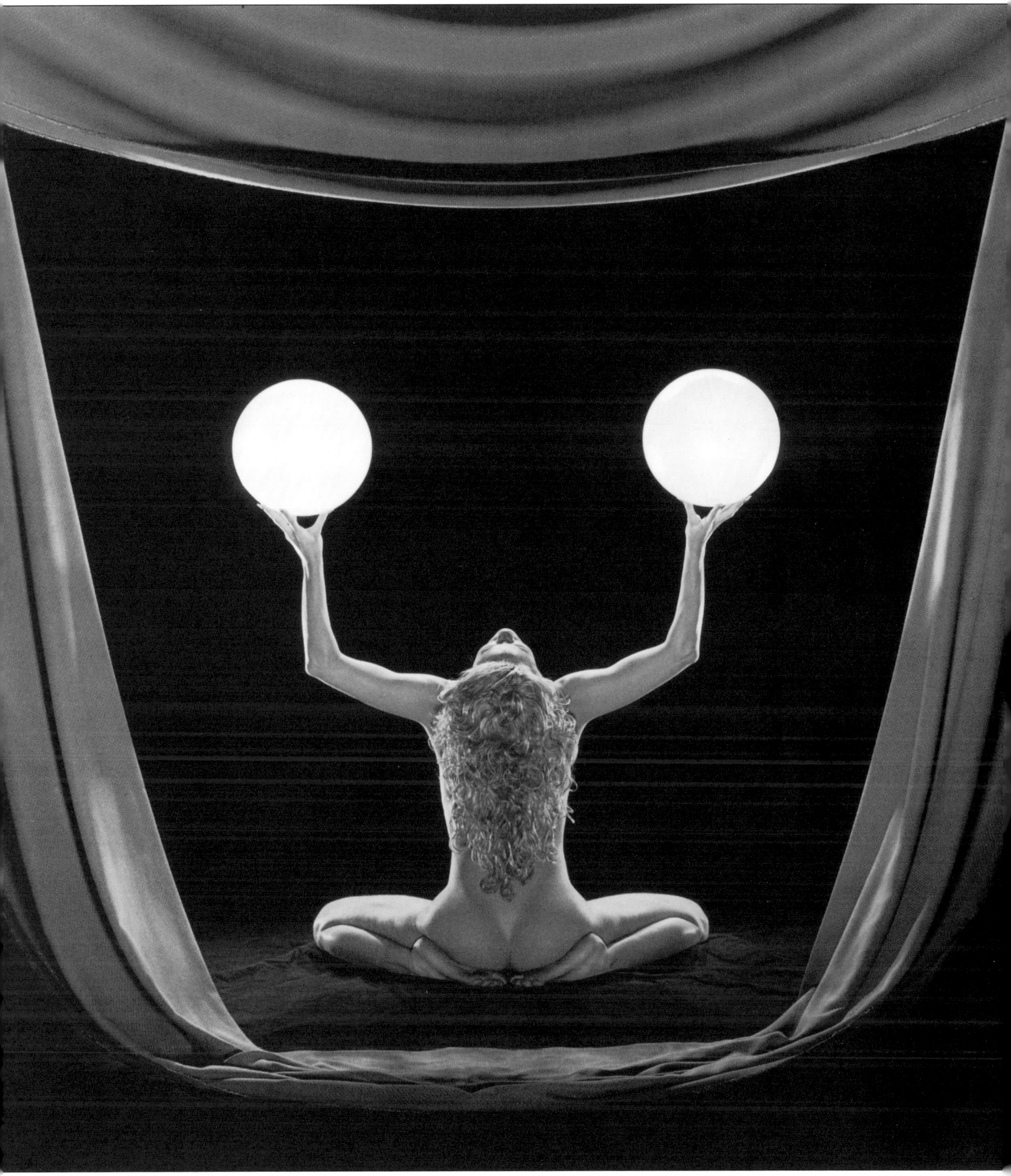

Shooting Nudes

My art nude work is certainly influenced by glamour nude work I have done in the past. After doing a lot of "automotive bikini-girl" work, then working with many of the models on glamour shots for their portfolios, I started getting interested in more dramatic, fine art images. Now I tend to do nude work with all different kinds of models and body types.

I find nude photography one of the most difficult and rewarding types of work I do. With nudes, lighting and posing requires attention be paid to the entire body, not just to the face as in portraiture. Also, by its very nature, nude photography is a sensitive subject and one which requires close attention to remain "art."

Lighting

This simple symmetrical pose was illuminated from each side by two skimmers. This is a basic element in much of my lighting, and depending on the subject and the look I'm going for, I manipulate the highlights by moving the skimmers closer to the camera, or closer to the background. The background of the image is seamless black paper, but this was taken way down in printing to create the impression that the model is almost floating in the frame.

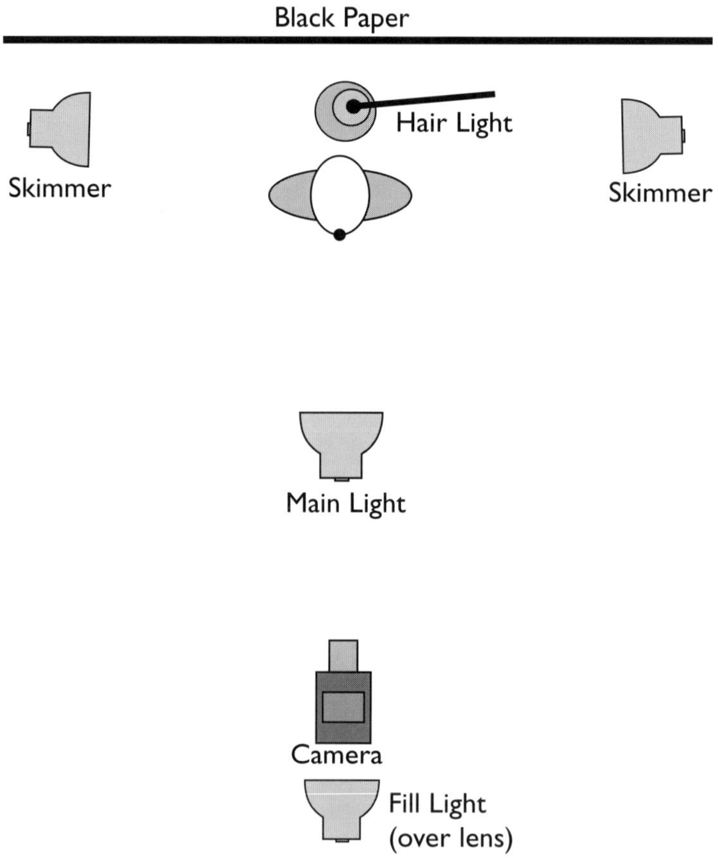

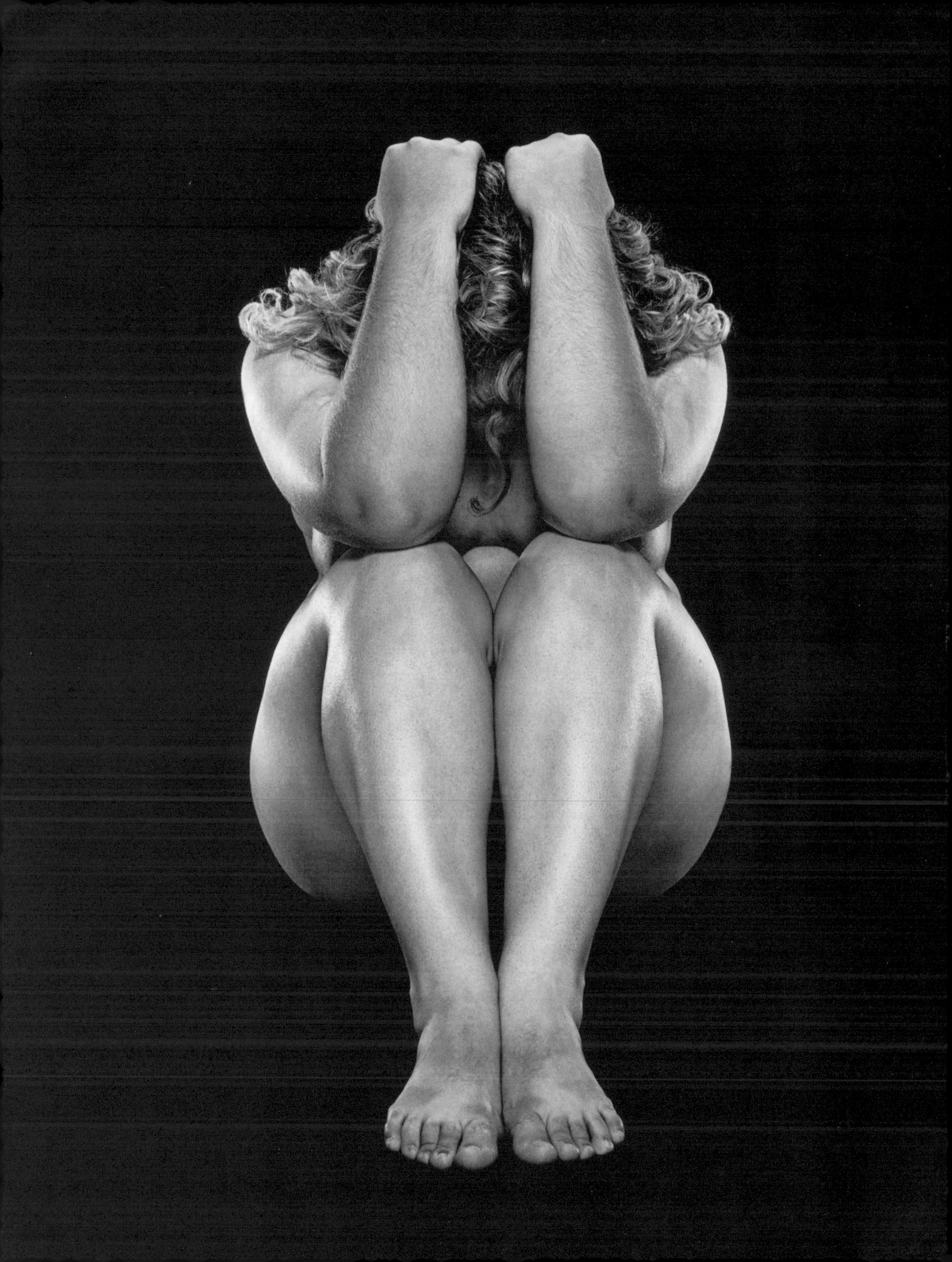

Composition

The idea for this image developed during the shoot. I had seen photographs of this model with her hair shaved on the sides in a sort of grown-out mohawk, and had her in the studio as part of a figure study session.

I had a hair-stylist help her arrange her hair in these long spikes. Then it occurred to me that I had on hand a chimney top I had made years ago while working as a designer. I put it in the picture and liked the way it worked with the composition, creating balance and complementing the model's simple pose (a pose which also lends an androgyny to her figure).

Composition has been harder for me to learn than any of the technical aspects of photography simply because there are so many contradictory ideas and theories. In some cases I take these guidelines, but ultimately I am more likely to follow the "Rule of Comfort" than the "Rule of Thirds." By this I mean, if I like it, I go with it – even if I can't explain it or label it.

In competition, people often consciously stick to the formal guidelines, and sometimes I am also conscious of the rules that the judges know and which are popular. Still, some of my award-winning images have been major rule-breakers. For example, I won Best Portrait in Southwestern Regional PPA competition with an image that depicted the subject in the center of the photograph looking directly into the camera.

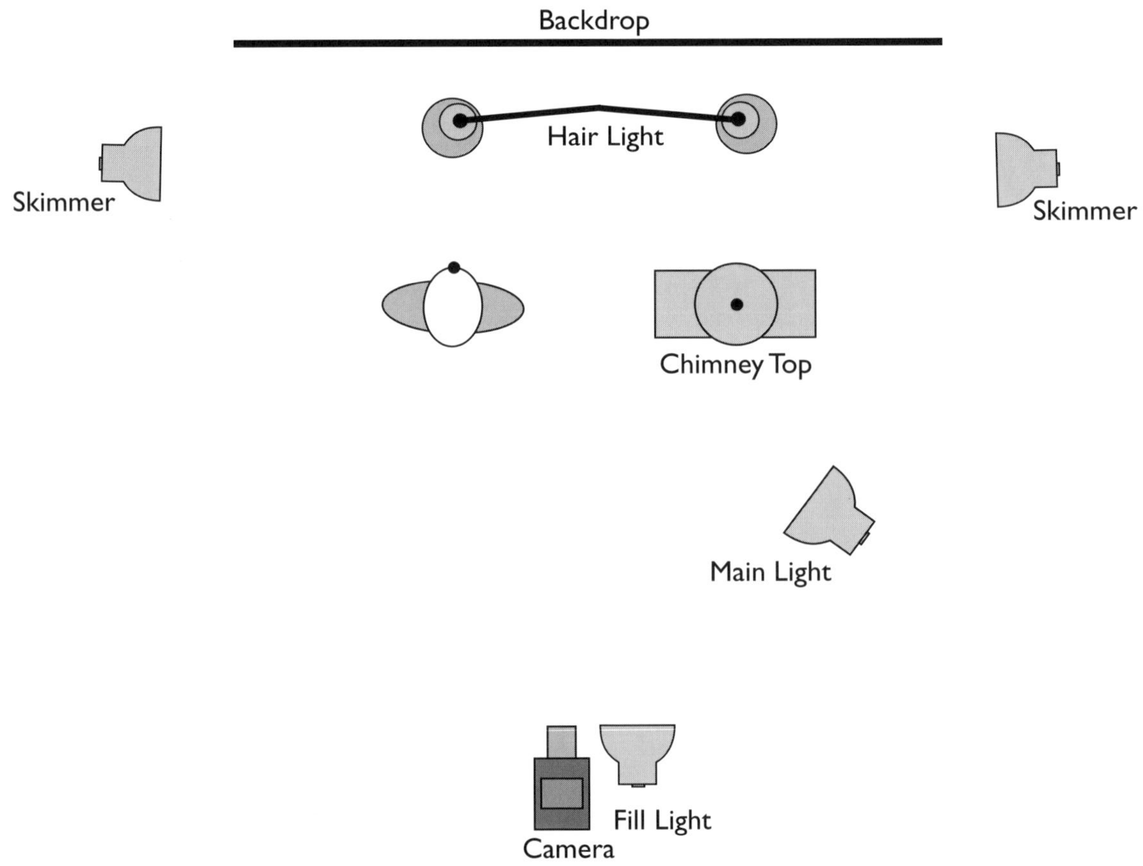

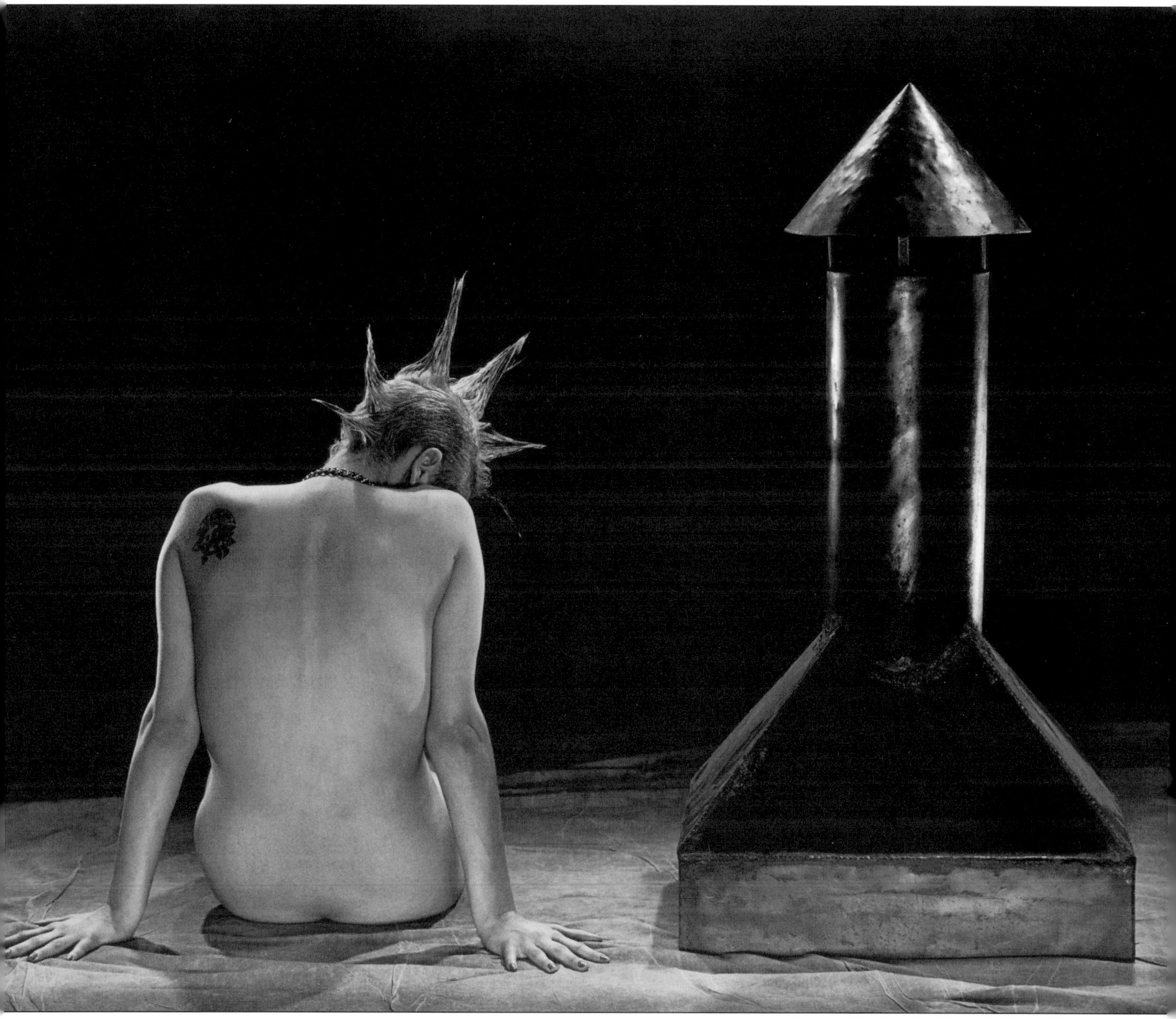

Model

This image was created for the model who is a singer, and also a favorite model of mine with whom I have worked for years. She was looking for something along these lines, so we settled on using white as the theme. She is posed on a white bench, with white scarf, pearls, sunglasses, cigarette and shoes.

Controversy

In the 1995 New Mexico State Fair, the censorship of this image hit the newspapers and evening news. In a juried show, the image was granted the honor of exhibition, but was then pulled from display by the fair's administration which claimed it was not "family" enough for the exhibit (although other nude images remained on display). Eventually the situation was resolved, and the next year "Cinderella at Midnight" won Best of Show and People's Choice in the same competition.

The experience has certainly colored the way I feel about nude photography. People sometimes have a hard time drawing a line between glamour photography and art nudes. They tend not to take seriously photographs they perceive to be "glamour" shots; apparently they can't see past the nude body to the workmanship of the photo. Experiencing this first-hand has made me very conscious of the social stigma still associated with nude photography.

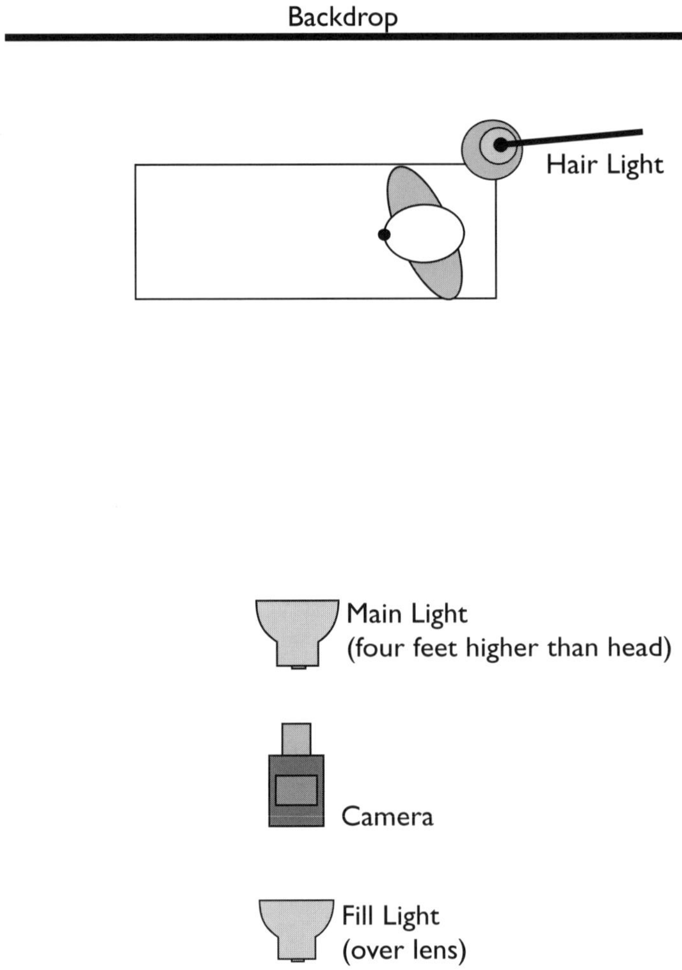

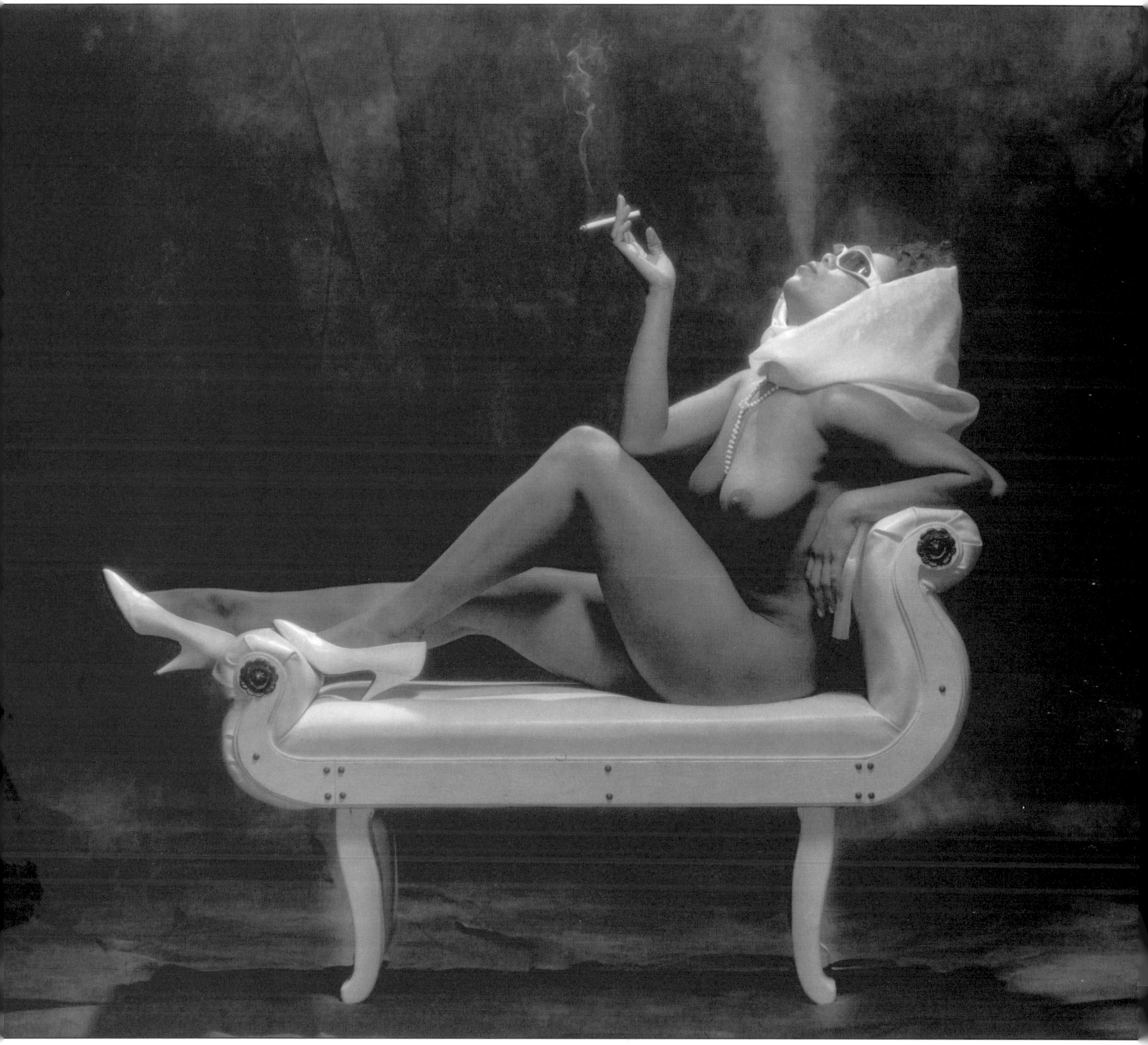

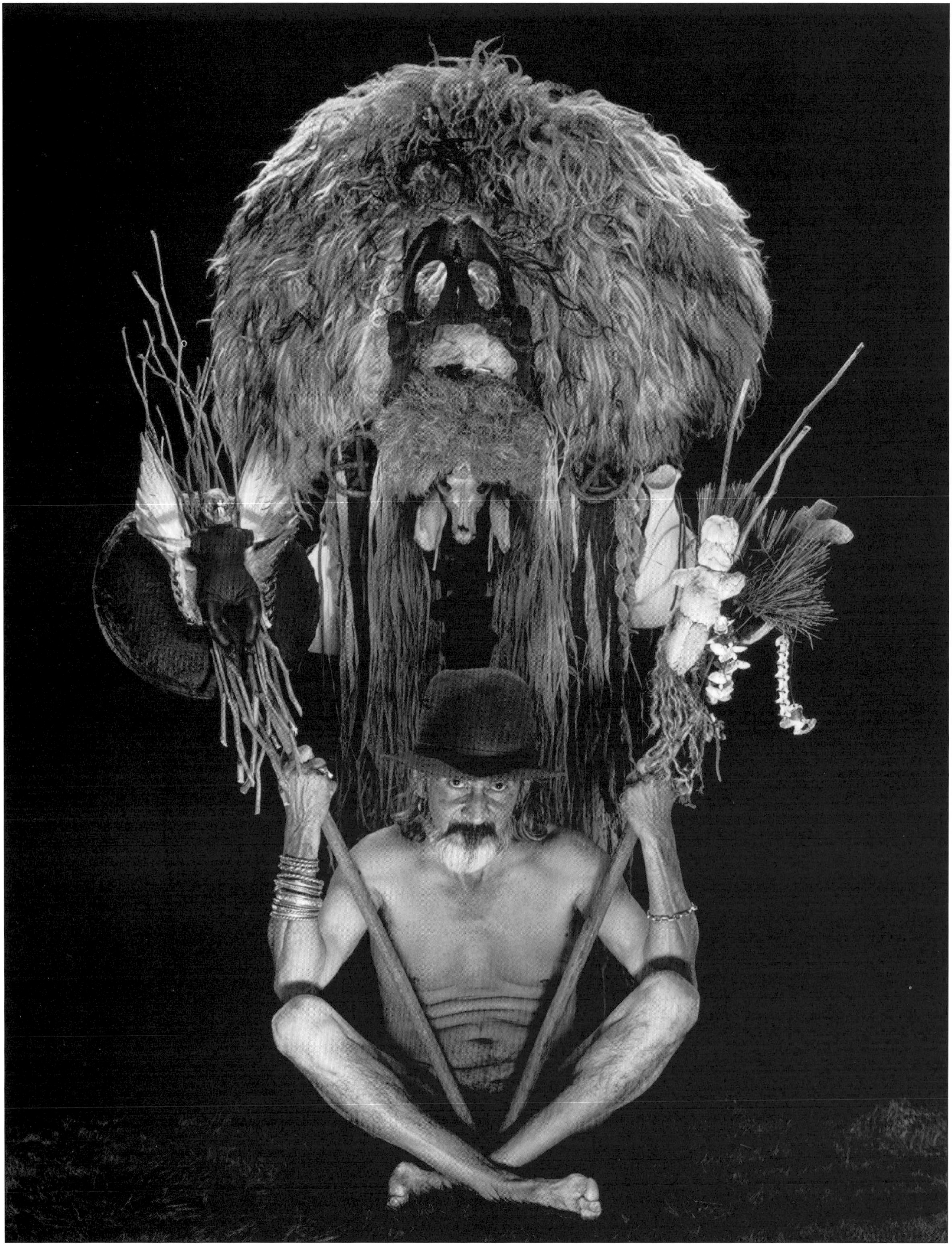

Model

This model, named Atocha, is an artist and a nudist who creates art that deals with death, sex and transformation. I saw his work during an exhibition at which my work was also displayed. I thought his art was amazing, but I also felt his features had really great character. He was just someone I knew I wanted to photograph. Therefore, we arranged a session and, in exchange for a model release, I shot photos which he could use for his own publicity.

Composition

The composition of this image is strongly symmetrical. When I went to visit him at his home to discuss the shoot, I saw more of his art and was able to select these three art pieces with which to shoot him. Since he is a nudist, he was naturally photographed nude, but as he does wear a hat, this was left on.

Lighting

The lighting scheme for this image had to illuminate both the art and the man. The artist is lit with bottom light, placed in front of him at a low angle. A light behind him illuminates the man and his work, preventing his body from casting a shadow on the art. A spot was placed above the artwork and brings out the dark pelvic bone in the center of the top piece. Skimmers were placed to either side of the subject and a fill light was used above the lens.

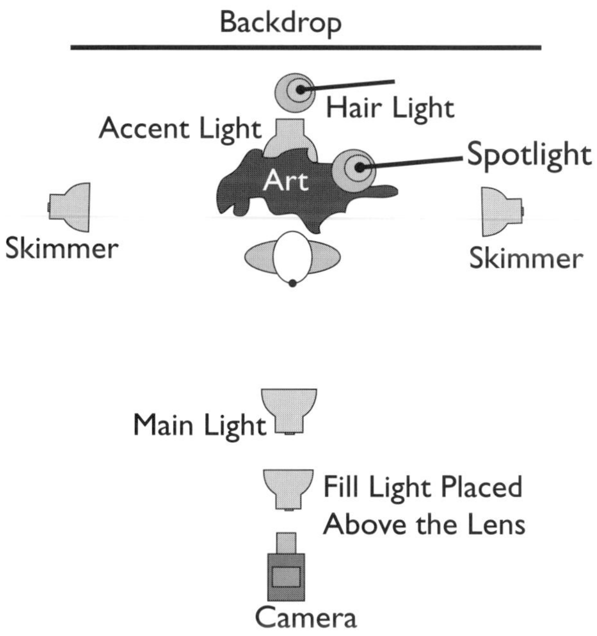

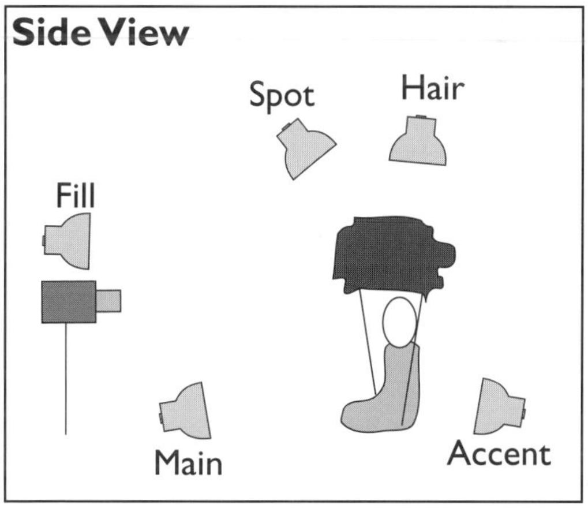

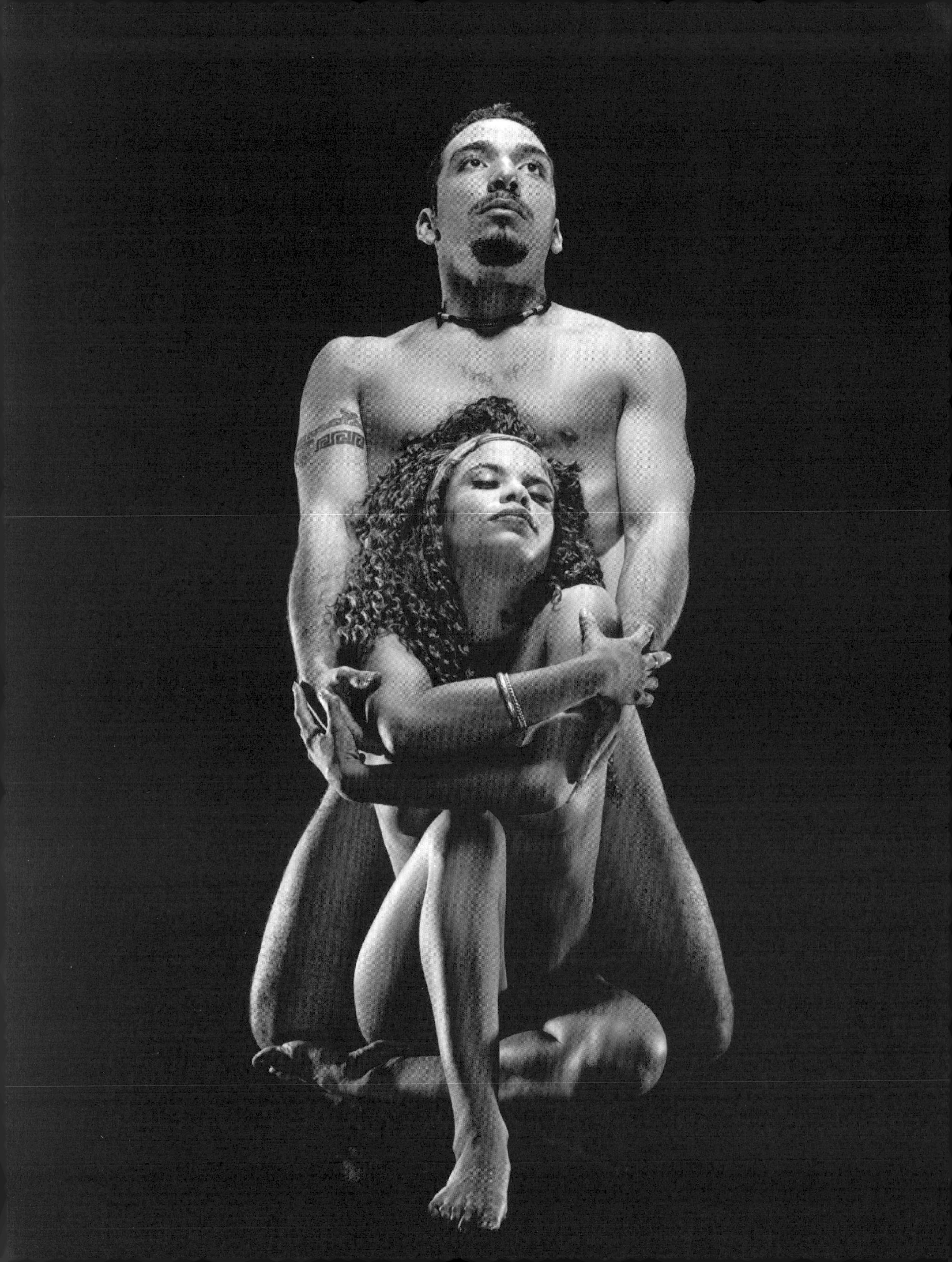

Models

The woman in this image is a model I work with frequently. I generally make it policy not to allow spouses in the room while shooting. I find it makes the atmosphere a little uncomfortable, and that the model may look to his/her spouse for approval or cues, instead of staying focused on what I'm trying to get him/her to do.

However, since I knew both halves of this couple, I invited the man to the shoot, and eventually asked him to pose in some of the photographs. The result was a few really good images.

Drama

To add to the drama of the piece, I concentrated on lighting on the top halves of the couple's bodies. On the lower part, the lines on the edges are retained but there is no detail. I love high impact, high drama, strong poses like this. They are what I like to look at, and what I like to create.

Lighting

The main light was positioned to the camera right, almost above and a little in front of the subjects. A hair light was added above the couple and skimmers were placed to either side of them. A fill light was used close to the lens.

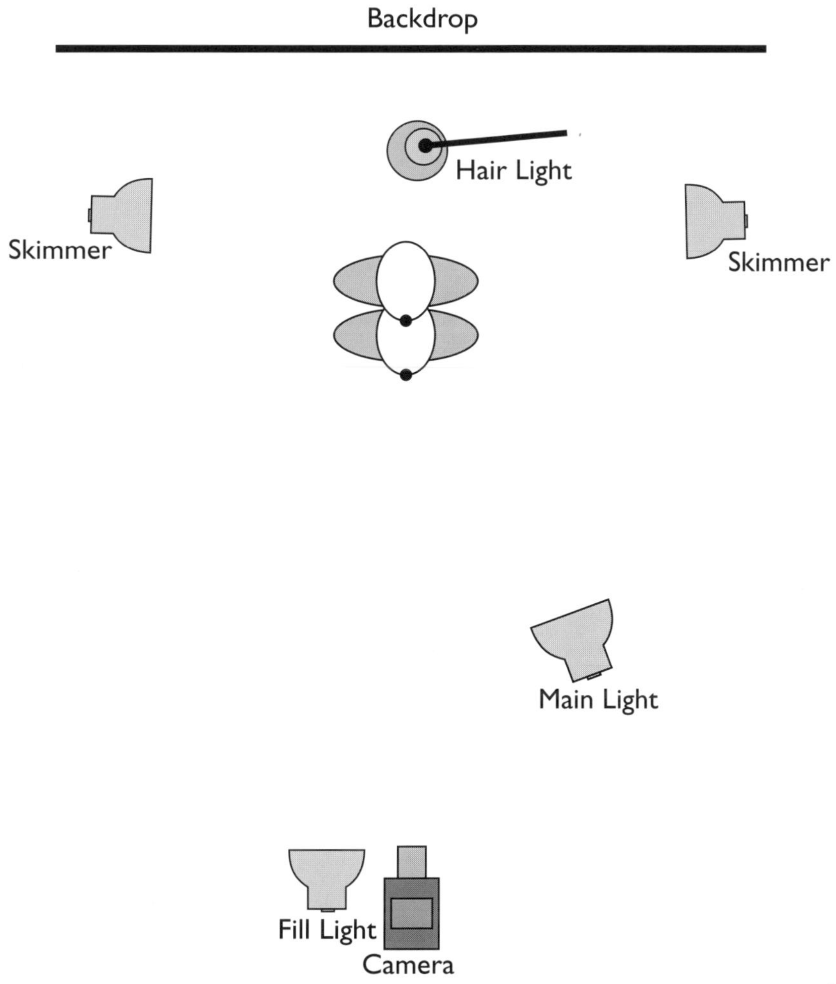

On Location

I went to González's studio for a calendar shoot, taking with me all of the equipment I could conveniently pack (since I had no idea what I was walking into). At the studio, I looked around to get a good sense of his work, who he is, and what he does.

Composition

After selecting the works that would appear in the photo, I arranged the line of the paintings so that they all pointed in toward his face. During preparation for the shoot, the artist also showed me a painting he was doing. I noticed some interesting distortion of perspective in the piece; this turned out to be based on a distorted photograph. Therefore, I decided to mimic this distortion in my photograph of González. A wide-angle lens was used to distort his leg and draw the viewer's eye from the right-hand corner to the center of the piece.

Lighting

A skimmer was placed behind the model to his right, and a main light was positioned above the model (to his left) to illuminate his face. A fill light was used on the lens axis. Finally, a light placed behind the large painting shines on the smaller painting on the wall behind the artist.

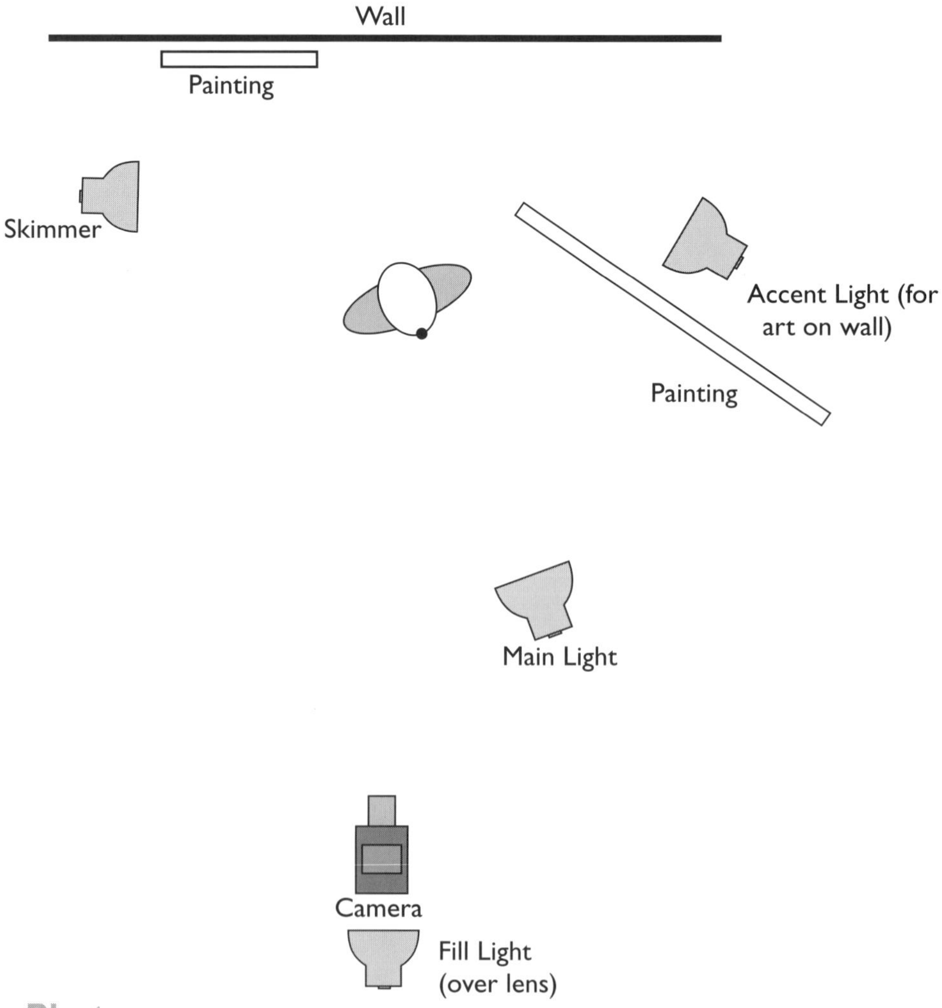

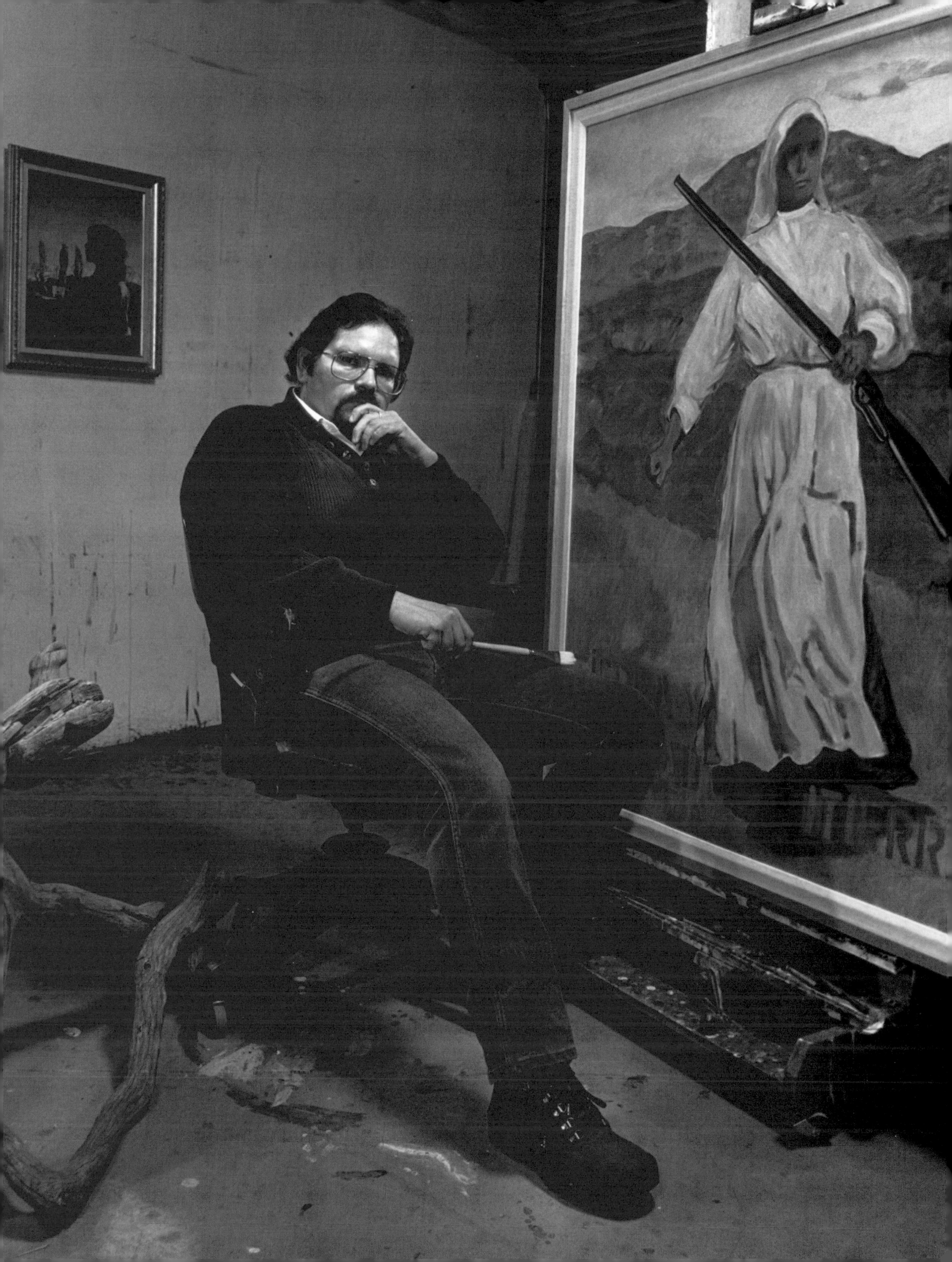

Rey Lujan Gaytán

Model

Rey Lujan Gaytán is a very talented artist with a great look who came to me for a publicity shot.

Composition

We decided not to go with a traditional approach, but instead to use a strong profile shot. When Gaytán spotted the bandolier in my studio, it struck his fancy, so we loaded it with his brushes. Above all, the image and its composition reflect the artist's personality: playful, comfortable, and not at all reserved!

Lighting

The lighting for this photograph was tricky since the model was wearing so much black, and because careful attention had to be paid in order to light the brushes (also mostly black) in his bandolier. We tried a few different poses, then fine positioned the lights for this shot.

A main light was placed almost in front of the model, but just slightly toward the background. Skimmers were used to either side of the subject. A hair light, and a fill light on the camera lens axis were also used.

The model's left hand picks up some nice specular highlights, the result of very careful positioning. Light also catches on the shiny surface on the brushes.

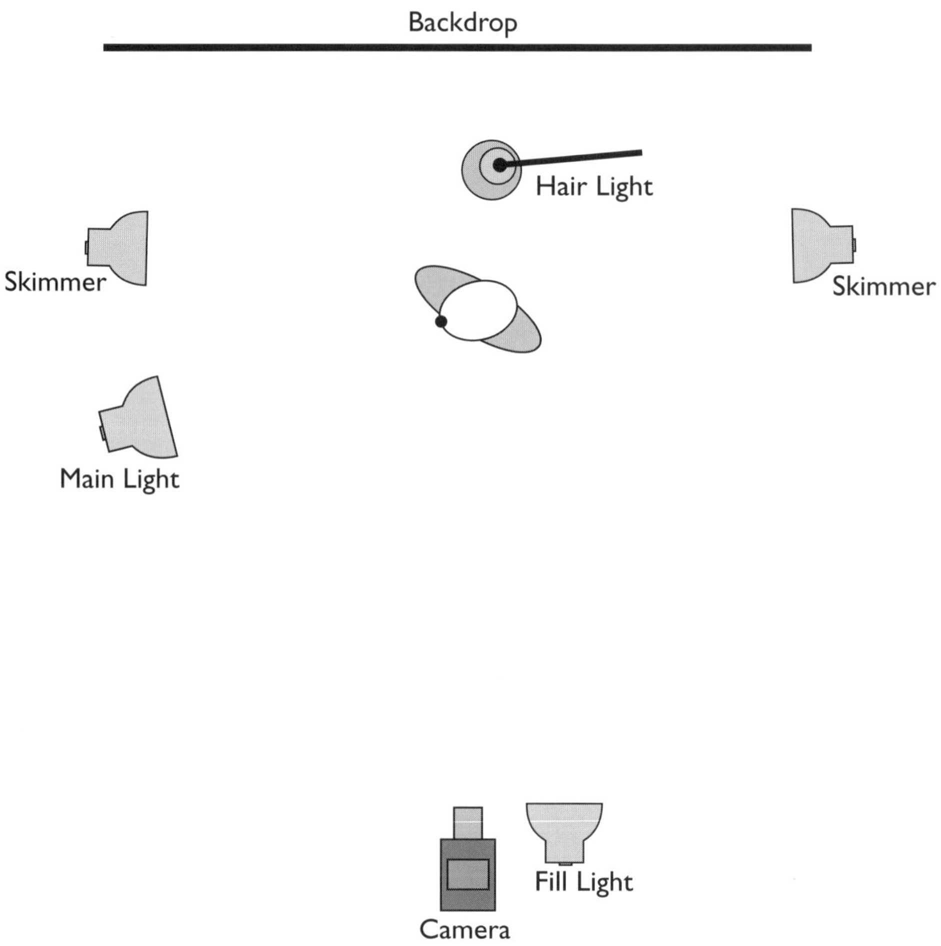

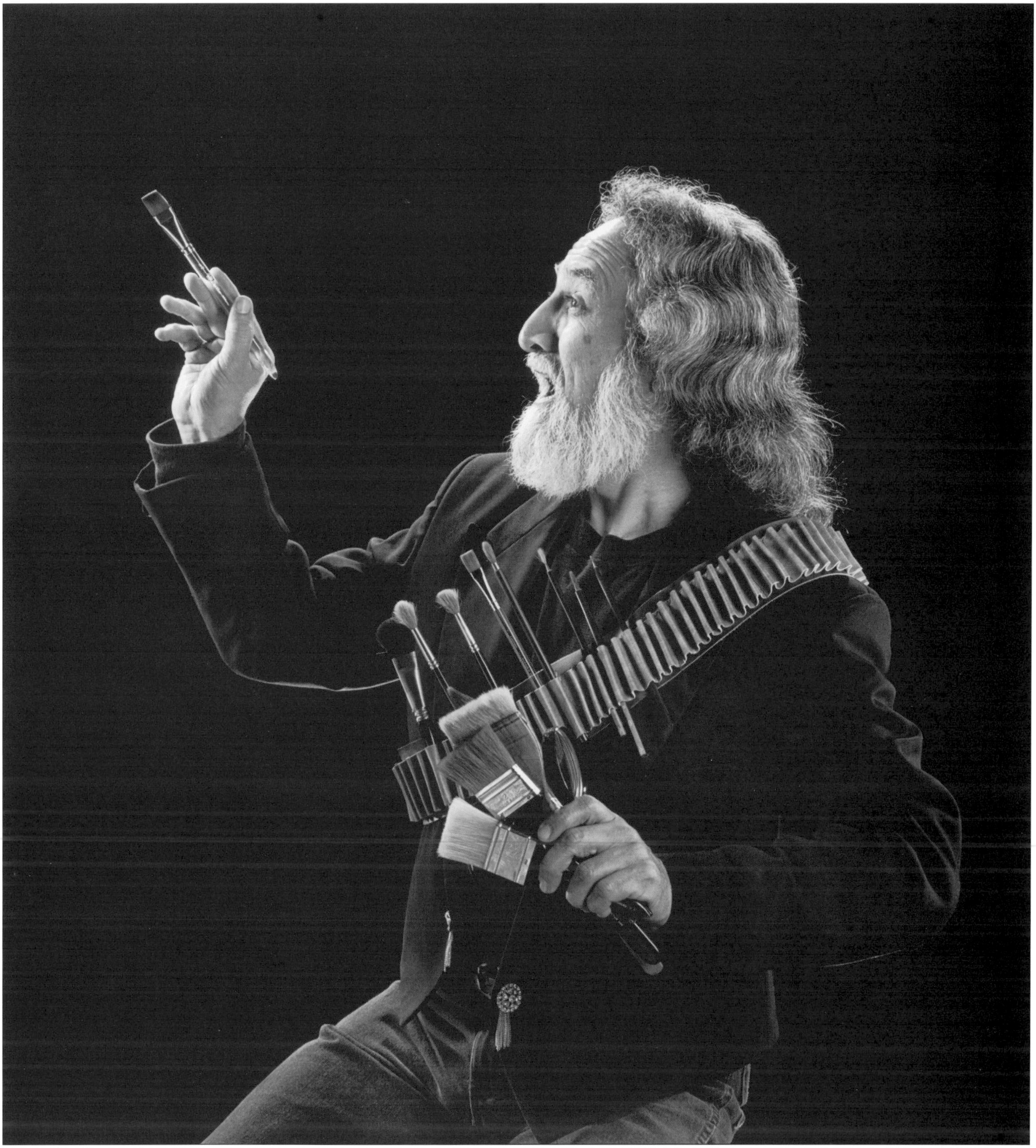

Micky Cruz

Model

Micky Cruz is a composer, musician and bandleader whose publicity I have been doing for years. This image was shot for a CD cover.

Clothing

Since he had no concept in mind, I asked him to bring several outfits with him to the studio. The rule of thumb is: better to bring clothes you don't end up using, than to realize you don't have something you want!

Shooting

The CD cover was to run in color and I also wanted to shoot some black and white. This is an instance in which having a camera with interchangeable film backs really simplifies my job.

Lighting

To create the dramatic look of this photo, one skimmer was used to the right and behind the subject. The use of a low power fill light left the shadows on the model's face quite dark. The main light was placed at a 45° angle to the model's right to create a Rembrandt lighting pattern, dividing the face and giving his features good shape and depth. A hair light completed the set-up.

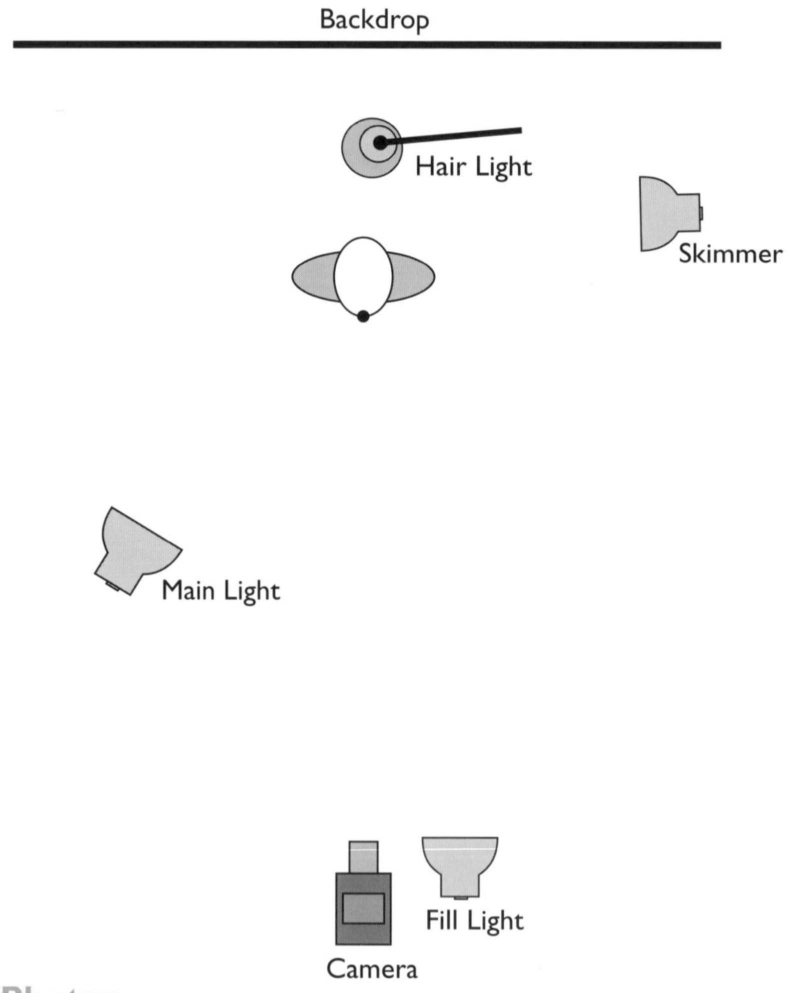

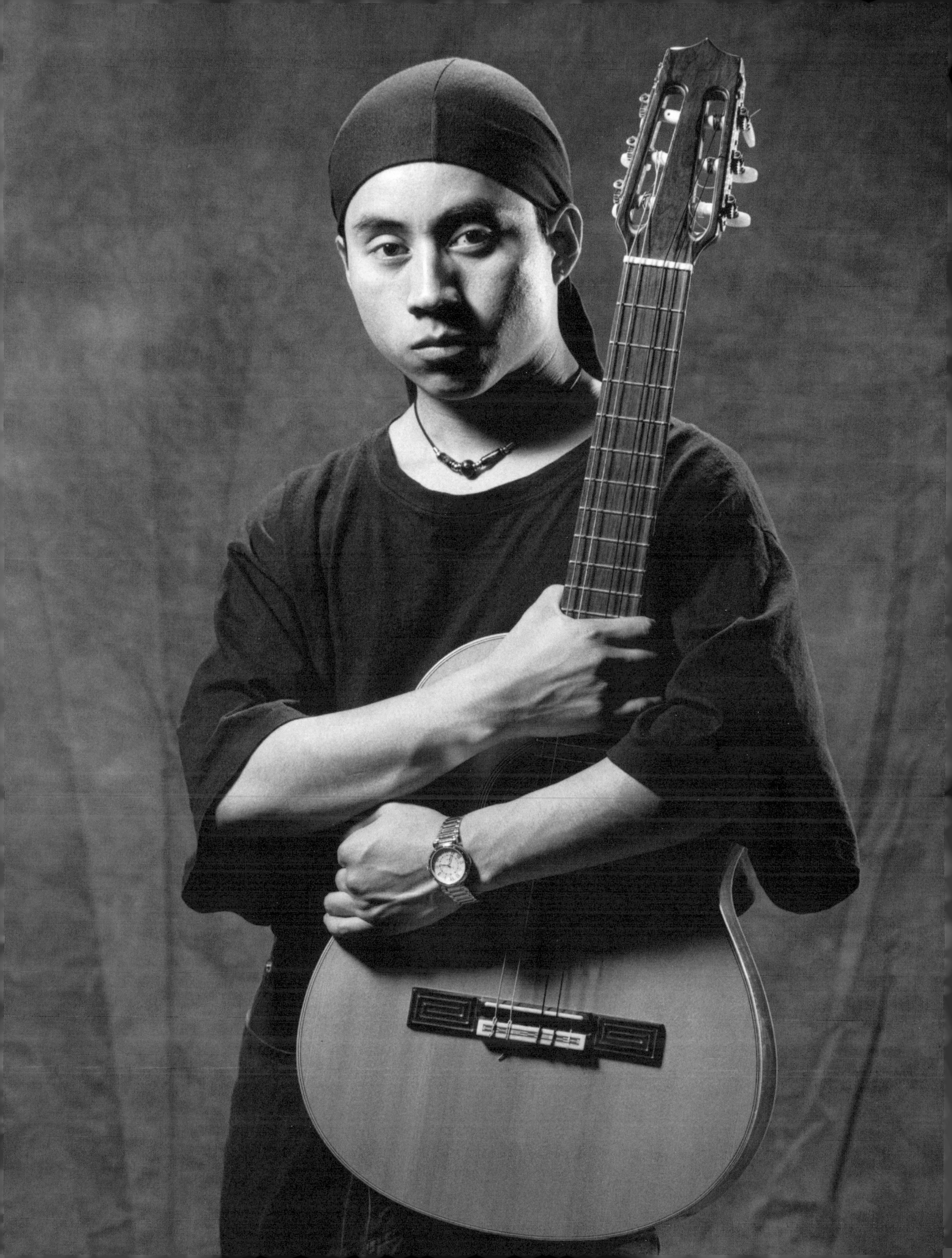

Artists and Their Work

When you see photos of artists or musicians in this book, they are almost always depicted with their instruments or art. Shooting an artist with his work and in his environment tells something about his personality that goes beyond the face. Rick Maisel, an escape artist here depicted in his shackles, handcuffs, and chains, is no exception.

I met this interesting man when *New Mexico Magazine* had me shoot color chromes for a story on him. Later, he came back to me for promotional shots. Although they look good in color, the "jewelry" of his trade was especially well suited to black and white photography.

Lighting

The main light was positioned almost directly above and a little behind the model's head. It's a dramatic effect which compliments the pose – both of which seem to say "I want to be free!" Two skimmers were also positioned to either side of the subject, and a fill light was used on the lens axis.

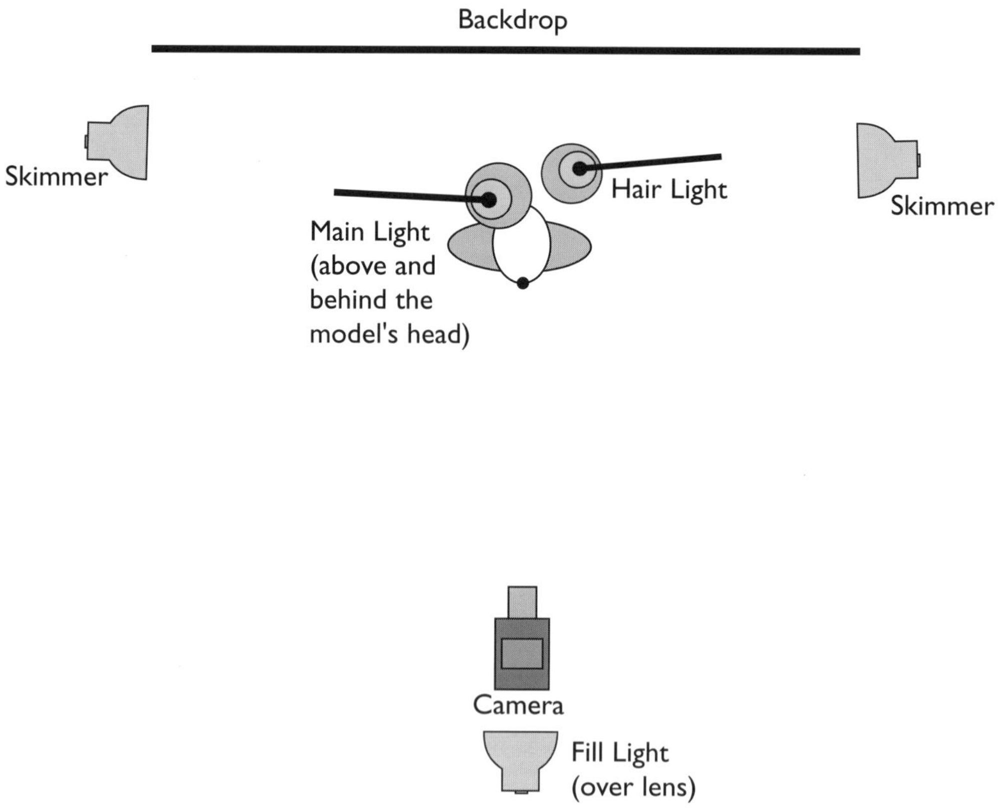

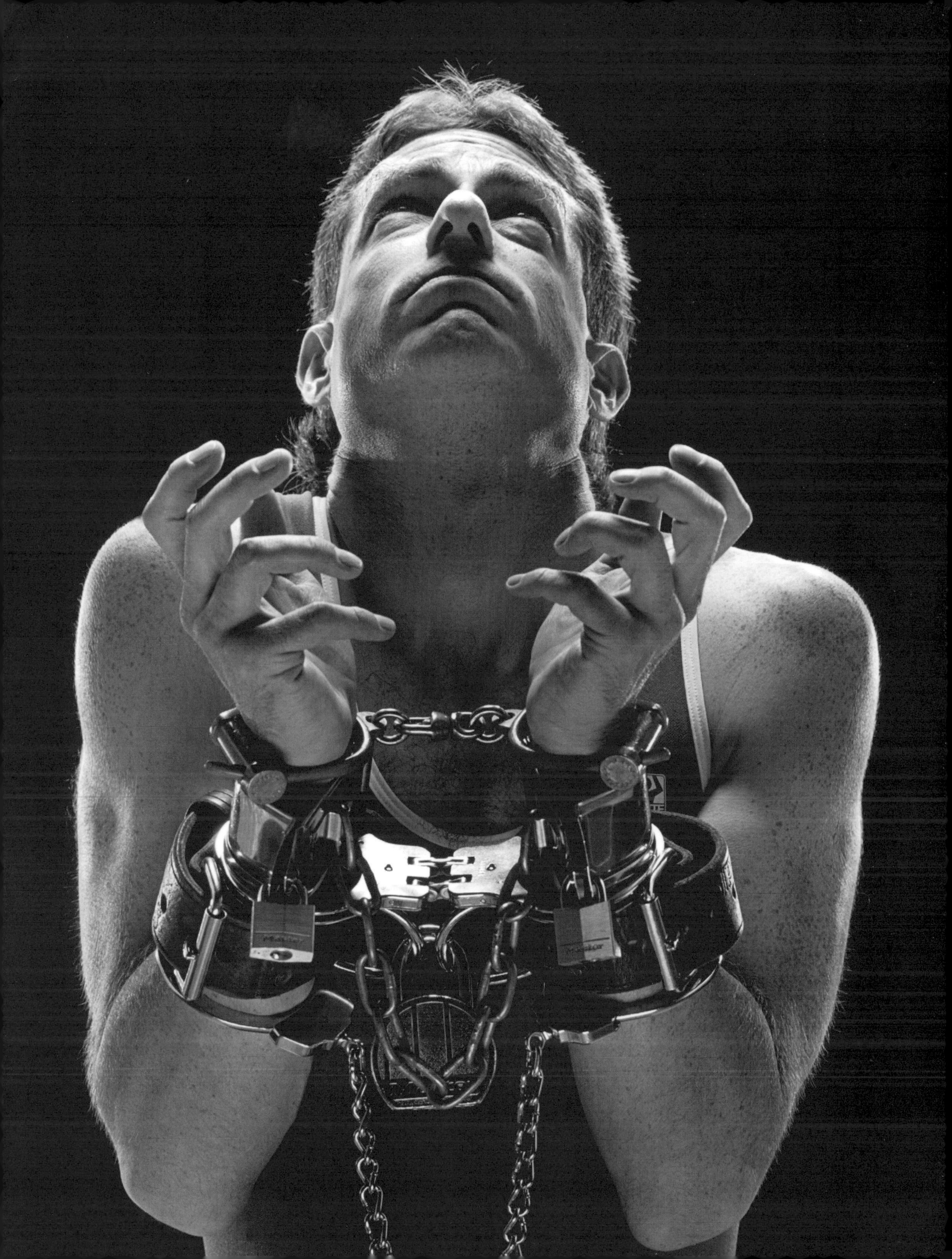

Model

This model, a well known Flamenco dancer who also teaches dance, was photographed for a calendar produced by the Hispanic Cultural Foundation. A major benefit of shooting artists is that they are hardly ever self-conscious and don't hesitate when you ask them to do something. They share a common goal with the photographer: the creation of art.

Composition

I had planned out the idea for this image well in advance, and had her bring her costume to the studio. I also arranged for an actor friend of mine to play the part of the guitarist. The guitarist an important element in the composition; the eye starts here, moves up the neck of the guitar and toward the dancer and onto her face and raised arm (positioned at a similar angle). This movement of the eye parallels the twirl of the dancer, movement captured in the uplift of her skirt.

Lighting

The main light was placed perpendicular to the dancer's face, just out of view of the camera. Two skimmers were placed on either side of the scene. A fill light was used close to the lens axis, casting the subject's shadow on the background and giving the background mixed tonalities. Very little light was allowed to fall on the guitarist since, for the purpose of this shot, he is essentially a prop.

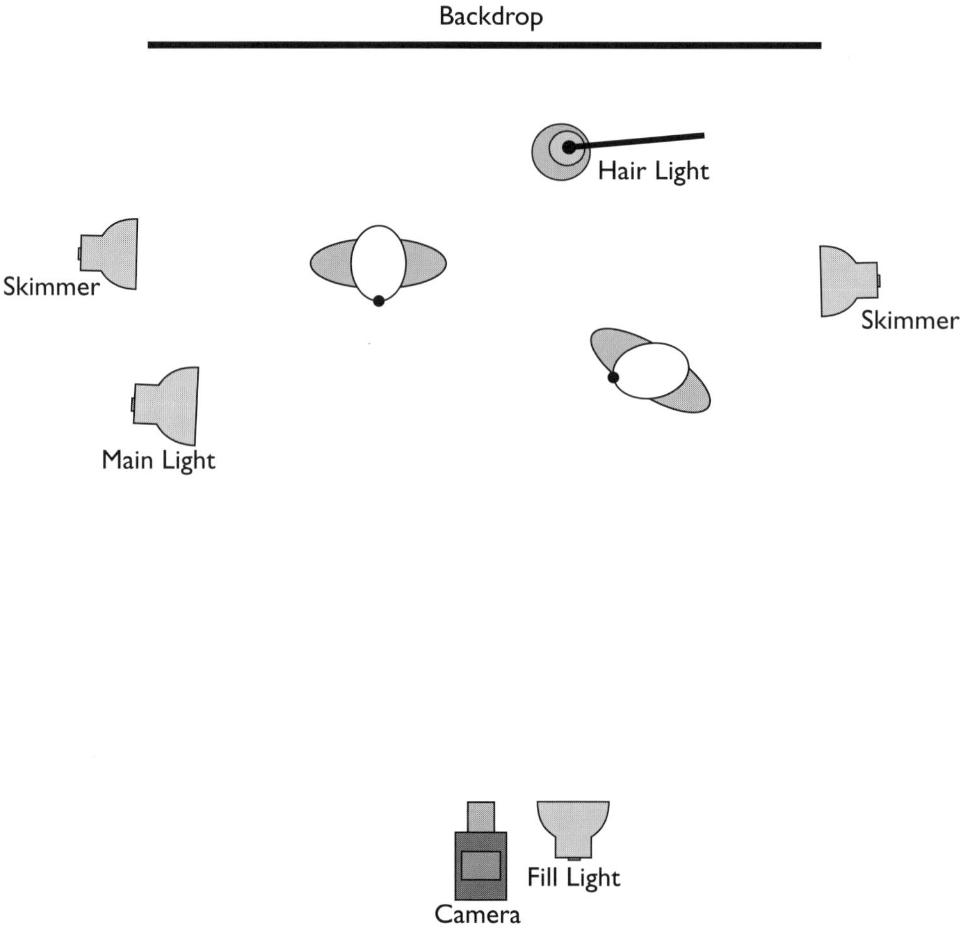

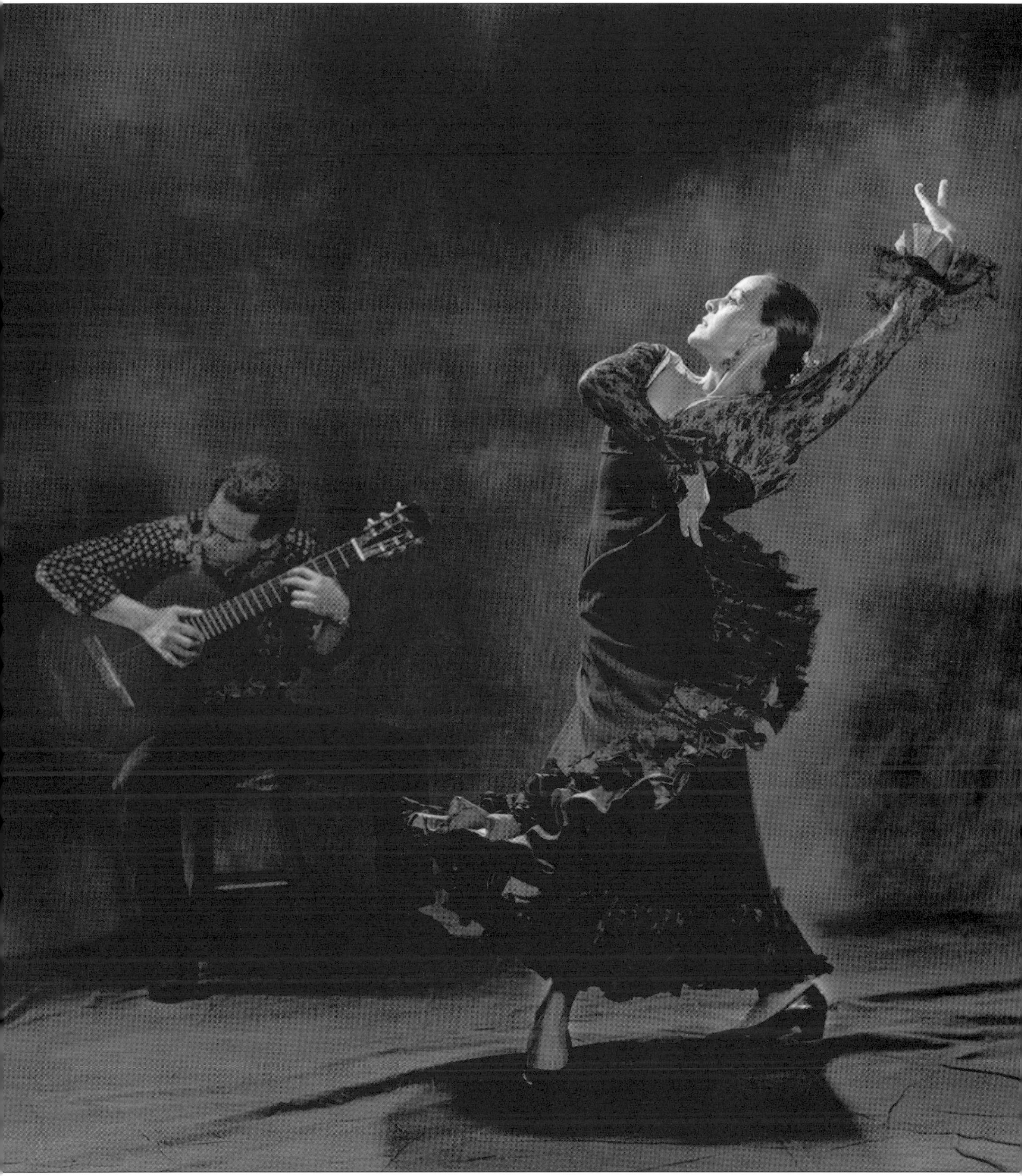

The Shoot

I had originally been scheduled to shoot promotional pictures for a guitarist, but when he was unable to make it, I figured there was no sense in letting a good set-up go to waste! I put on my suit (purposely adding the bright white socks to throw white into the tonal arrangement), and used the pose for myself that I had had in mind for him. Of course, instead of a guitar, I shot myself with a camera.

Self Portraiture

When shooting a self portrait I generally set everything up and have a friend click the shutter. Usually it take a few tries to get things right since I tend to be preoccupied with all the technical considerations and have to "guess" what things look like through the camera.

I wasn't originally crazy about the idea of self-portraiture, feeling like I belong behind the camera and not wanting to seem conceited. Still, being in front of the camera has been a good experience for a few reasons. First, I accidentally discovered there is a real collector's market for self-portraits, and so I have been able to sell quite a few of these. More importantly, I get a chance to experience what it's like for my models. This gives me a better understanding of how other people feel as subjects. Finally, it gives me a little leverage. After all, I'm not asking models to do anything I wouldn't do myself!

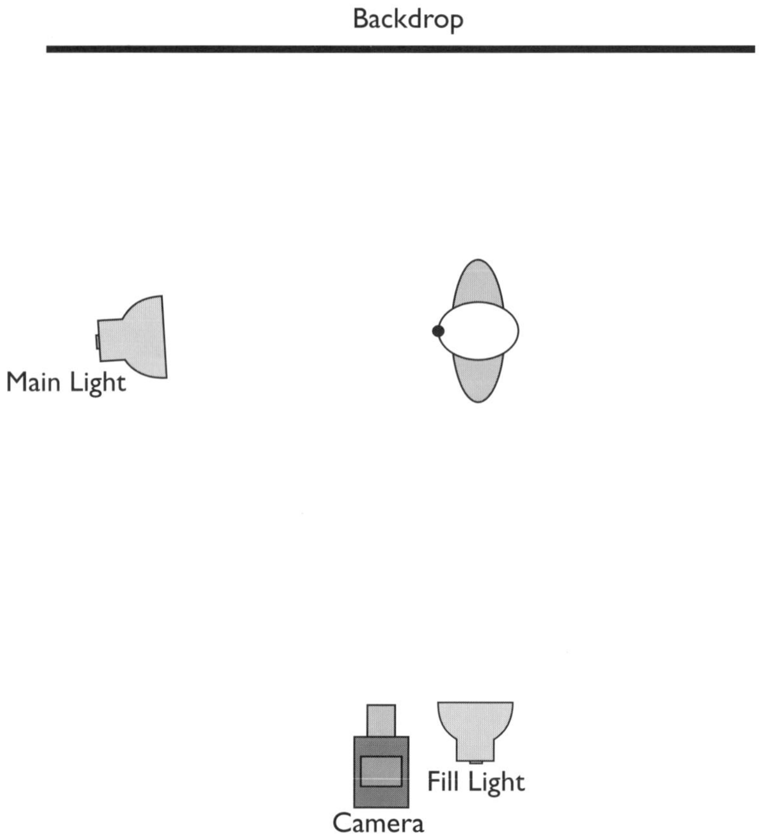

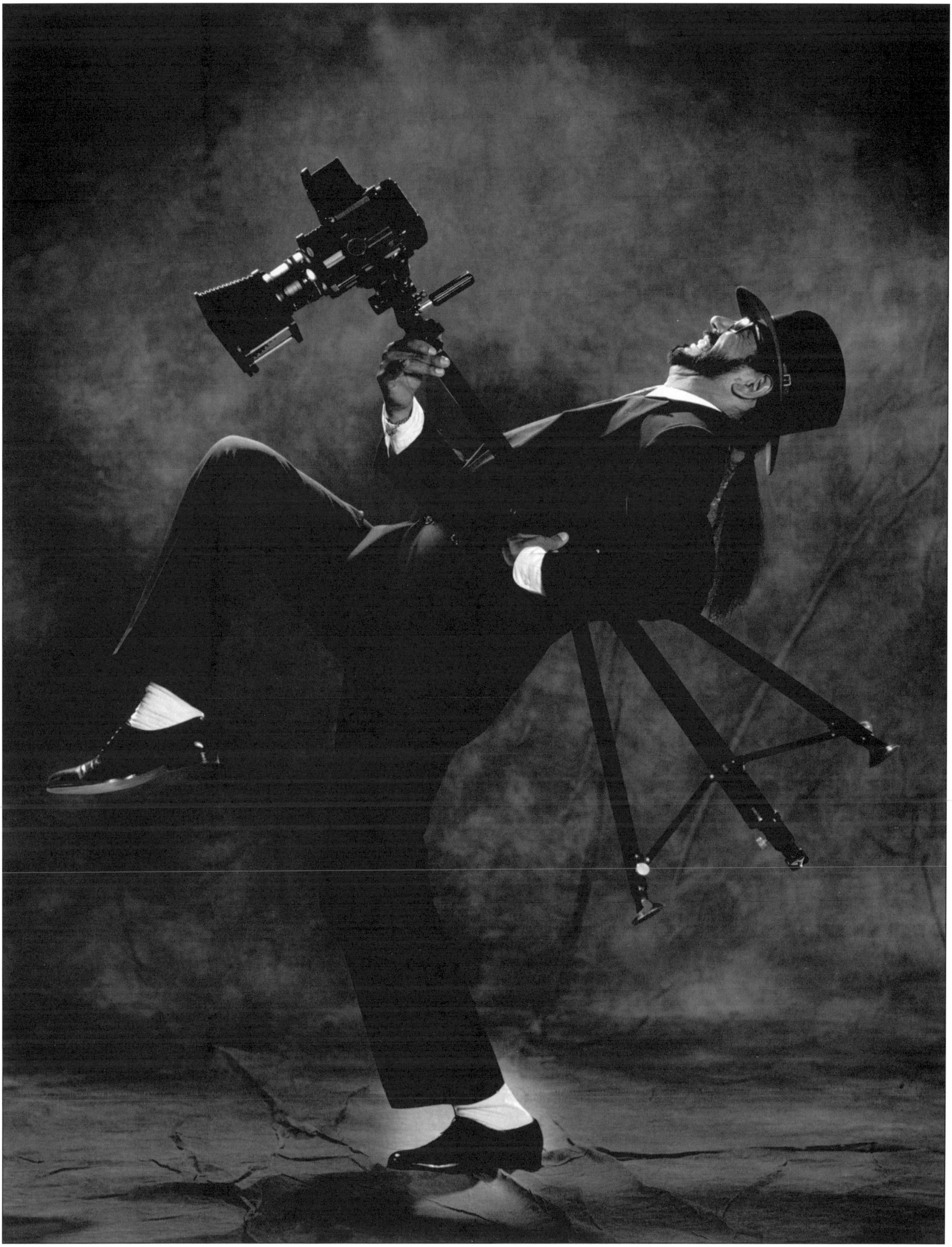

Familia Pimentel

Models

This group image was also shot for a calendar featuring Hispanic artists. The Pimentel family runs a guitar making shop, and manufactures high quality guitars used by many famous performers. This image was shot on location in their shop, an intimate area in which the subjects were placed close together to show family unity. Guitars in various states of completion were used as props.

Lighting

Since we had a small space to work in, light was used to make the photograph more dramatic. Two main lights were placed on either side of the group. A hair light was added above and fill light was added close to the lens axis.

Shooting Groups

Taking pictures of groups is always harder than taking pictures of individuals simply because there is more to consider technically. There is also endless posing – the first person posed has moved by the time the last one has been posed. Therefore, it's almost impossible to get everything posed exactly right; you're better off trying to eliminate the faults than achieving perfection.

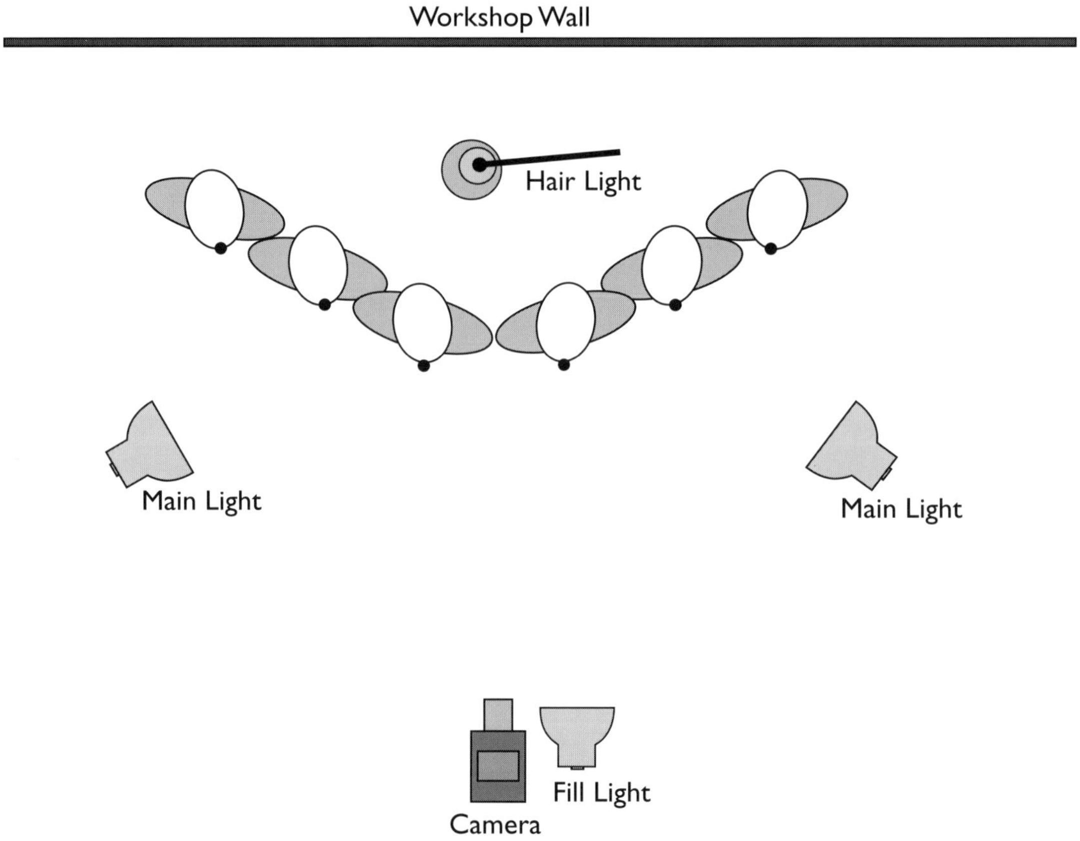

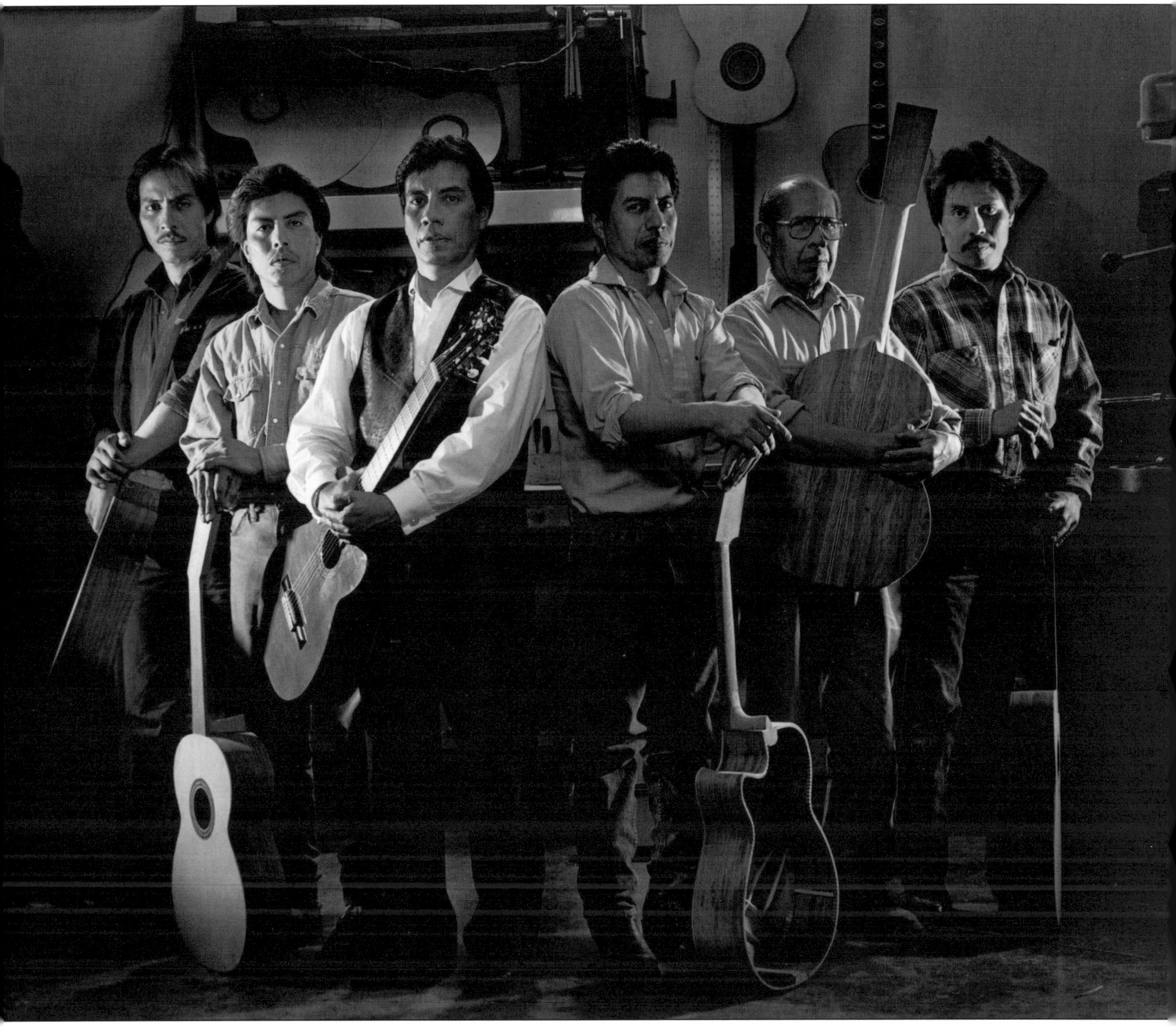

Models

Mezcla is a group of visual artists with whom I exhibit. We present themed exhibitions of painting, visual poetry, photography, etc., all having to do with Chicano (Americans of Mexican origin) culture.

The Shoot

As a former professional musician, one thing I miss most about playing is the jam. Photo sessions like this one, where everybody has a part, come close to capturing that feeling.

This shoot was arranged to take a publicity shot for an exhibition. Everybody brought lots of junk to use for props and we put it all on a table so everyone could grab what they wanted and switch off frequently.

Lighting

Since this was a good sized group, a broad main light was used in front of the subjects and just out of camera view. Two skimmers were used on either side of the group, and a hair light was placed above. Fill light was used near the camera.

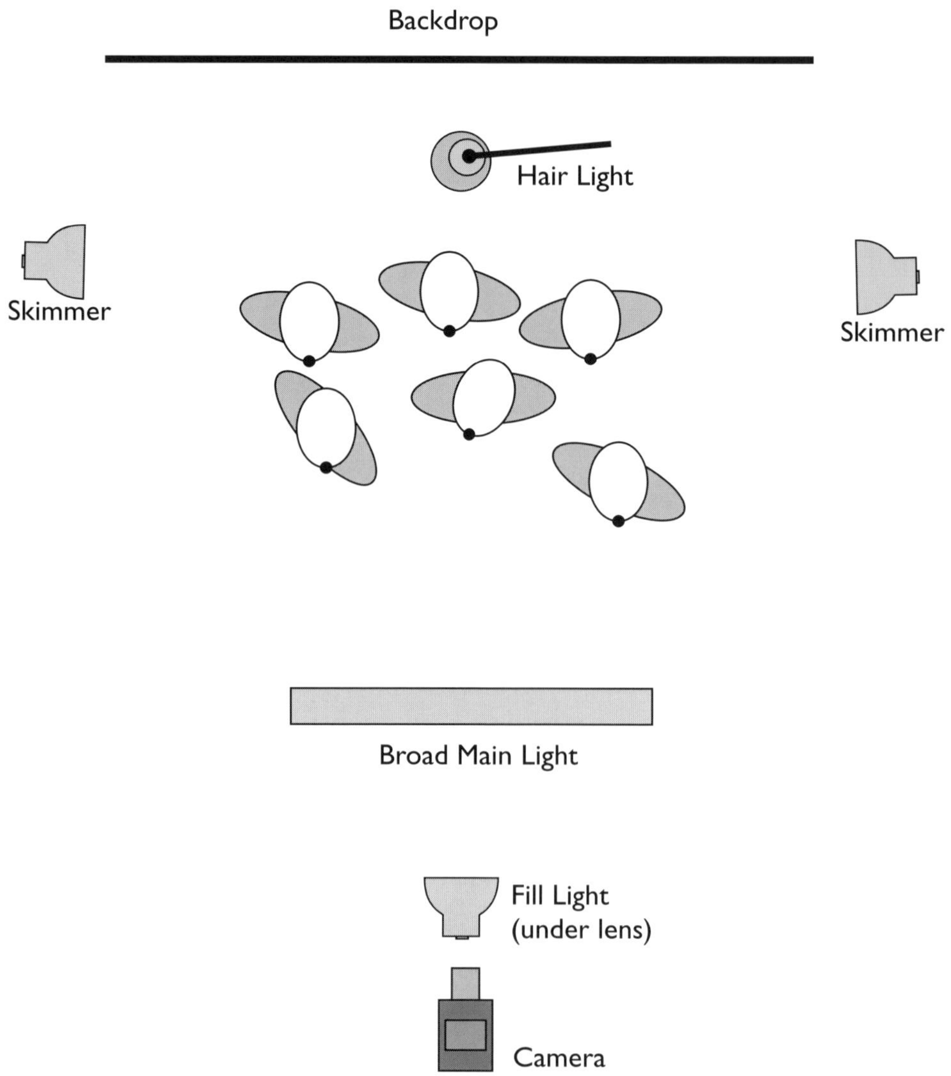

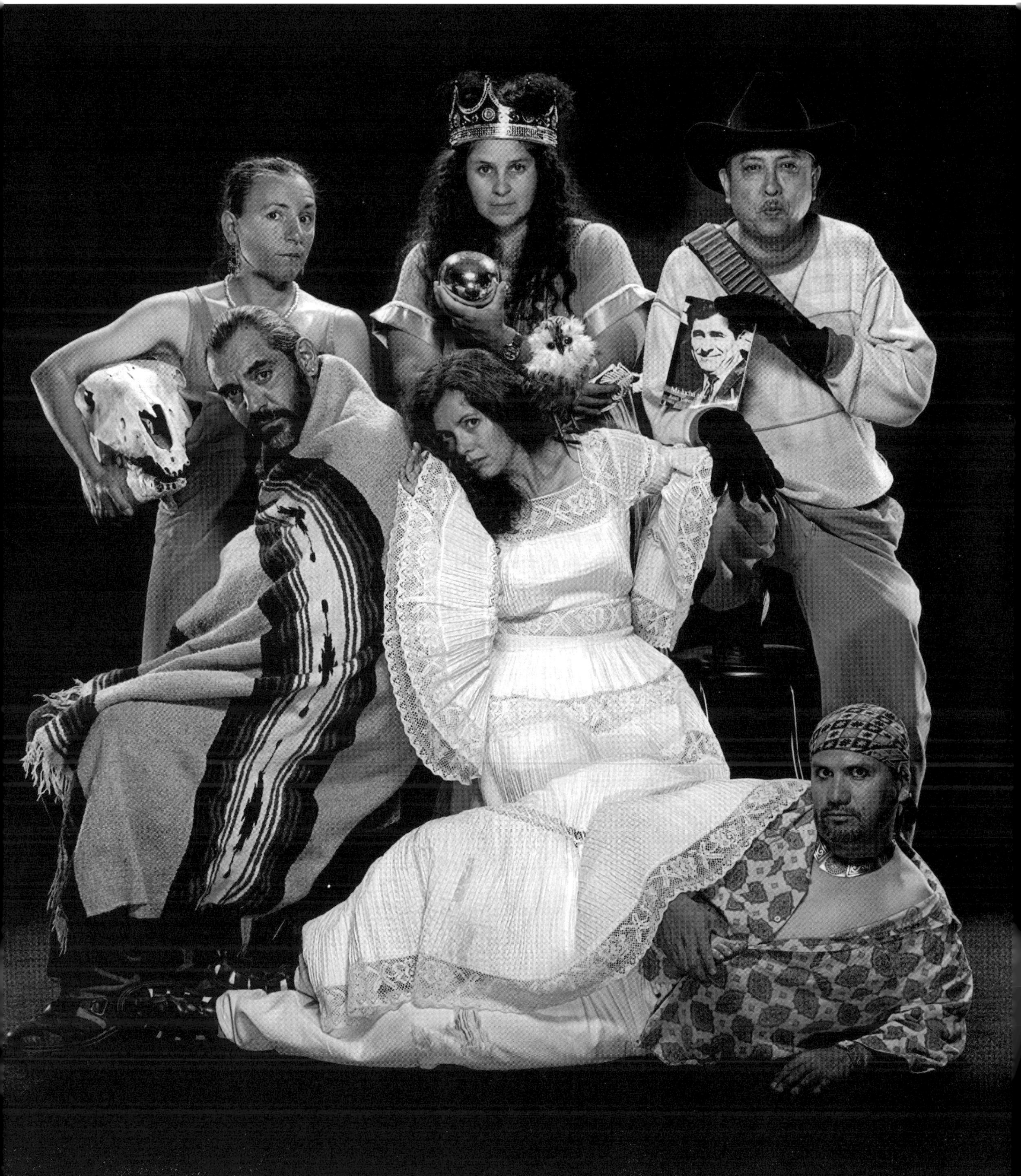

Rey

Inspiration

This is the same model as appears on page 57. The artist had brought with him to the studio a minifying glass which I saw before the shoot. As we got to the end of the session, I kept thinking about the minifying glass, and for the last shot I put it in his hand and positioned it to catch a little face in a big face.

Lighting

Skimmers were used on either side of the subject, but were moved a forward to create specular highlights on the noses and faces. This also helped keep light on the minifying glass and prevent it from shadowing the model's face. The main light was positioned above and to camera left. A hair light and fill light placed next to the lens completed the lighting set-up.

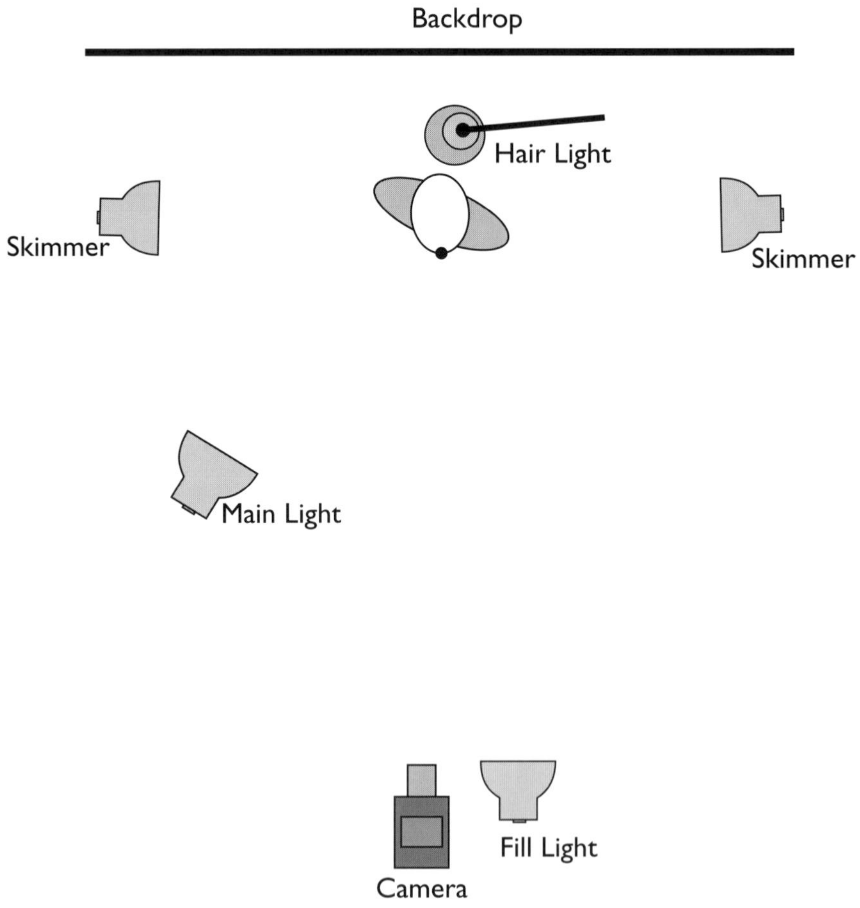

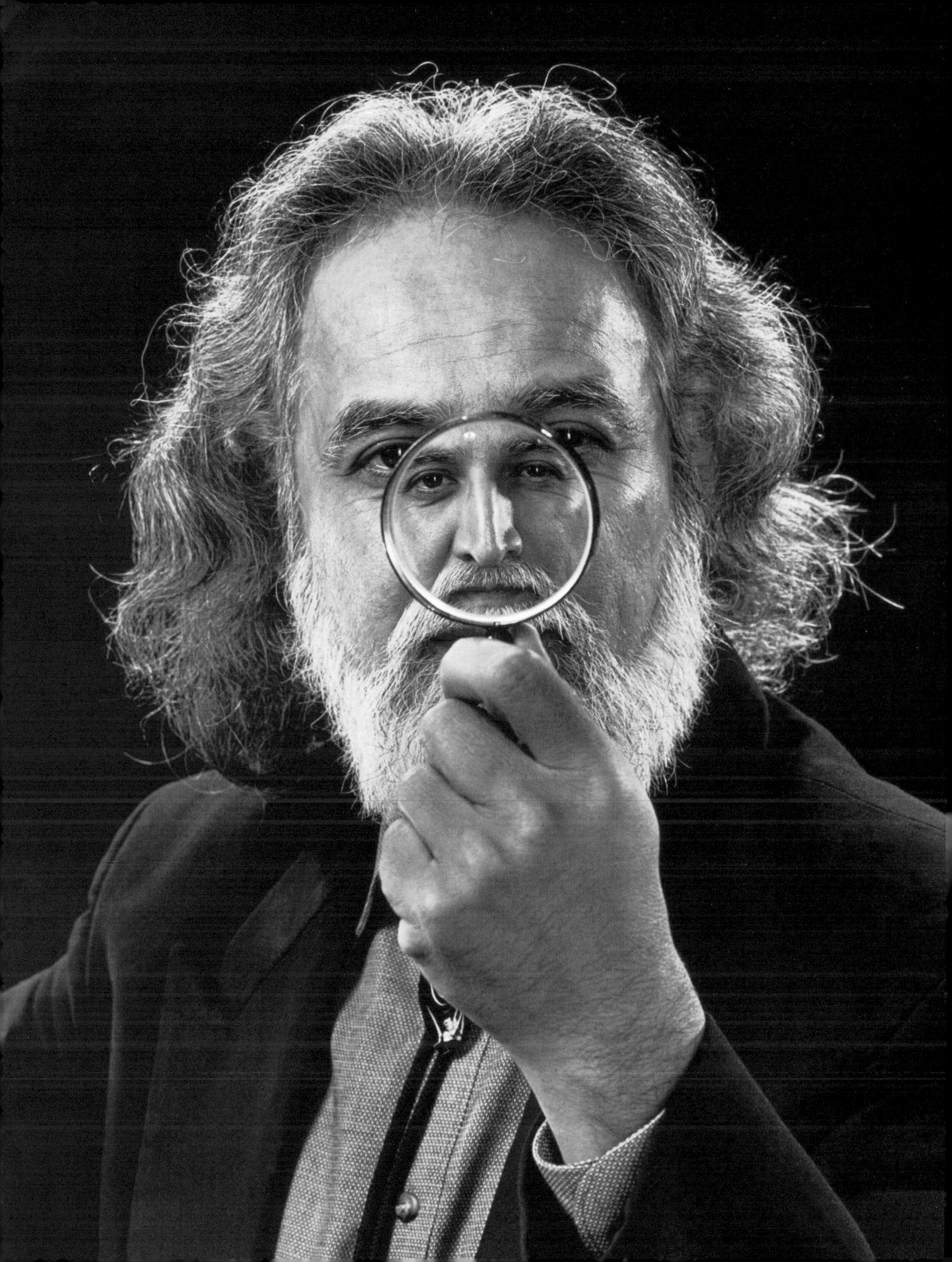

On Location

This image was taken for a museum which was exhibiting Armijo's wood, steel and stone sculpture. I shot it on location, a challenge I love since it forces you to think on your feet. Although photography on location doesn't allow you the same degree of control you can have in the studio, the act of responding to the unknown can produce very interesting photographs.

In this case, I shot the image on location in the artist's studio and had to work with the elements available. I saw this piece of unfinished sculpture and decided to use it in the image. It had to be placed in a vise to display it in the manner seen here.

Lighting

After selecting the art with which to shoot the subject, I placed him in front of it. Because the studio behind him was very cluttered, I used light fall-off to remove all detail from the background of the image.

The main light was placed almost in front of the model's face. Skimmers highlight the back of his shirt, his hair, and the front of his body. A hair light shines on the subject and a reflector also bounces this light onto the artwork. A fill light was added near the camera lens.

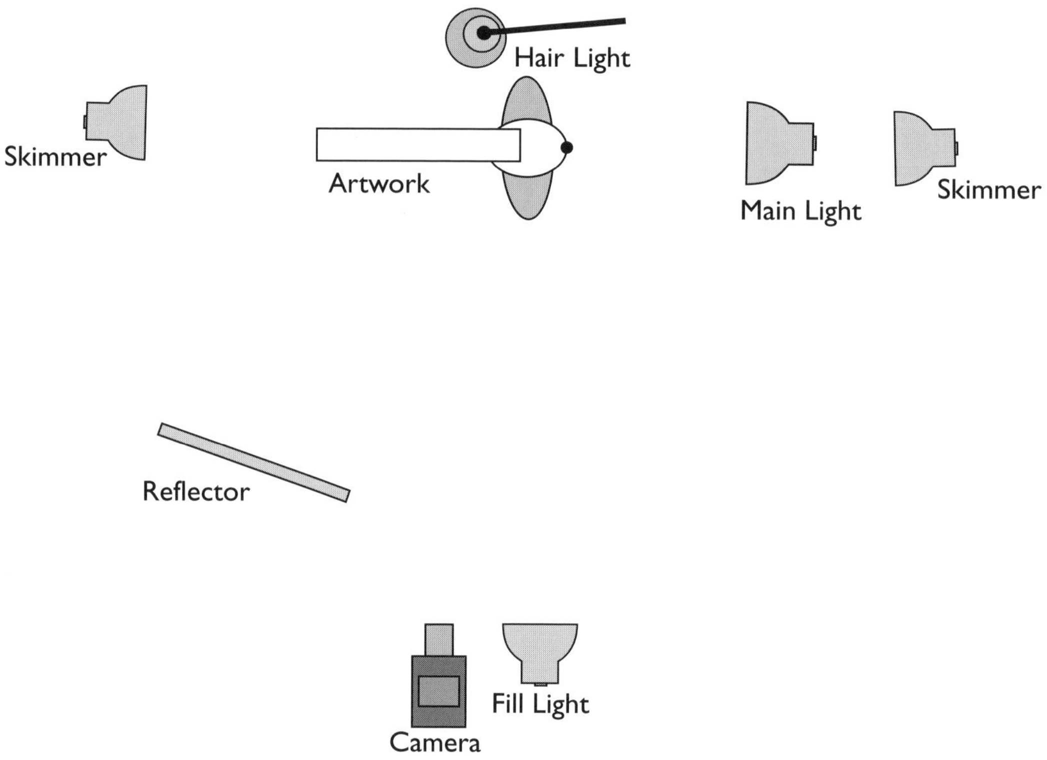

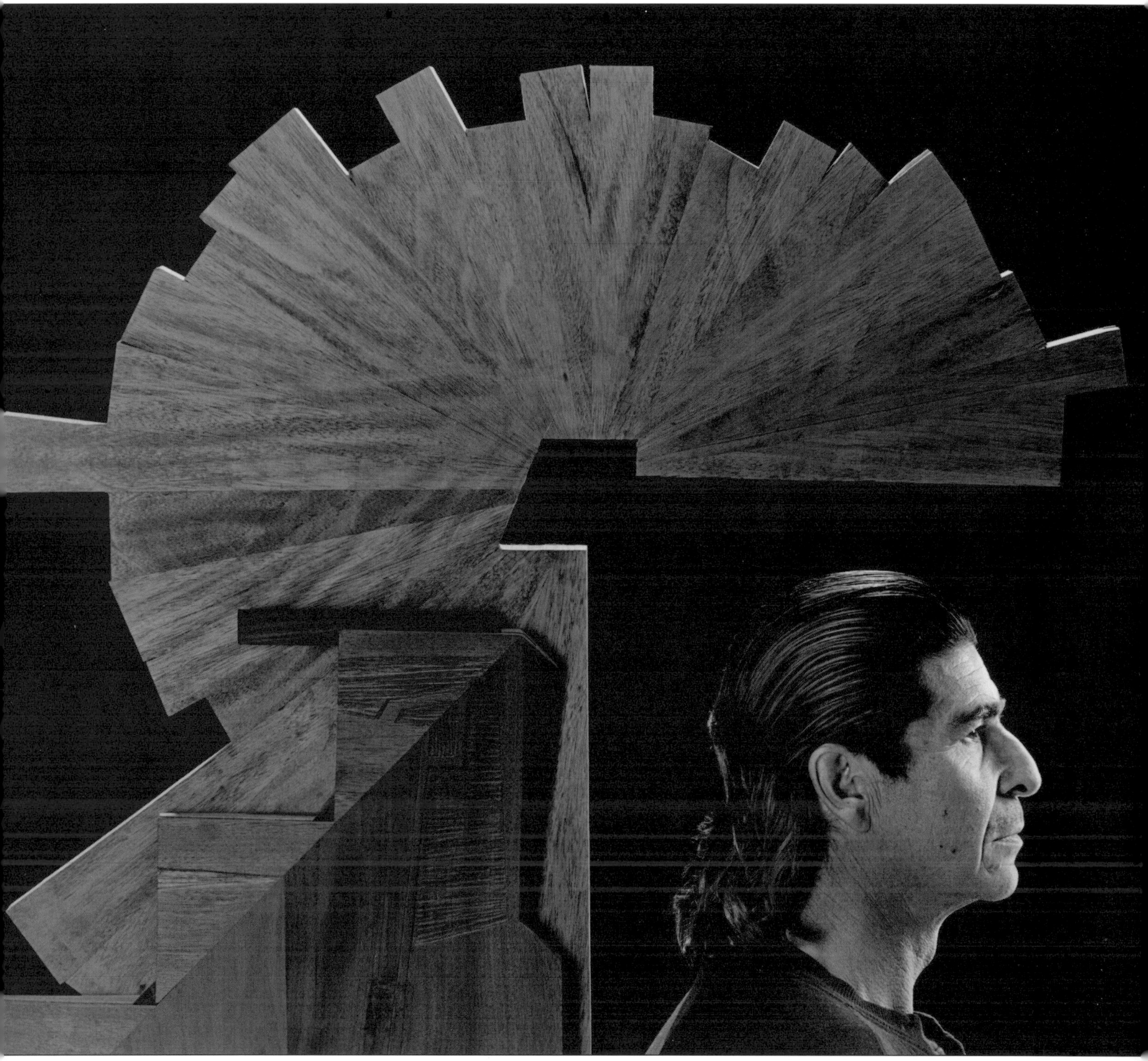

The Shoot

This photograph of artist Luis Jiménez was taken in his studio for the Albuquerque Museum. I used two assistants on this shoot. We would move the art around to set up a nice composition, then call him in periodically from where he was working to shoot a picture. The whole shoot took hours for us, but only a few minutes for the artist!

Lighting

The lighting for this image was especially complex since it involved lighting both the artist and large pieces of his work.

The main light was placed to the left of the model, and a fill light was added at the lens. A strong skimmer was placed high behind the model to his right. Another was placed behind the model, angled up to light the bottom of the horse sculpture. A third skimmer was placed behind the subject and to his left. The plant in the foreground was illuminated by a Morris Mini Slave, placed to light a dark spot. An additional accent light was placed on the camera left to hightlight the edge of the plants. Another accent light hits the sculpture behind the model.

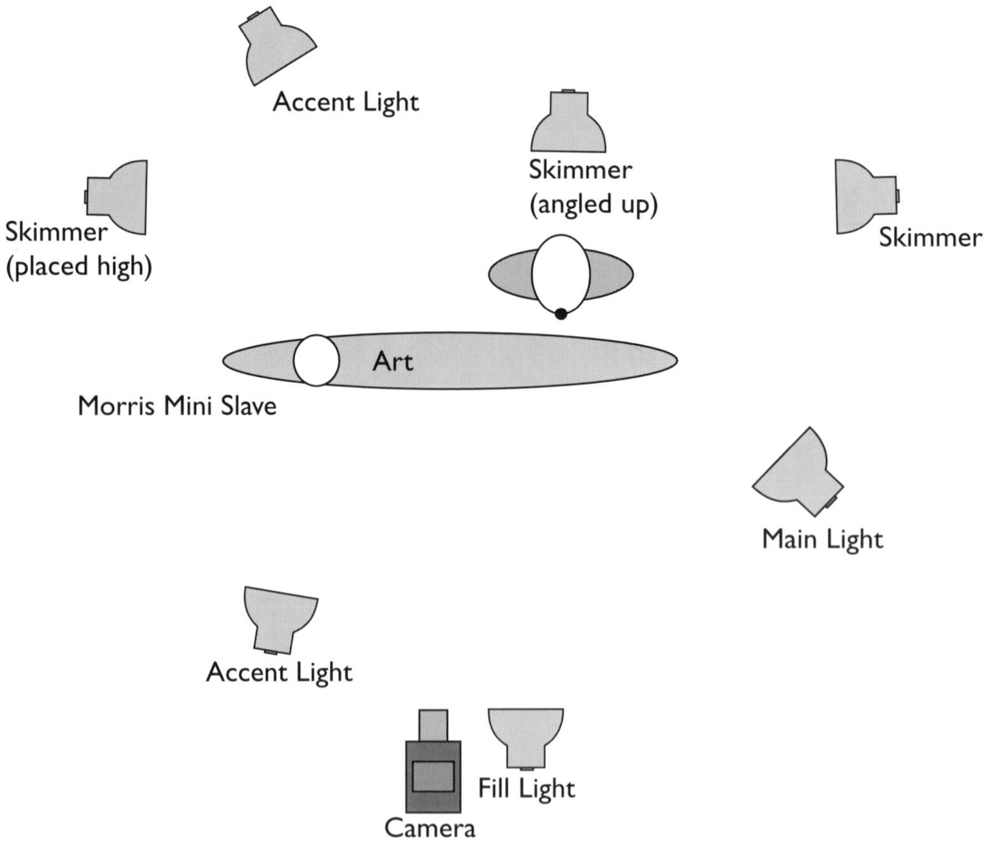

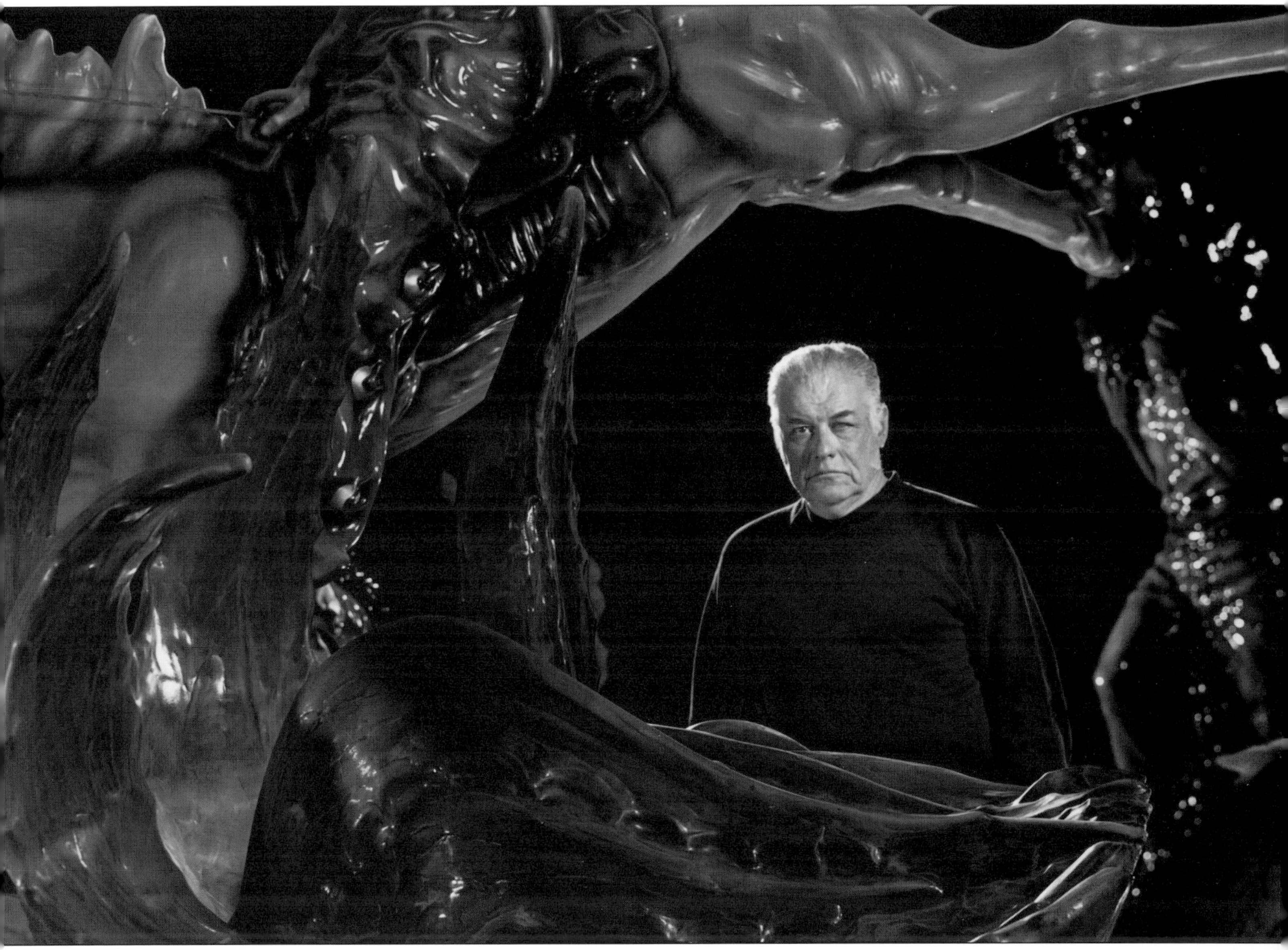

Alia and Candles

Working with Models

This photo was taken during a shoot for an album cover. The girl's mother was the singer in the band with which I was working. The band had wanted a very dramatic image, and when I found out about their love of candles, I incorporated these for a high impact look.

One of my favorite parts of my job is getting to know the people I shoot. I love people (probably one of the reasons I like taking pictures of them), and most importantly, I like listening to their stories and learning who they are. I think this is an important element in creating great photos of them. First, it means that I'm no longer a stranger behind the camera, but a friend. This invariably puts people more at ease. Second, knowing my subjects helps me to capture more of who they are (if that is what's desired in the session). People photography, to me, is more talking to people than shooting them.

Lighting

Since strobe lighting was used, it had to be balanced out with the continuous light from the candles. A 3:1 light ratio was used on the skin, and the shutter was really dragged.

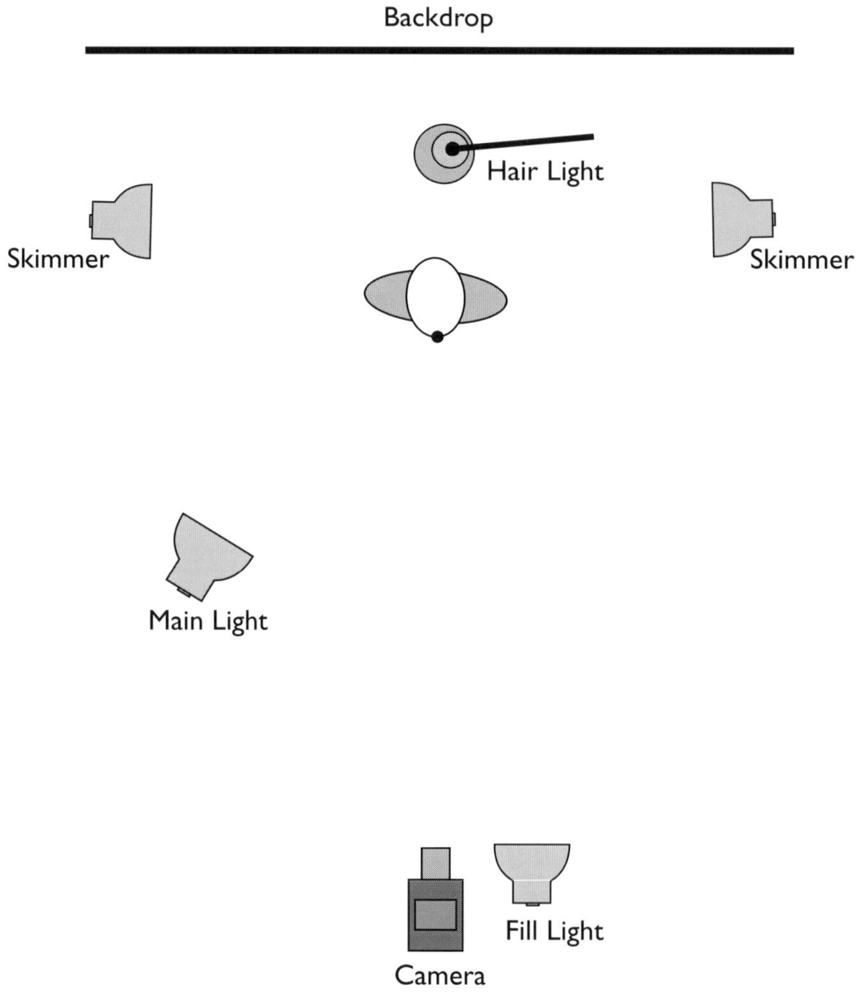

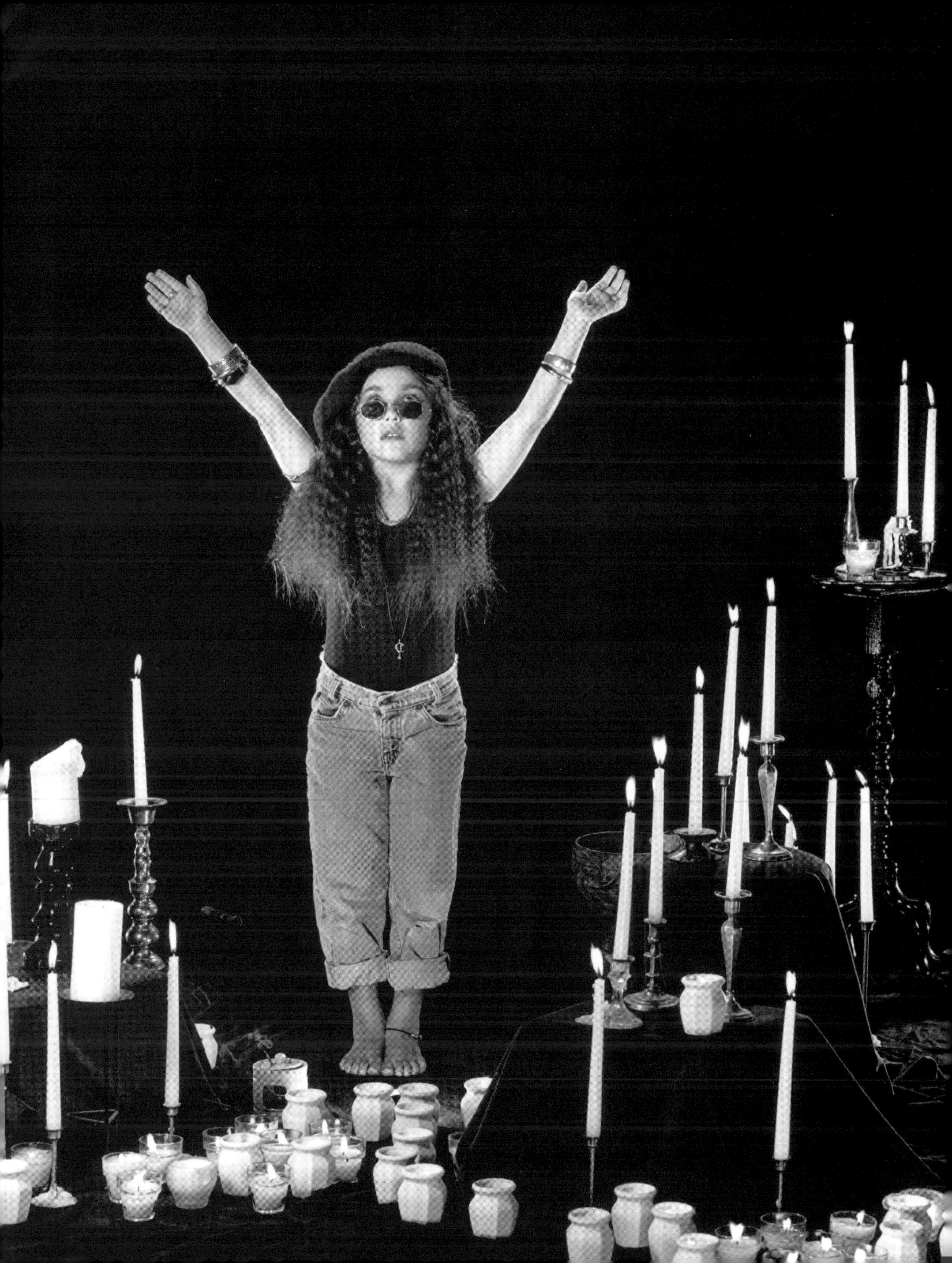

Diane the Magicienne

Model

Diane came to me for publicity shots for lithographs and posters. She's a natural performer (which certainly shows in this photo!), and brought her own supply of tricks to the studio.

Lighting

Two skimmers were placed on either side of the subject. A hair light was used above, and a fill light was placed next to the camera lens. The main light was positioned to the camera left, just above head level. This creates short loop lighting on the subject's face (shadow from nose falls just below the nose).

Hair Light

The hair light should be geared to match the hair color of the subject you are photographing. Blonde hair requires a rather low intensity, medium hair needs slightly stronger light, and dark hair requires the hair light to be quite intense.

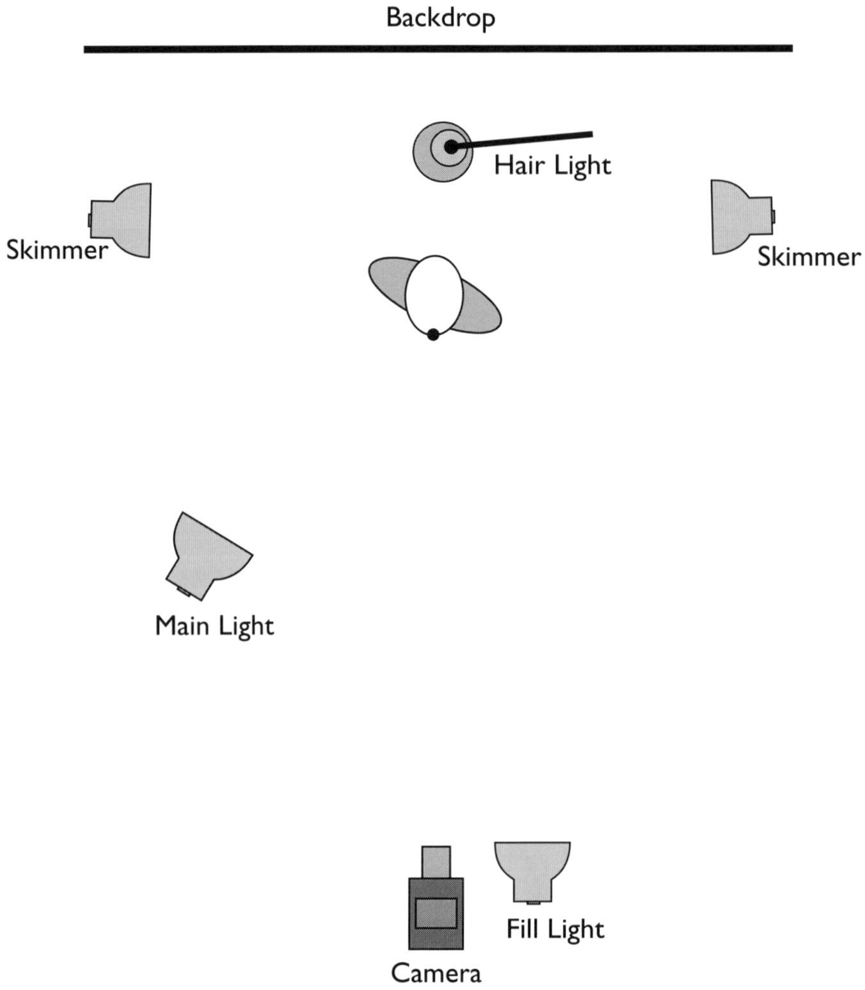

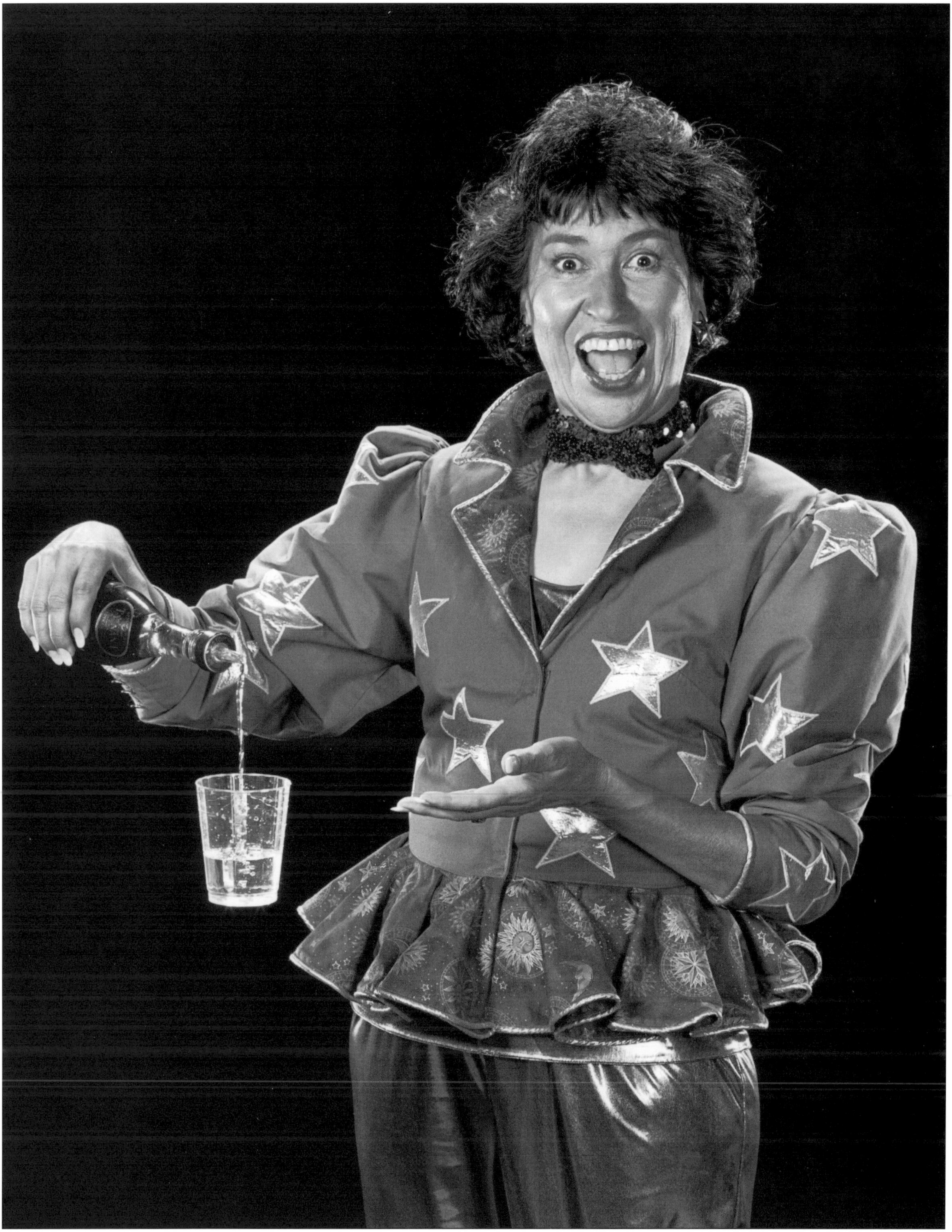

Piador

The Shoot

Piador is a very talented *a cappella* group (who treated me to a little concert prior to the session!). They came to the studio to shoot publicity photos for the group, and wanted a very simple shot.

Lighting

To photograph this rather large group, I used a broad main light centered above and in front of the subjects. A skimmer placed on either side of the group helps to separate the group from the backdrop. A fill light was used next to the camera lens. A hair light was also used above the group.

Learning Lighting

Although I have studied design and worked professionally as a designer, I'm pretty much self-taught when it comes to photography. Lighting is one of the aspects of photography that has fascinated me the most, probably because it appeals to the technical, mathematical side of me, as well as the artistic side. Learning the theory of light and the laws of physics that govern is something I did mainly by reading lots of books. Understanding these principles is crucial to using light creatively without being inefficient, since it helps to eliminate endless trial and error.

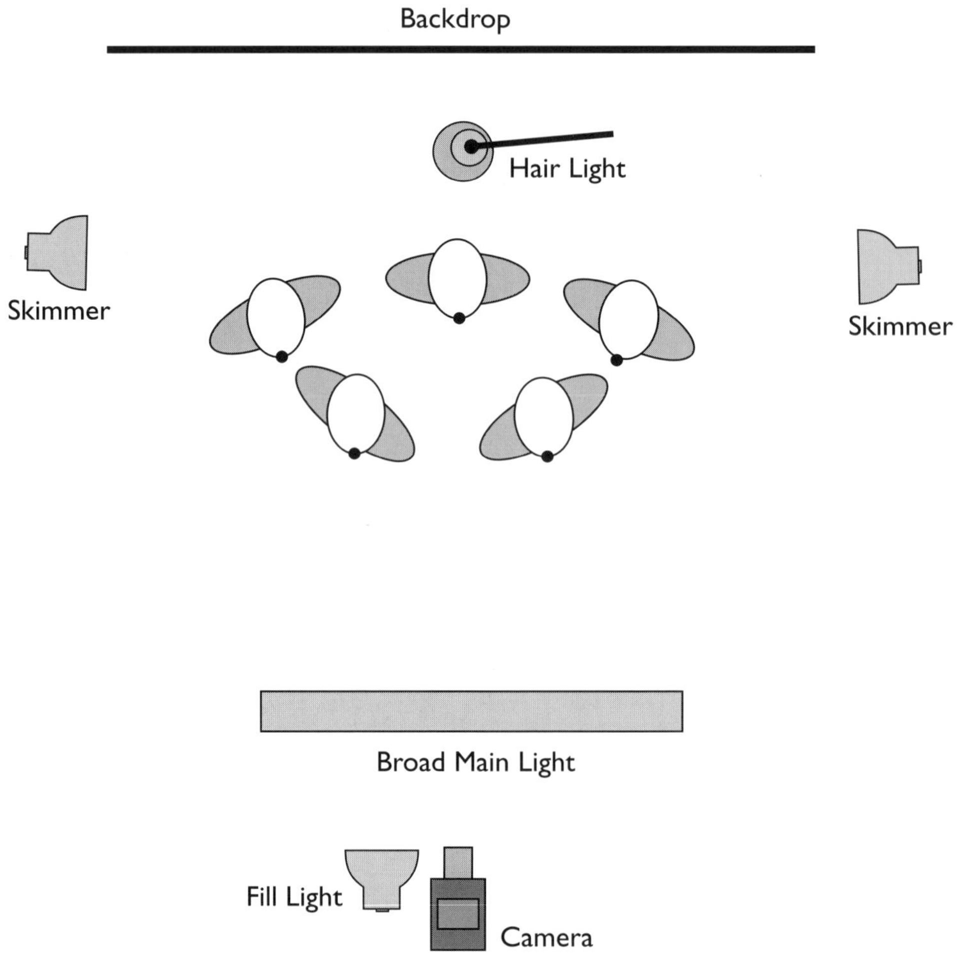

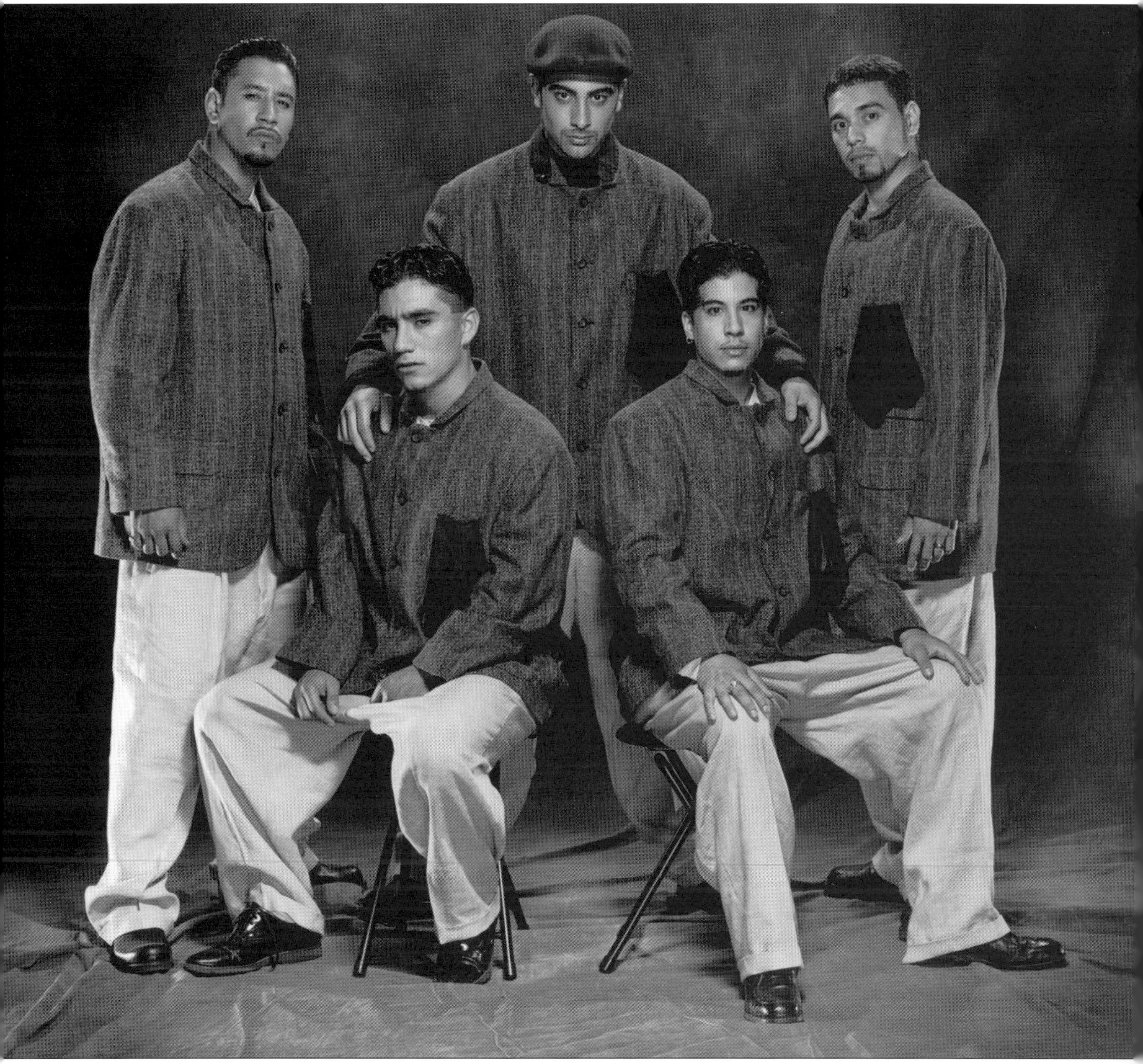

Casa Blanca

Studio

The set-up of my studio helped me to accomplish this publicity shot for a salsa band called Casa Blanca. My studio is constructed with a disappearing staircase and a catwalk with a trap door in the ceiling. Shooting from this point allows me to shoot straight down without having to set up scaffolding or a ladder every time. The ceiling also acts as an automatic gobo!

Lens

A wide angle lens was used here to exaggerate the sense of depth. It also creates the interesting distortion of the faces in the back (which are disproportionately large when compared with the faces in the front).

Lighting

Skimmers were placed on either side of the group and help separate the edges from the background. The main light was placed on the ceiling, right below the camera lens. The fill light was actually then placed below the main light. A hair light was positioned above the group.

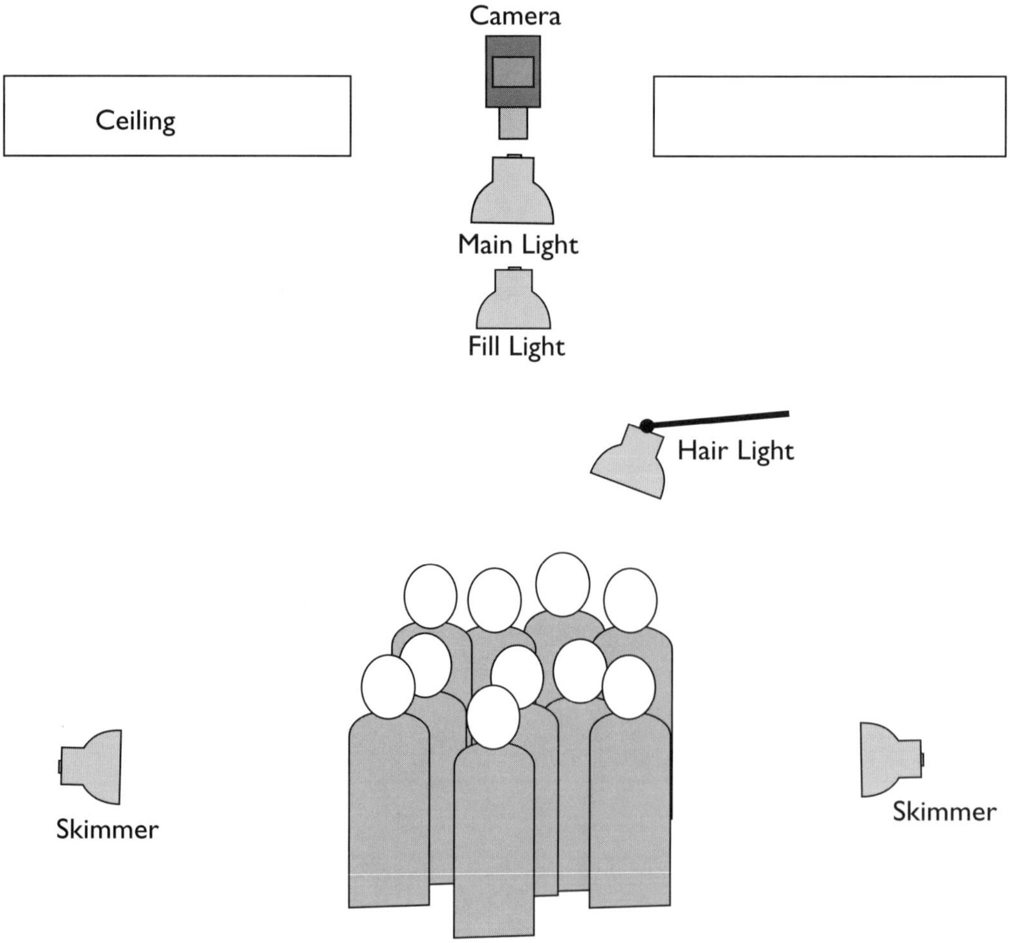

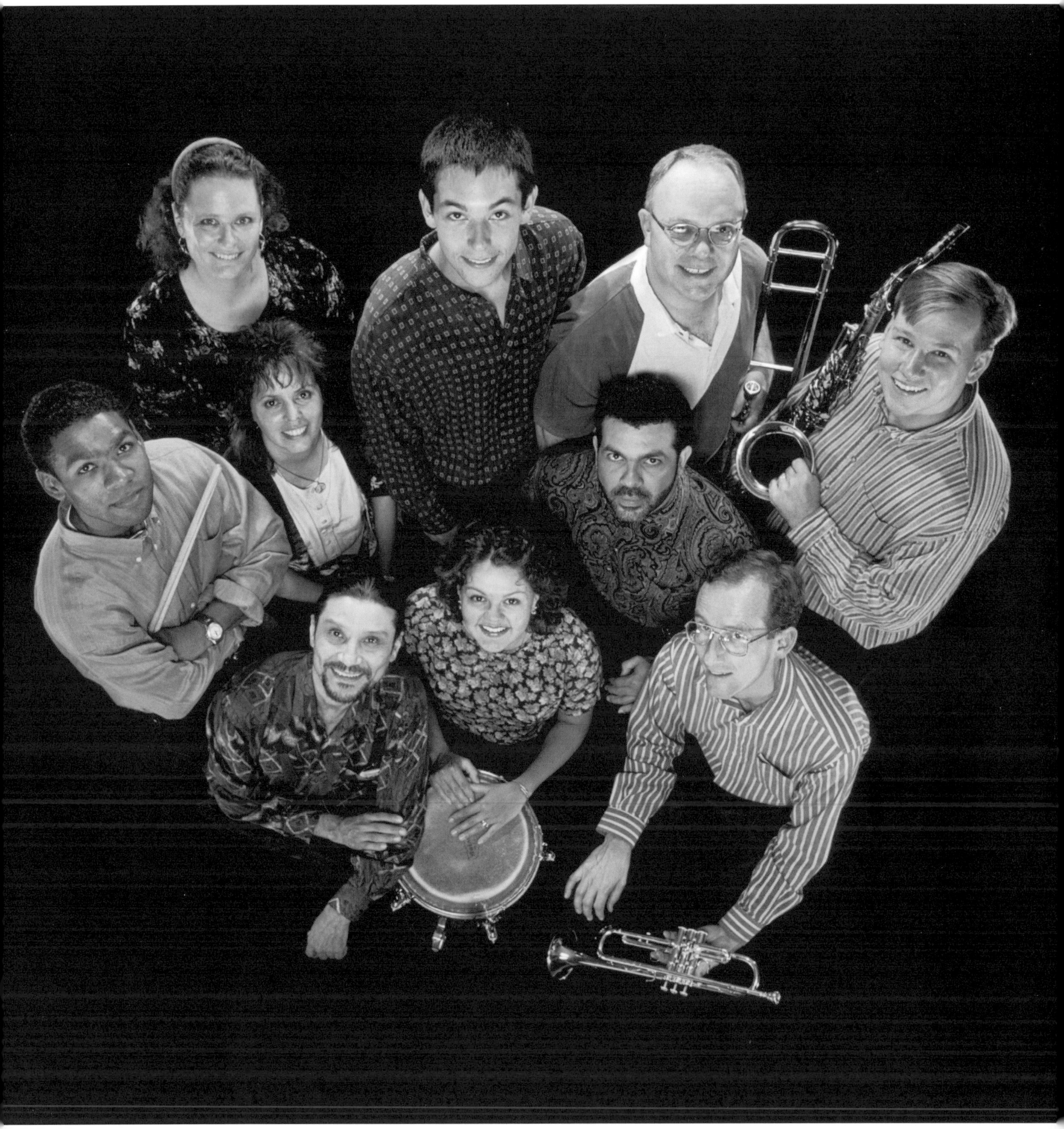

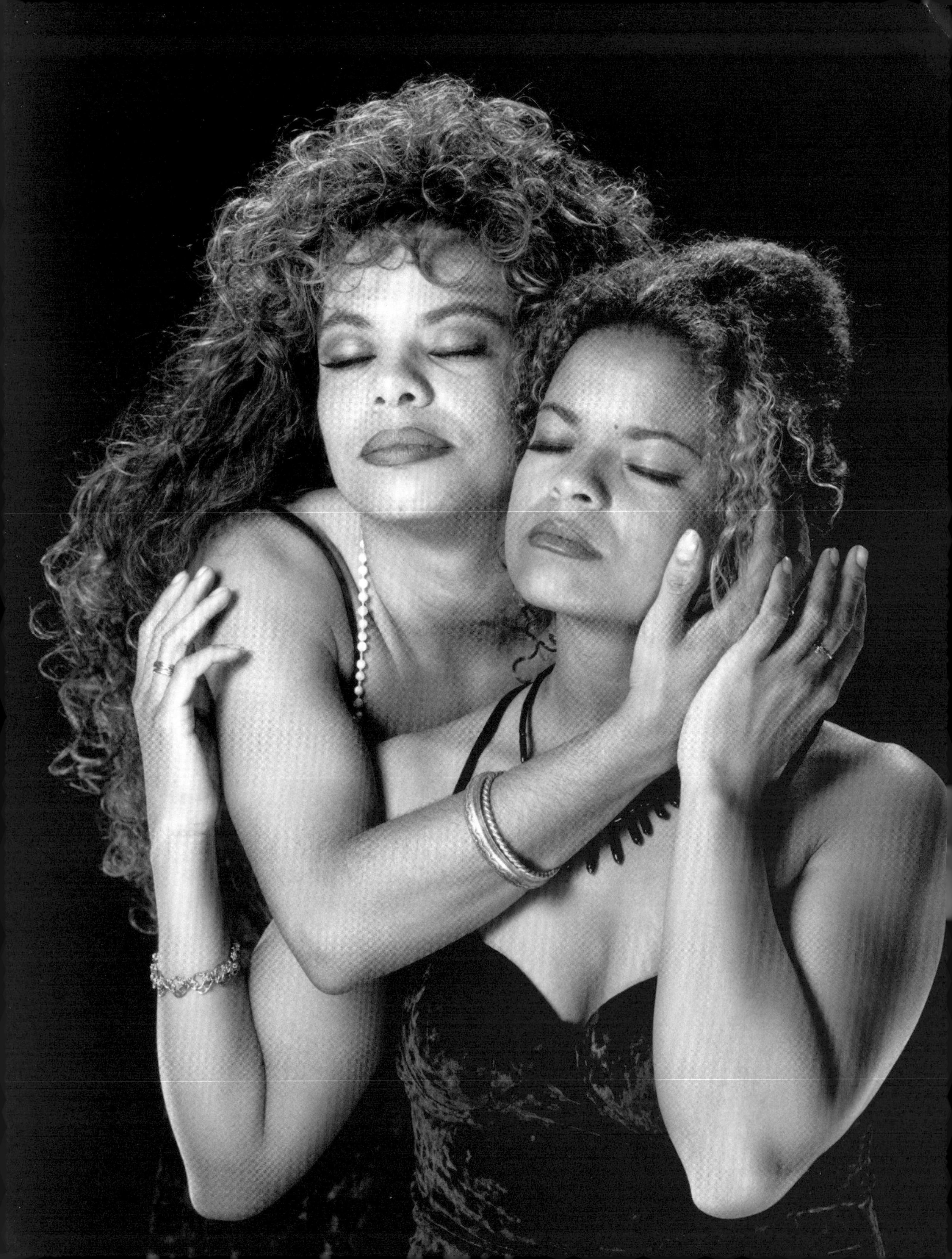

Sisters

Models

Twin sisters Didi and Dolly, a pair of singers and dancers, arranged this session as a publicity shoot. The image that resulted is reasonably like a regular portrait, but shows much more interaction.

Posing

This pose was selected to show the relationship between the two sisters. The models were photographed with their eyes closed, a facial expression that reflects intense emotion, but also mystery (it begs the question, "What are they thinking about?"). Adding this little element of mystery and emotion helps make the portrait more interesting.

Lighting

The main light was positioned to the camera left and kept relatively low (face level). This arrangement produces no loop on the nose. A fill light at camera level helps pick up the texture and adds definition to the subjects' black dresses. Two skimmers were placed to either side of the subjects, and a hair light was used above them.

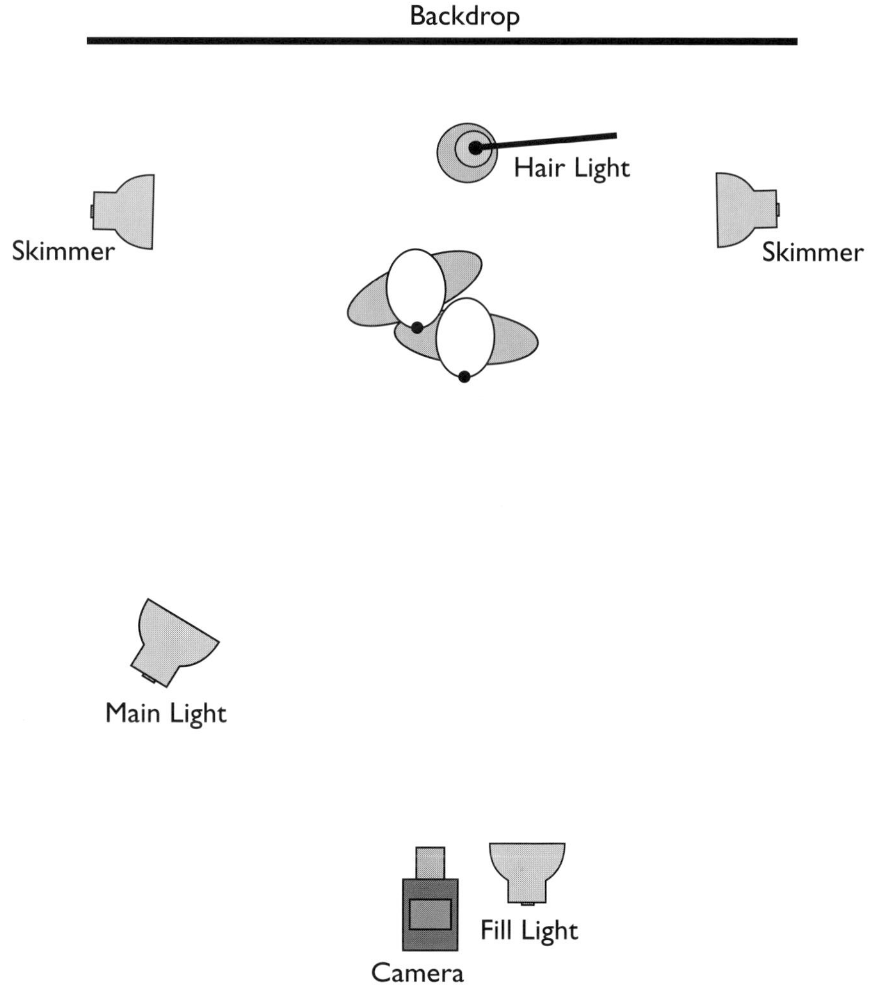

Gaspar Garcia

Model

Gaspar is an artist who creates paintings and sculpture, but who is also a very fine builder who has helped to restore historical buildings in my area. Knowing this detail about him, I decided to try to capture the "builder" side of my subject in this publicity shot.

Lighting

The main light was positioned 90° to camera left to create loop lighting on the subject's face (the shadow from the subject's nose falls on the cheek just above the lip line). The fill light was placed close to the camera. A hair light was used above the subject. Two skimmers were used: one behind the subject, and another weak one to the camera left.

Lighting for Hats

Shooting subjects who are wearing hats can be tricky. If the main here had been adjusted too high, the shadow from the hat brim could have caused the shaded area to lose definition. Since the hat was also light in color, it was important not to let this bright area overpower the subject. Therefore a scrim was added in in front of the main light to prevent too much light from falling on the hat.

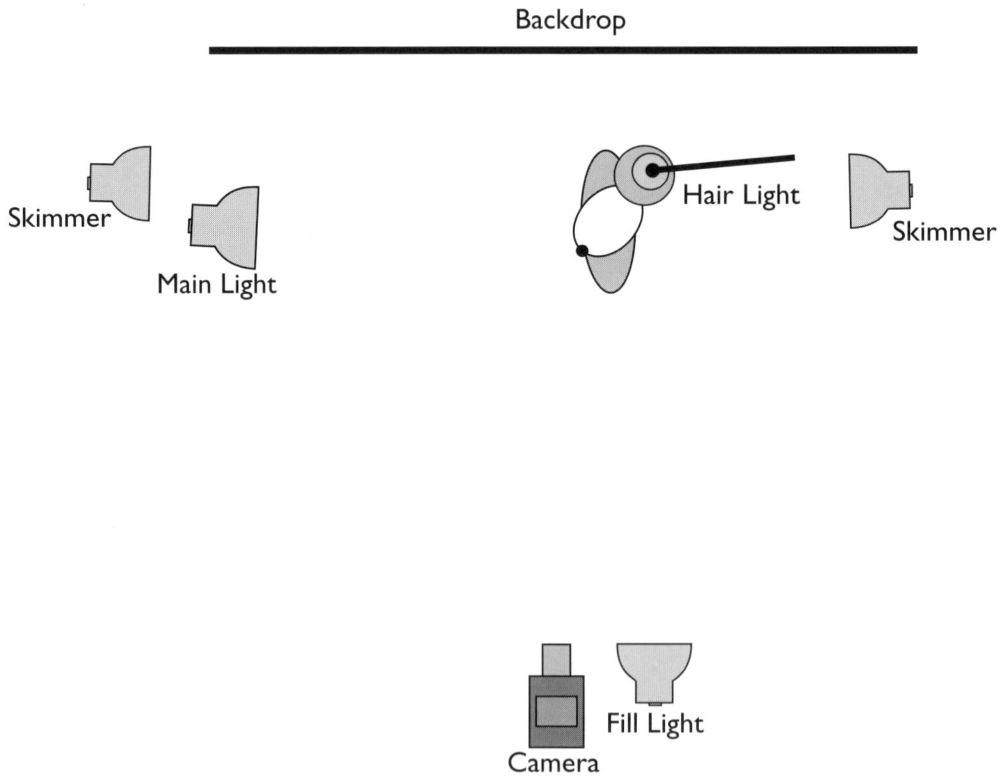

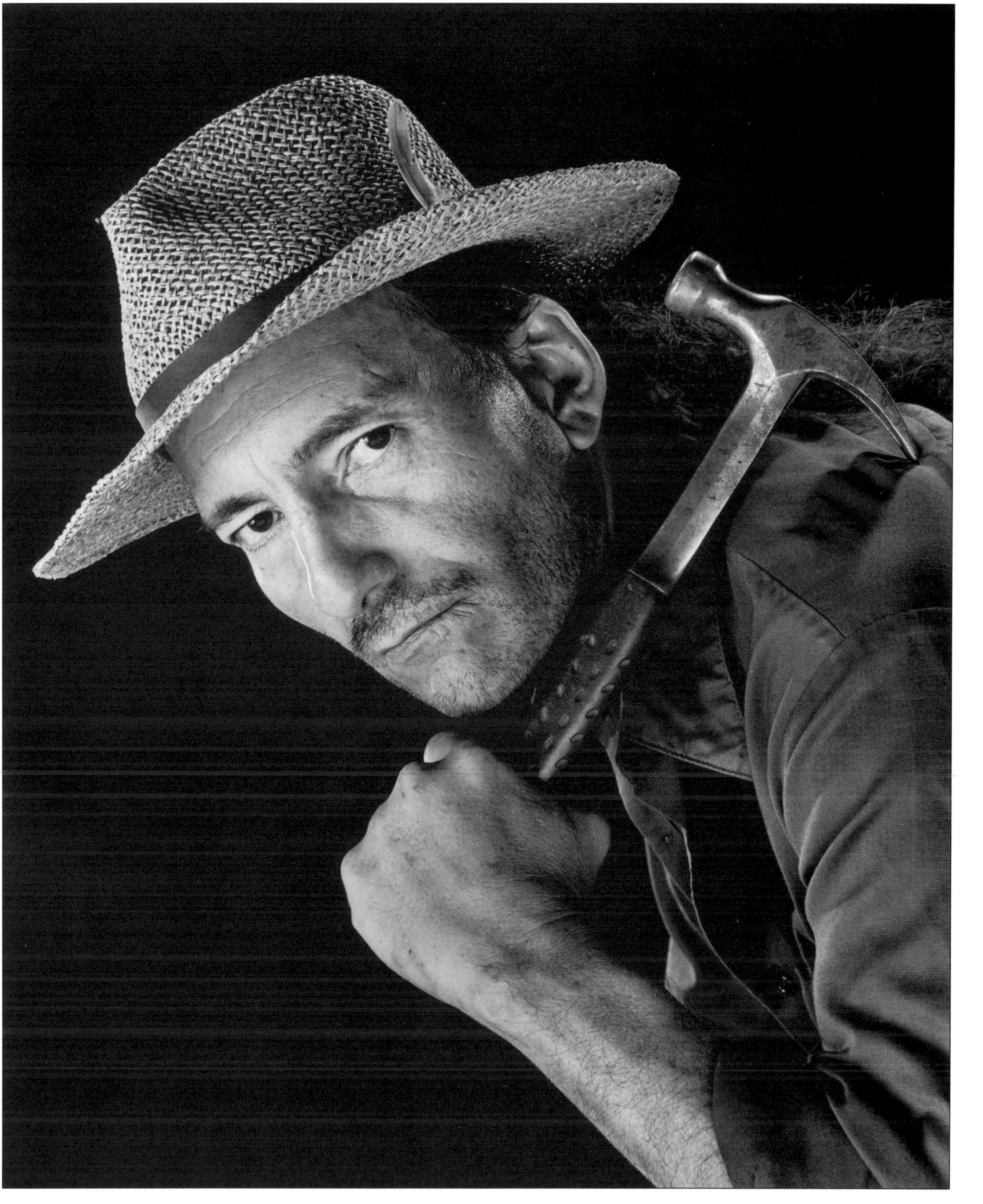

Publicity Shot

Since I do a lot of lecturing, I often receive requests for publicity shots. Most often I use "Foto Vato" (which appears in this book). Sometimes people want a head shot, though. That was the reason for taking this image. I also took some more conservative, "traditional" images, but after consulting with photographer friends about which to use, decided on this shot.

The Session

Basically, I did a photo session with myself to create this image. I took some rather mellow photos with my hair back, but then decided to try a different look. I let my hair down and placed a fan under the lens to blow it up. I put on a 70's-style, shiny shirt, and purposely allowed my cross necklace to show (since people often wrongly associate some of my photos with the occult). I had my assistant trip the shutter.

Lighting

The main light was placed to the camera left, high and far back to create a split light effect which divides the subject's face into two equal parts. A skimmer was used to the subject's left to add specular highlights. Fill light was used at a dramatic ratio with the main light, and a hair light was placed above.

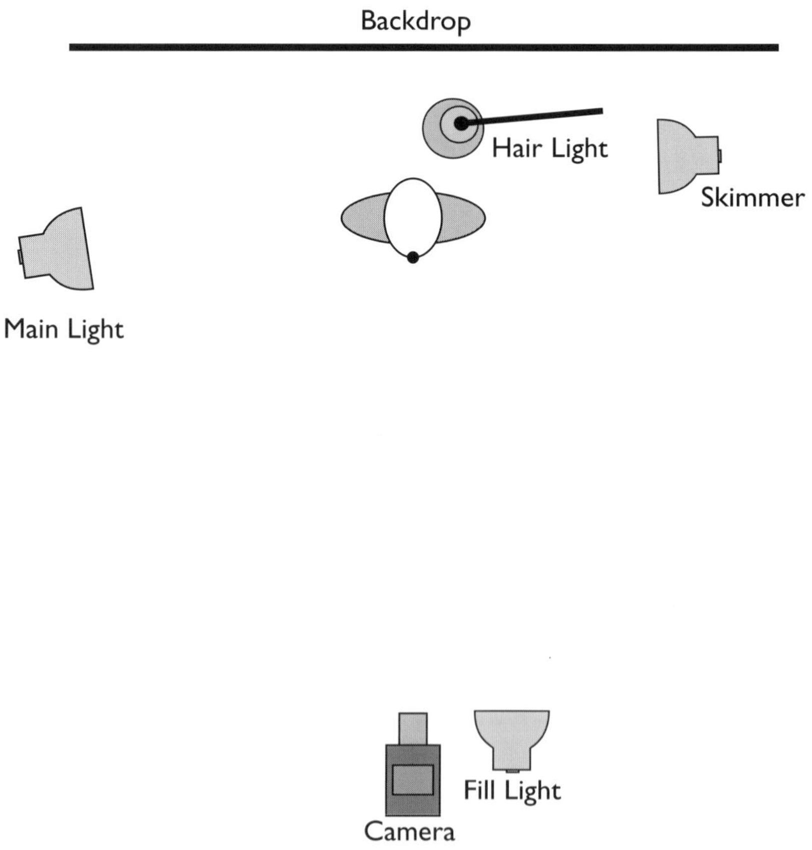

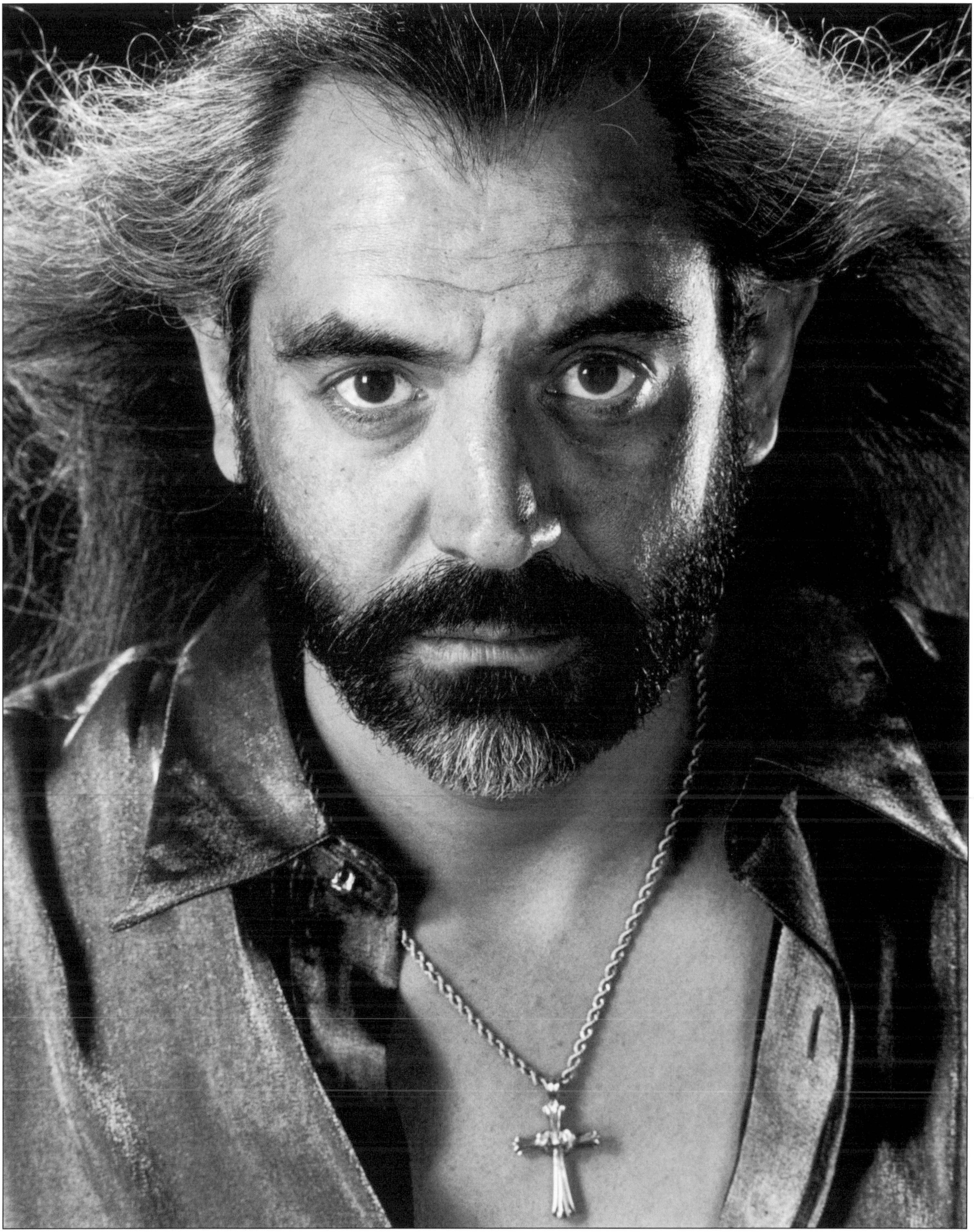

Steven Maes

Model

Steven Maes is a musician and producer who owns a recording studio. He came to the studio for a publicity shot. He came in with his band, and I shot images for them, but I also did some individual work with him afterwards.

Lighting

The main light was positioned high, back away from the camera. This allows his eyes and face to go into shadow. A skimmer was used to the left of the model, and a hair light was placed above him. Fill light was used close to the camera lens, and a little to the right, to add catch lights. When I feel there are too many distracting reflections in the eyes, I touch them out, leaving only one in each eye (usually the reflections from the main light).

Smoke

Several of the photos in this book depict people smoking. I use this as a prop, even with non-smokers, on occasion. As you can see in many of these images, the smoke adds a photographically interesting element.

Contacts

As a former musician, I'm fortunate to have a lot of contacts established in that career on which I can now draw as a photographer. Another means by which artists and musicians learn about my work is simply through photo credits. When people like what they see, they tend to seek it for themselves!

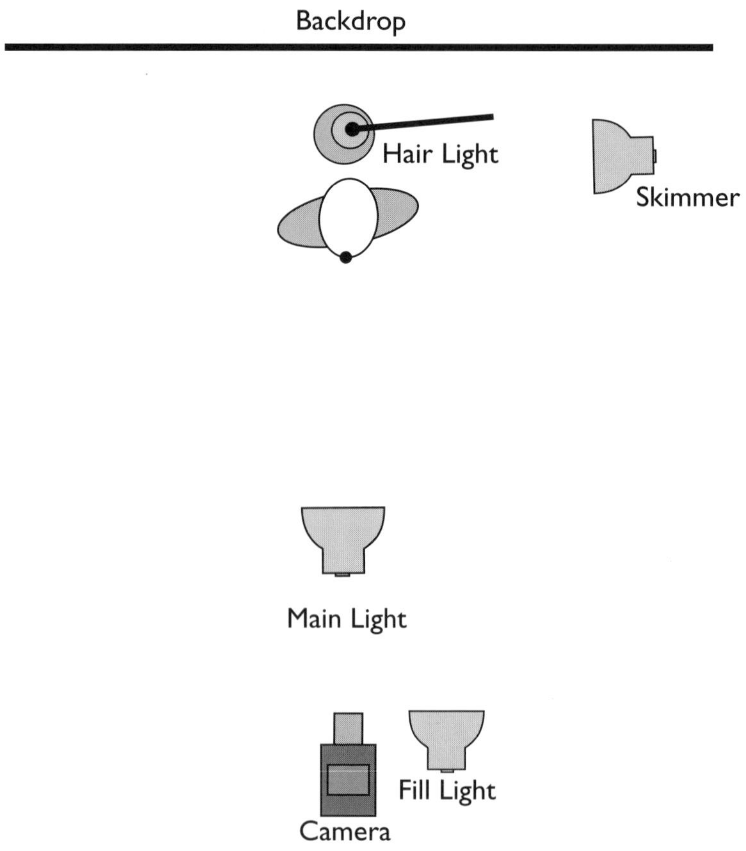

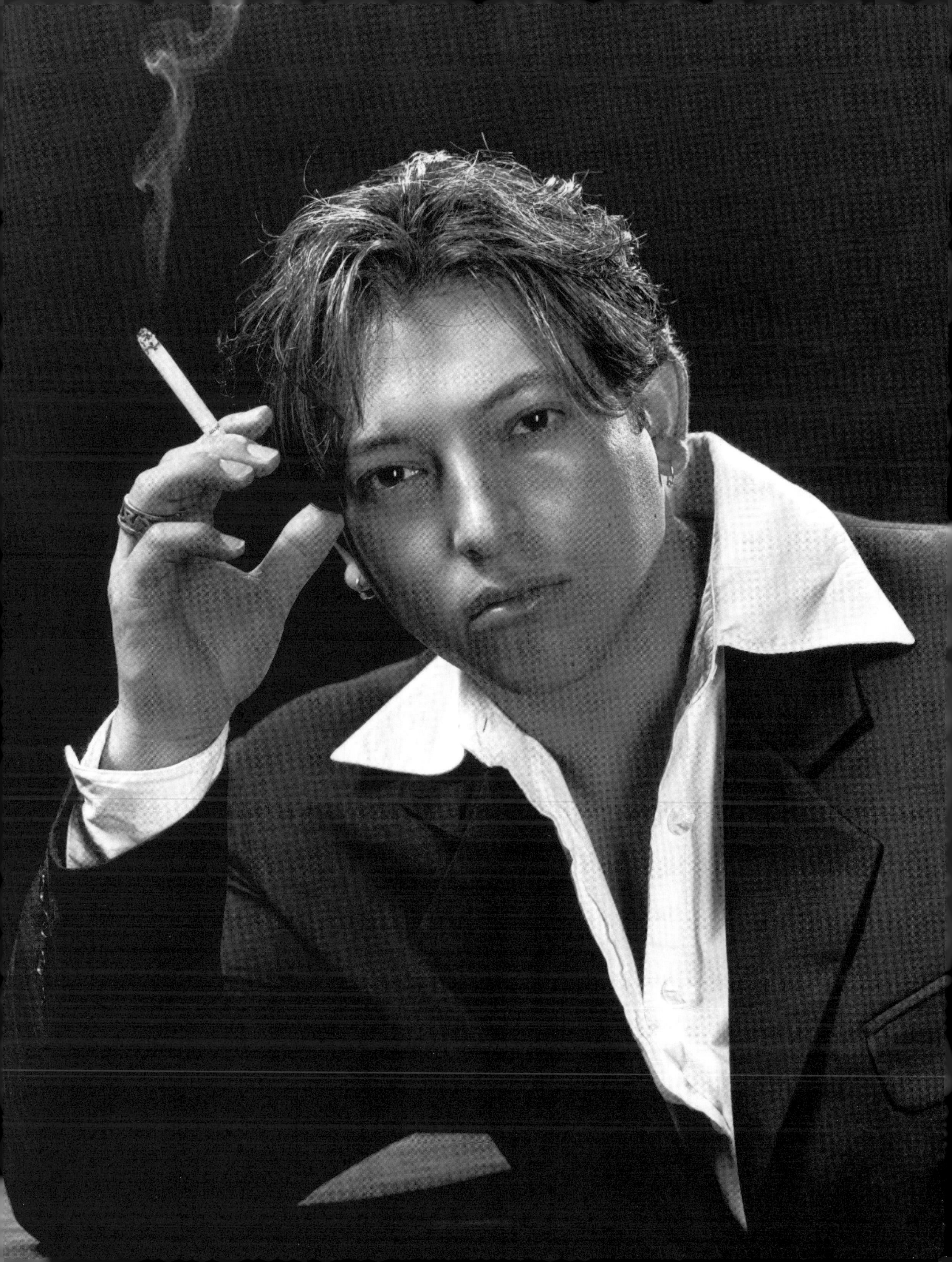

Duke and Pam

Model

The main subject, Duke, is a photographer and good friend who came to me for a publicity shot. He had in mind a 1940's inspired image using a female model in the background and a camera (one of my old ones, here) as a prop.

Lighting

The faces of both characters were lit by means of continuous theatrical spots. Skimmers light the edges of either side of the subjects. A fill light was placed to the right of the camera, and a hair light was used above.

Narrative

Telling a story has become more and more important to me, and today I find that just taking a "nice picture" isn't enough. Adding narrative to an image can make a controversial subject (such as a nude) more acceptable (especially in competition), but it also simply functions to make a picture appealing. People like to look at a photograph and see something there to interpret, a story to read. Creating narrative can be as simple as the relationship shown in this image, where the viewer asks "Why is the woman walking away from him?", but even simple narrative devices attract (and hold) the viewer's attention.

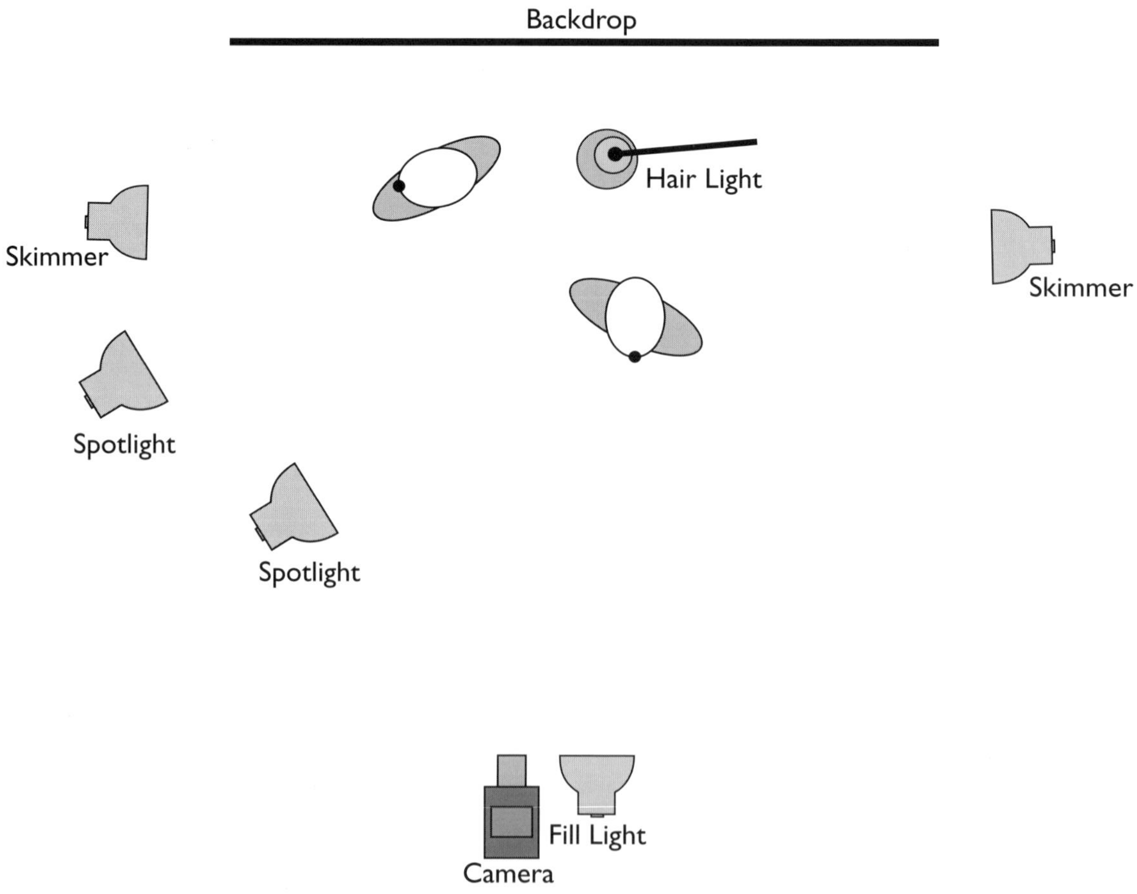

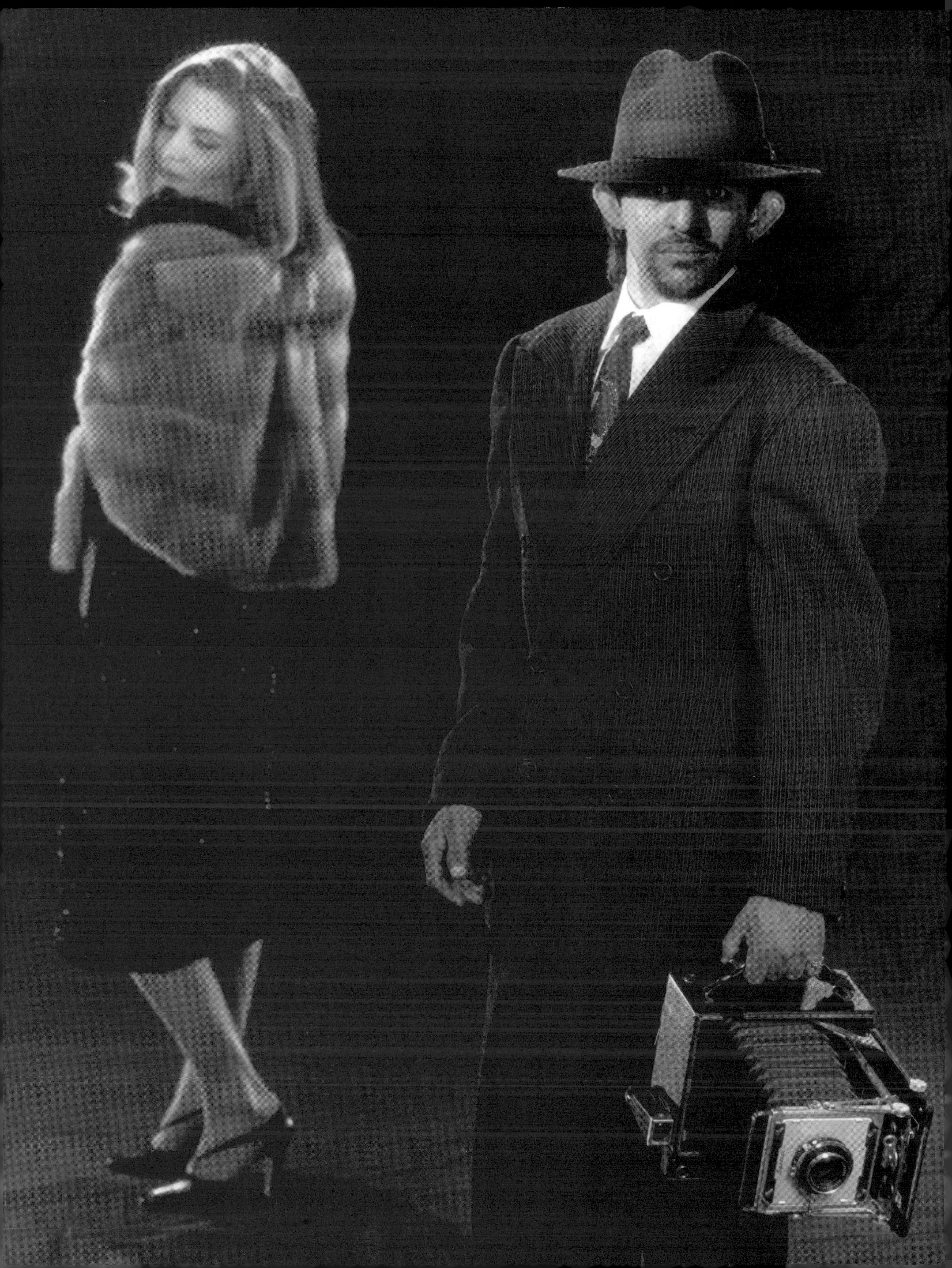

David Crespin

Model and Posing

The model in this image is a performer who works in carnivals, music videos, movies, etc.. He came in for a portfolio session and played with many different looks.

He was a natural performer and really got into the shoot. For this image I told him to "Look pissed!" – as you can see he did a fine job of it!

Lighting

The main light was positioned to the right of the subject. Fill light was used next to the right side of the lens. Skimmers were placed to either side of the subject, and a hair light was used overhead.

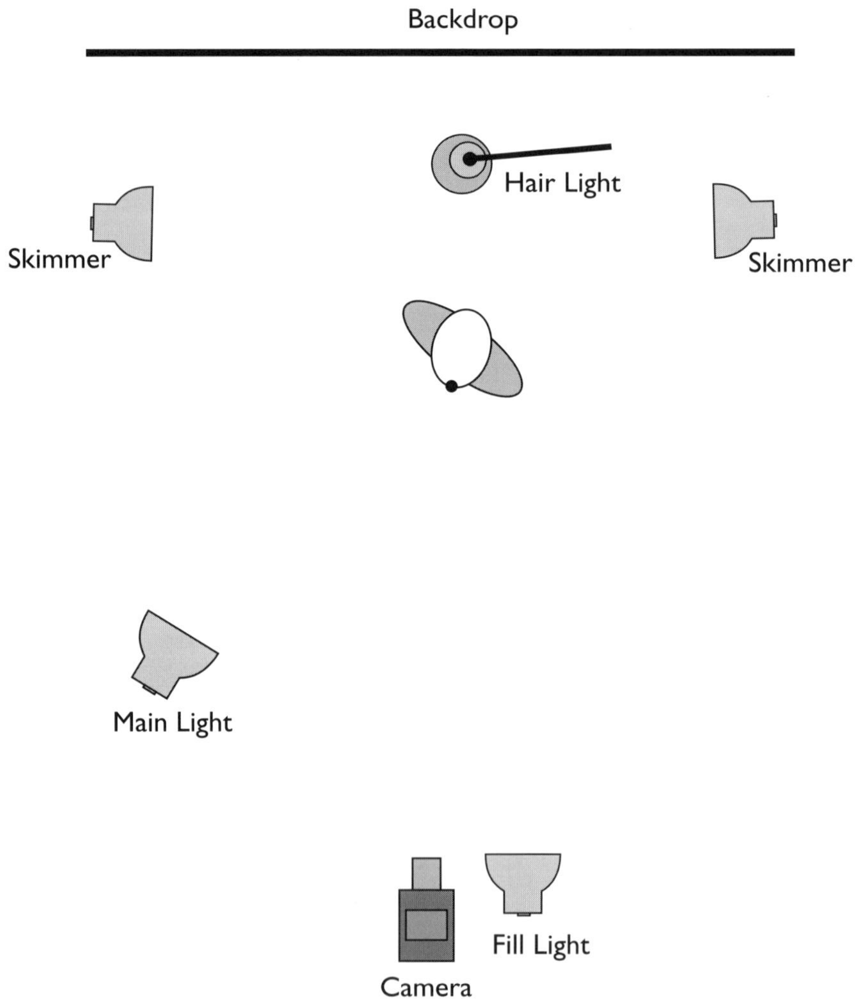

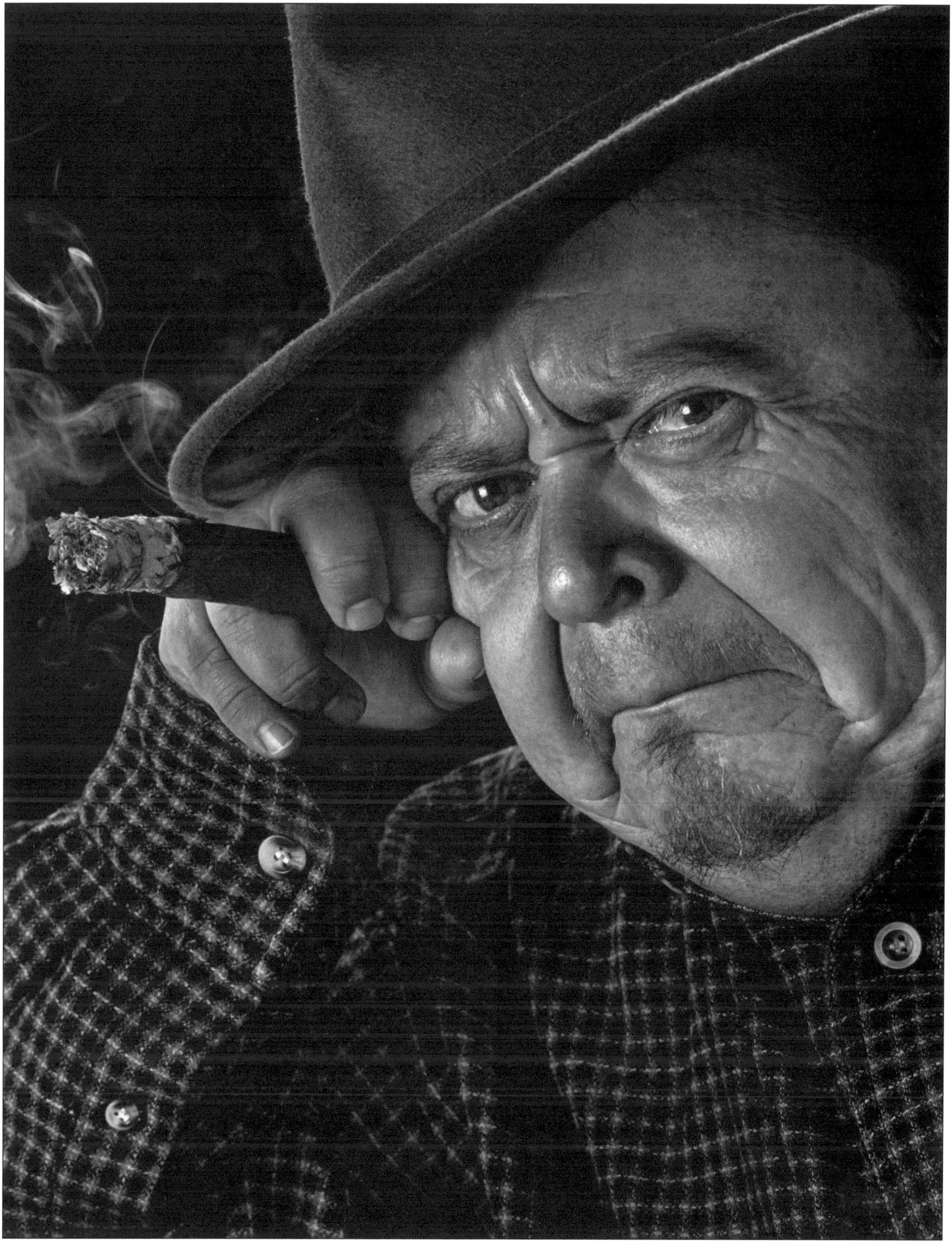

Robin (Expecting)

The Model

The model in this photo is a good friend who is also a photographer. She wanted some photos of herself while expecting, so we shot several art nudes, and several clothed images.

Lighting

Here, the model's body is silhouetted, but in low detail due to the low intensity of the fill light. Continuous light was provided by a theatrical spot placed to the camera right. This light was at a low angle to the subject, something evidenced by the horizontal nose shadow. A back light was placed behind the model's head, and a little below, to create the halo effect you see in this photograph. This same back light also silhouettes her stomach. A skimmer was used to the camera right.

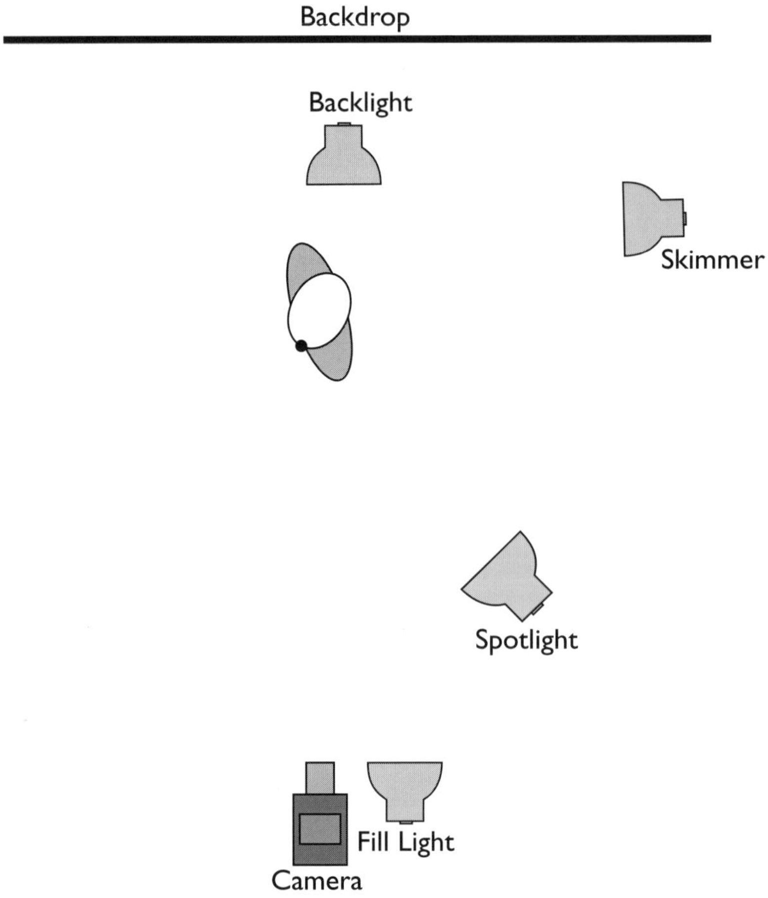

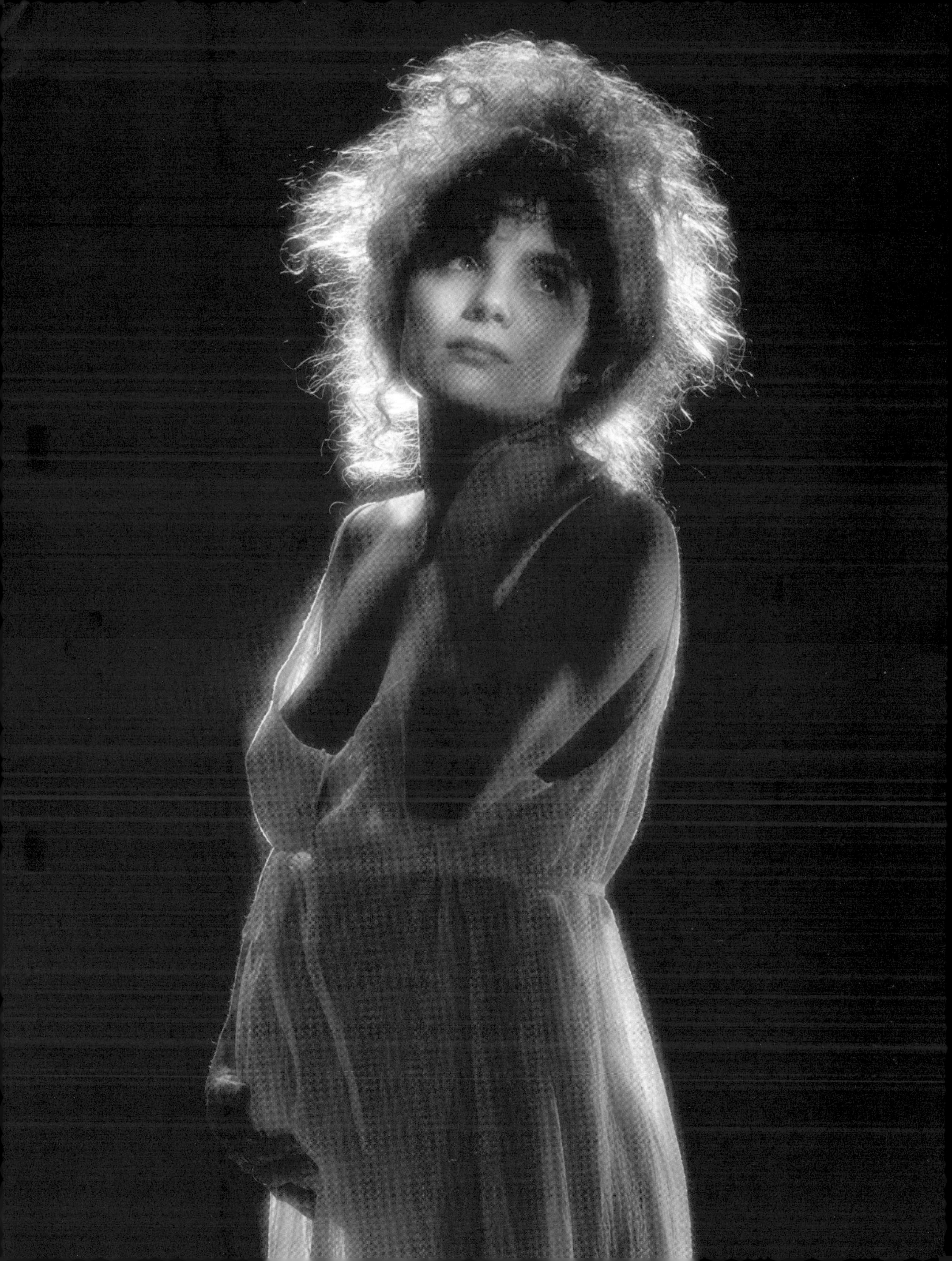

Pam (1940's)

The Shoot

This photograph came out of another session in which Pam was a secondary character. Since she was dressed up so elegantly, we decided to shoot a few more images!

Lighting

Since the image mimics a 1940's style when popular lighting for glamour images was quite a bit harsher than that preferred today, I used a theatrical spot to accent her face.

Period Style

1940's style is something that really appeals to me, and a look that you'll find in many of my images. I especially like the hats (of which I have a collection) and the baggy look of the suits (a style that is still popular). Capturing this period look convincingly also requires careful attention to lighting, as mentioned above.

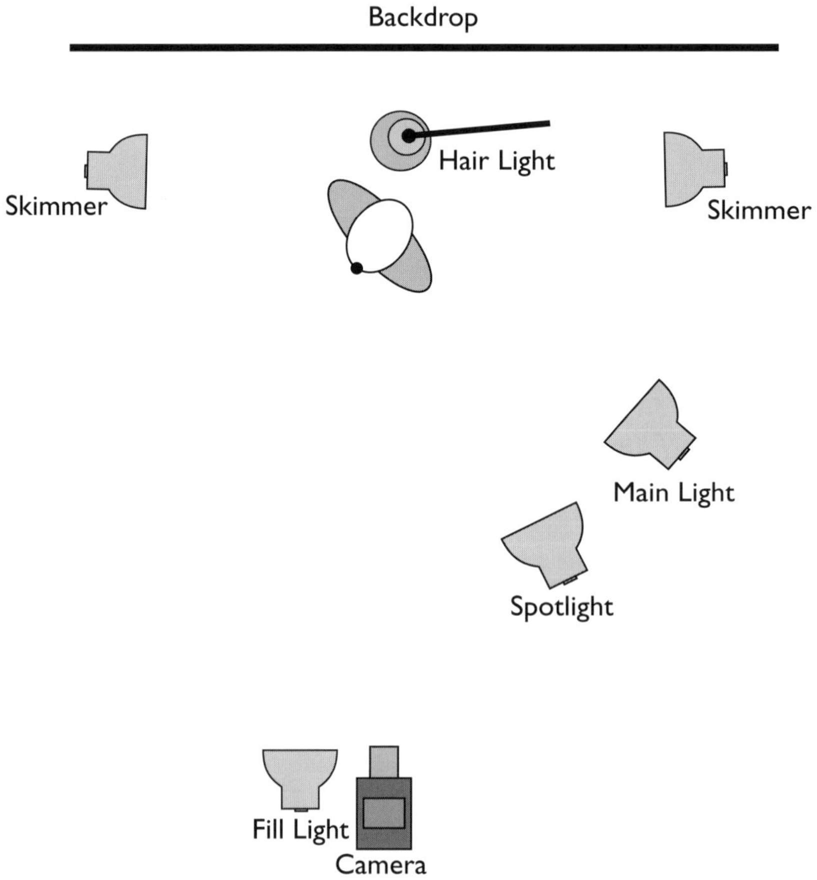

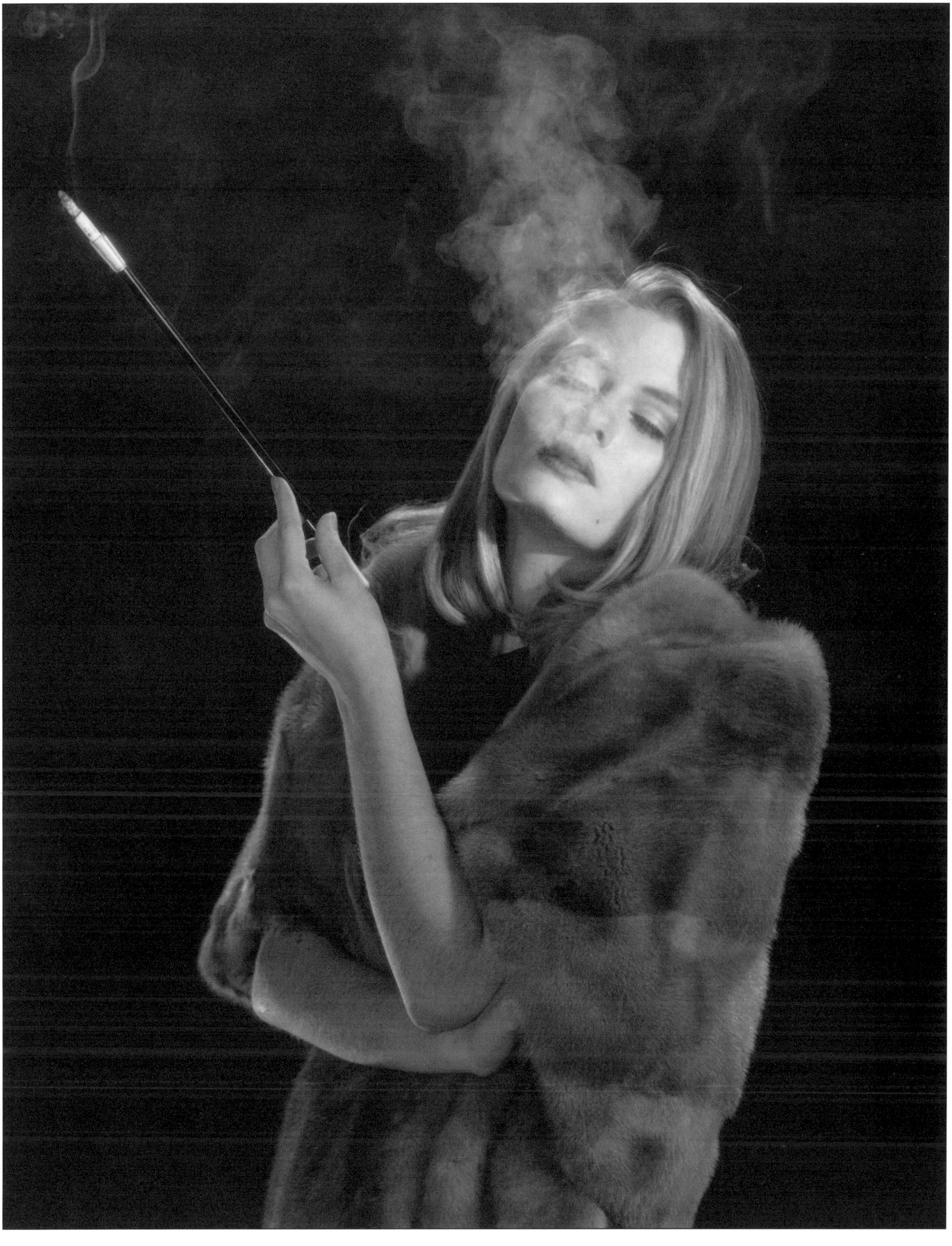

Mama's Surprise

Concept

This photo of my son and his mother was based on her concept. She wanted a photograph showing "mom and her main man" in a small, cozy setting.

Personally, I like working with client's ideas, and I really go after them whenever possible. I think it helps to really depict who the subject is; it's honest and real.

Lighting

The lighting was provided by two main lights. One was placed behind the mother, and one was placed behind the son. A continuous theatrical spot was used on the background.

A hair light was used above, along with a fill light next to the lens. Skimmers were placed on either side of the scene.

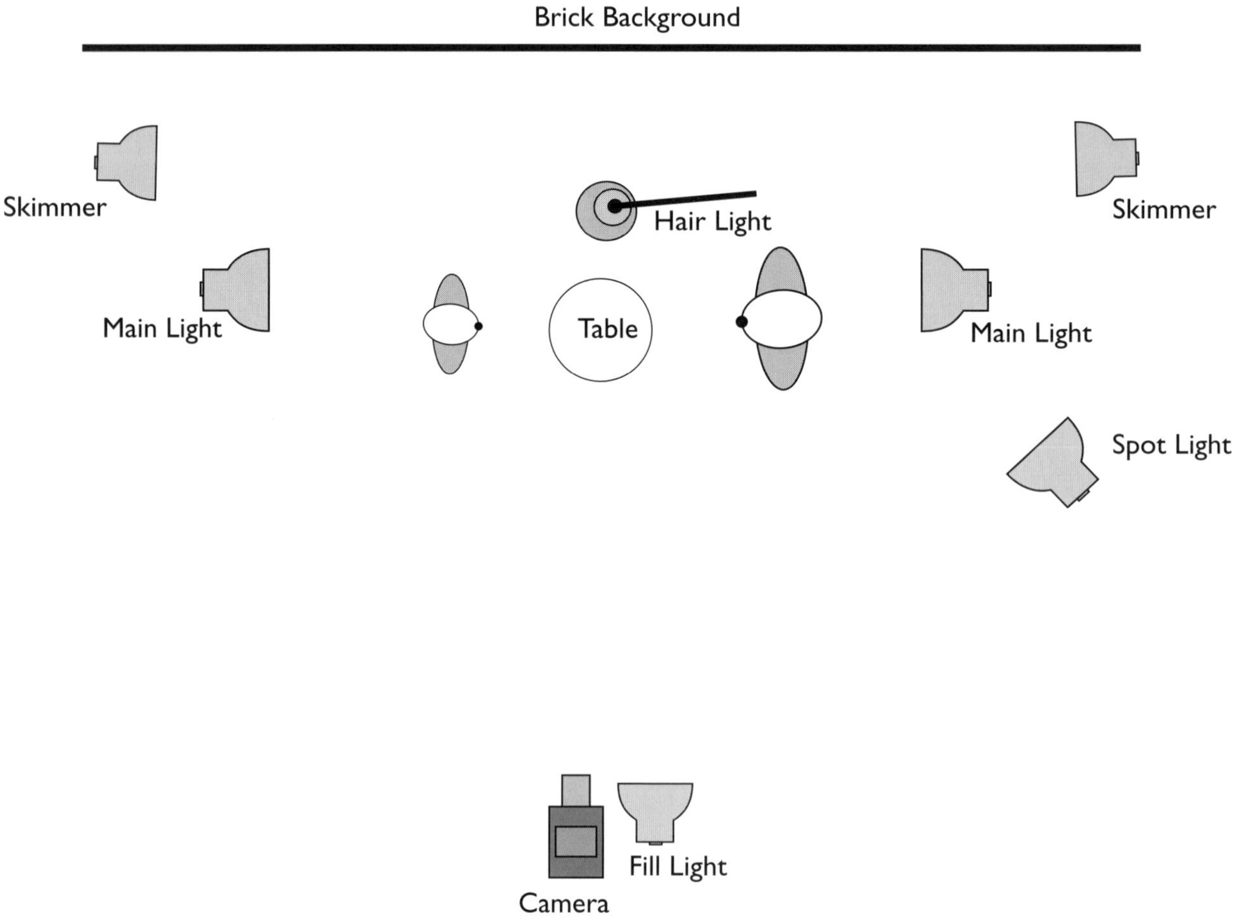

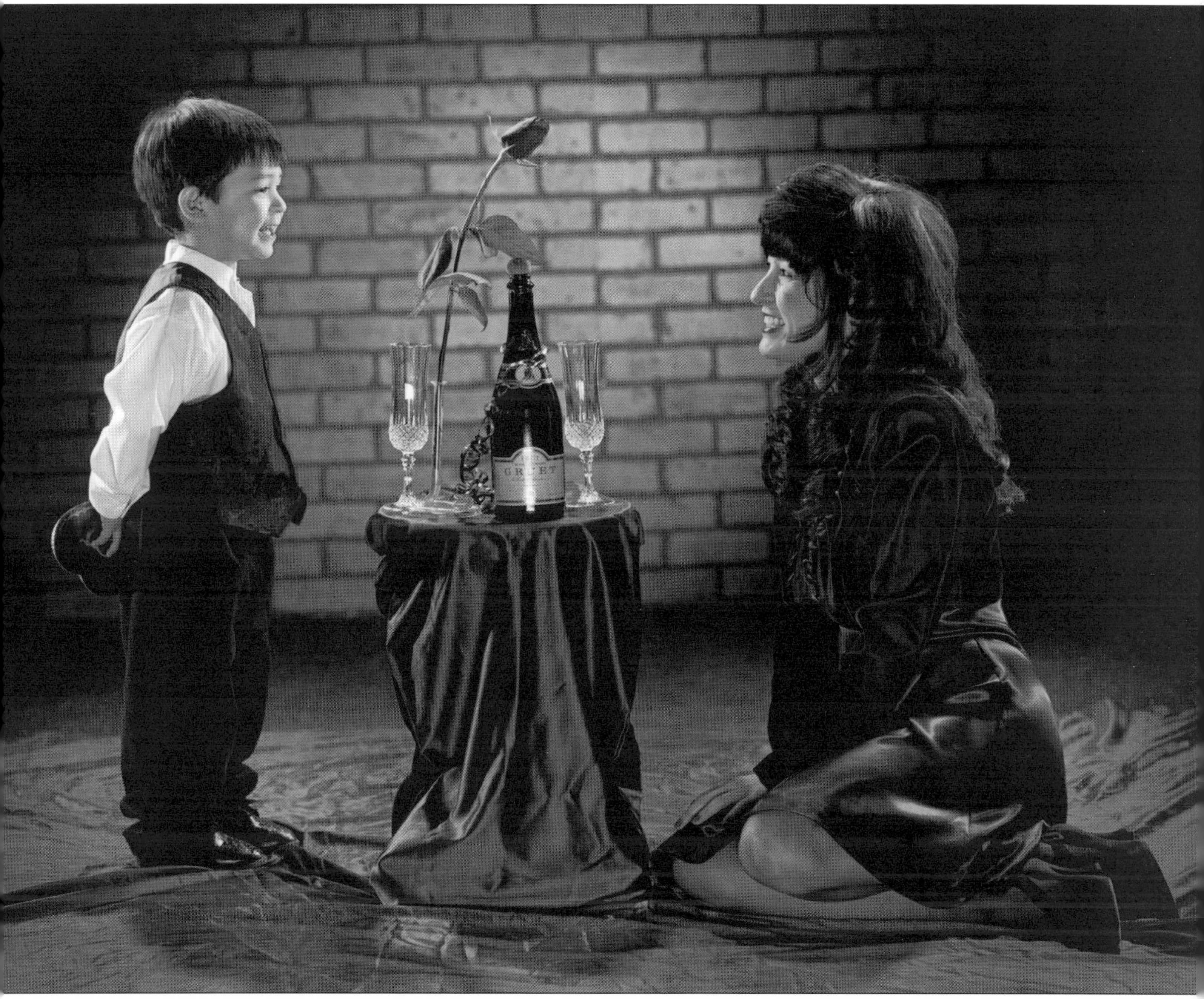

Jan Vidra

Image
For this photograph I tried to create a very serious look. To this end, I used traditional hand posing.

Lighting
The main light was positioned to the right of the model and far back to create a split light effect (in which half the face is left in shadow). Fill light was used next to the lens. A skimmer was placed to the left of the model to add texture to the part of his face that was left in shadow by the main light. This skimmer also adds specular highlights to his fingers. A hair light was also used.

Hair
The lighter the hair, the less light is needed on it. Even the fill light will pick up some detail on very light hair, while it will yield almost no detail on dark hair. With very light or white hair, the hair light should be equal to or less intense than the main light.

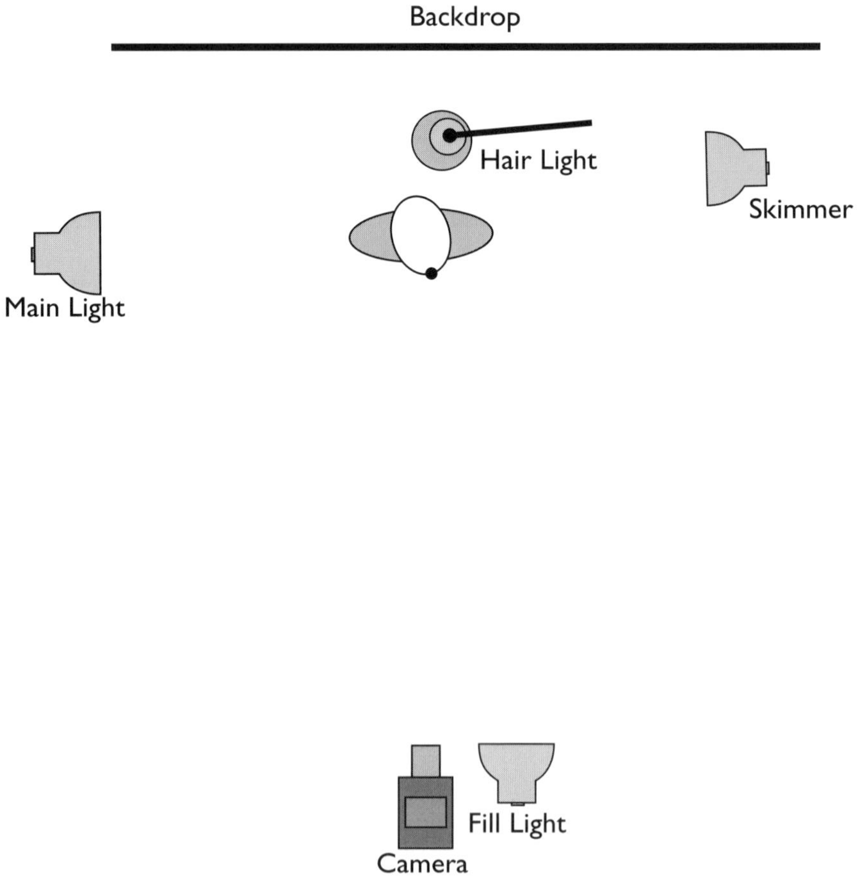

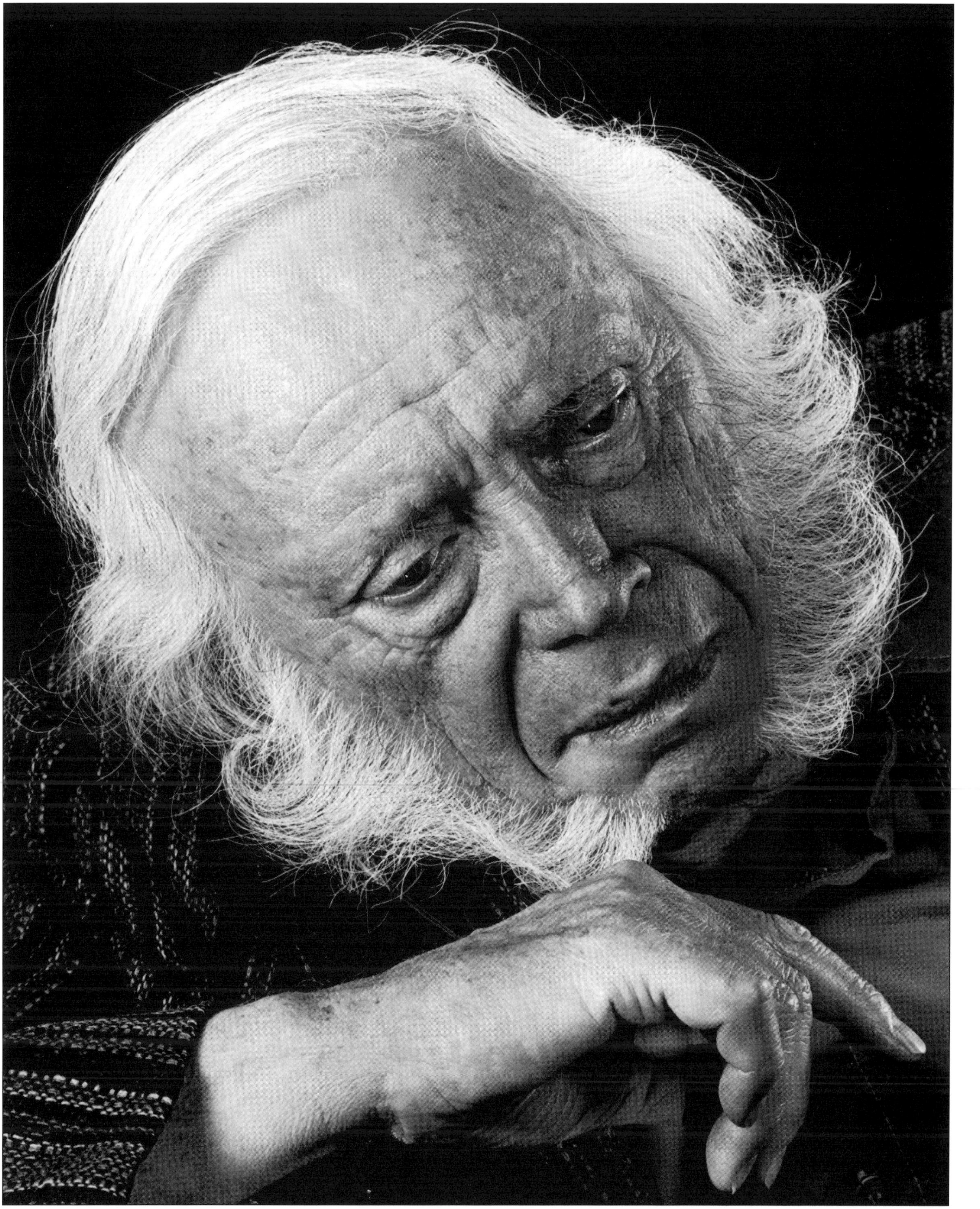

Clothing and Hair

To create this image, we got rid of the patterned jacket completely and draped the model in black cloth all the way to his neck. We also played with his hair.

Composition

I shot this picture with only the face at first, but then decided that adding the hands helped give the photograph a stronger foundation.

The basic compositional element here revolves around the positioning of the hair, pointing down, and the hands, pointing up. This arrangement, and the overall symmetry of the image, create a strong composition.

Lighting

The main light was positioned above the model's head to create a look of deep eye pockets and strong light on the brow and nose. A fill light used to the right of the camera functions almost as a second main. The hands are lit by the light from the main overhead and the fill light. Skimmers were used on either side of the subject.

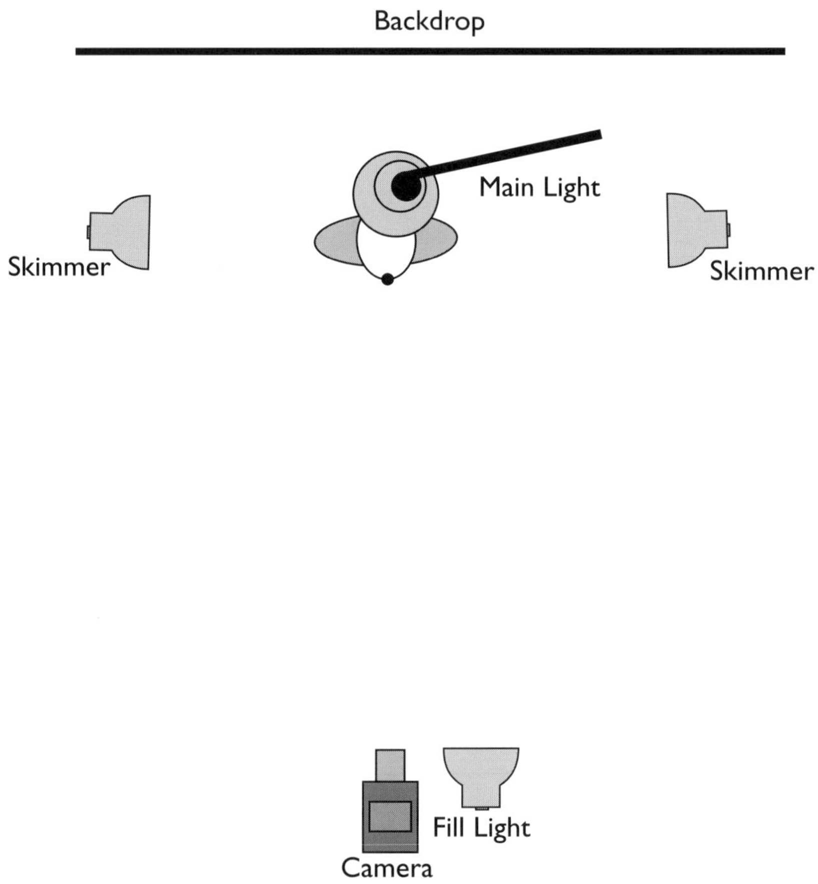

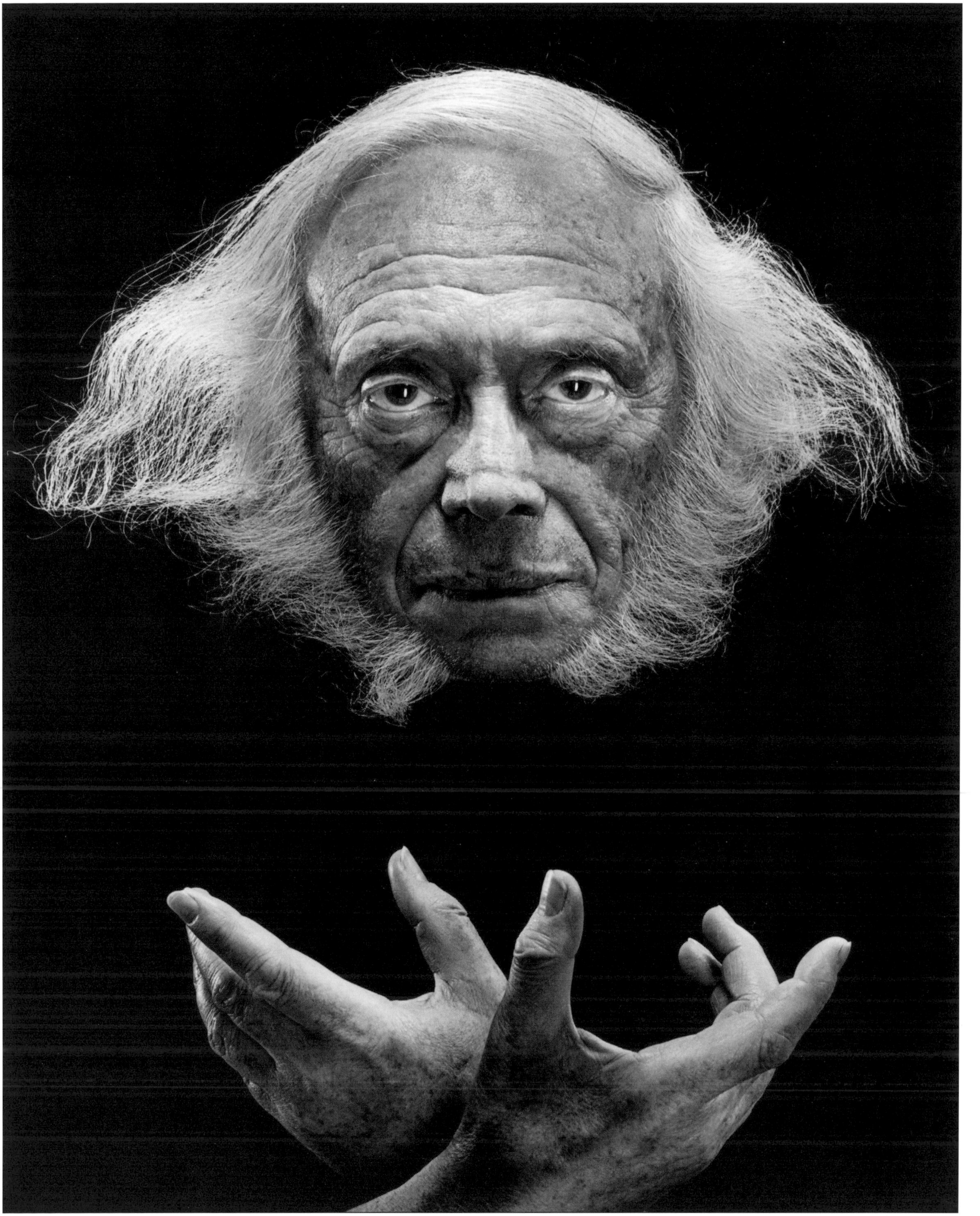

Monongye

Model

Monongye is an Apache lady I met in my neighborhood. She has an extremely interesting face that made her a great subject. I photographed her as part of a series on street people.

Lighting

The main light was positioned to the right of the model, and rather high. Fill light was used to the right of the camera. Two skimmers were used. The skimmer to her right helps to keep light on her dark hair and the fur she is wearing. The skimmer to the left creates specular highlights in the shadow due to the lack of illumination from the main light in this area. A hair light was also used.

Photographing Seniors

When shooting character studies such as this, the images don't have to be flattering in the traditional photographic sense. These images aren't about perfect skin and youth, but rather they reveal the character of the subject in lines and textures and tonalities.

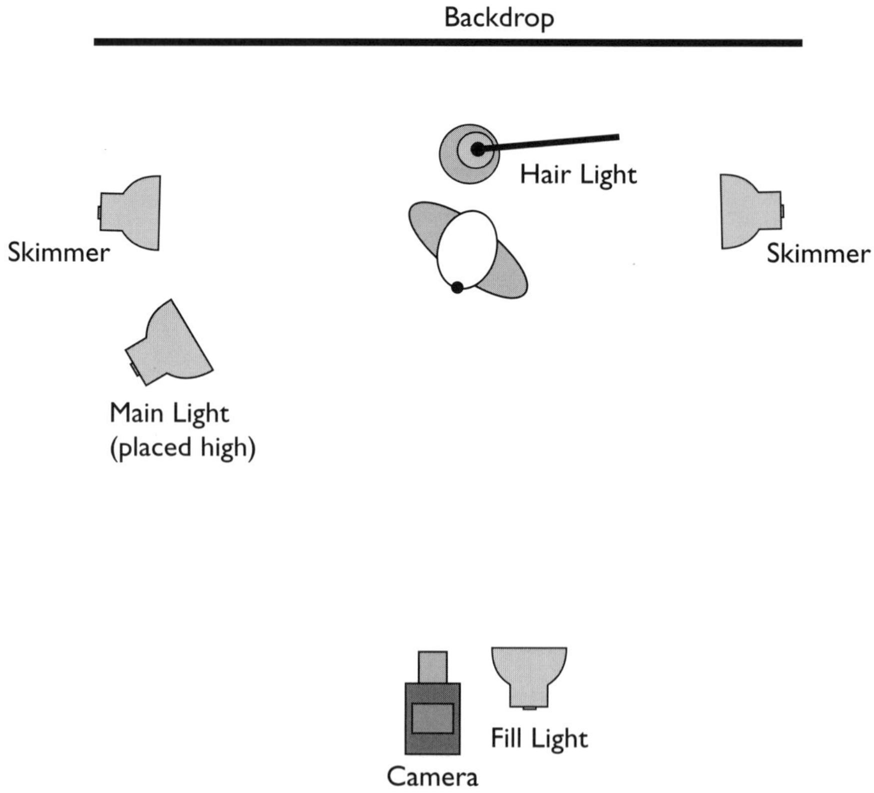

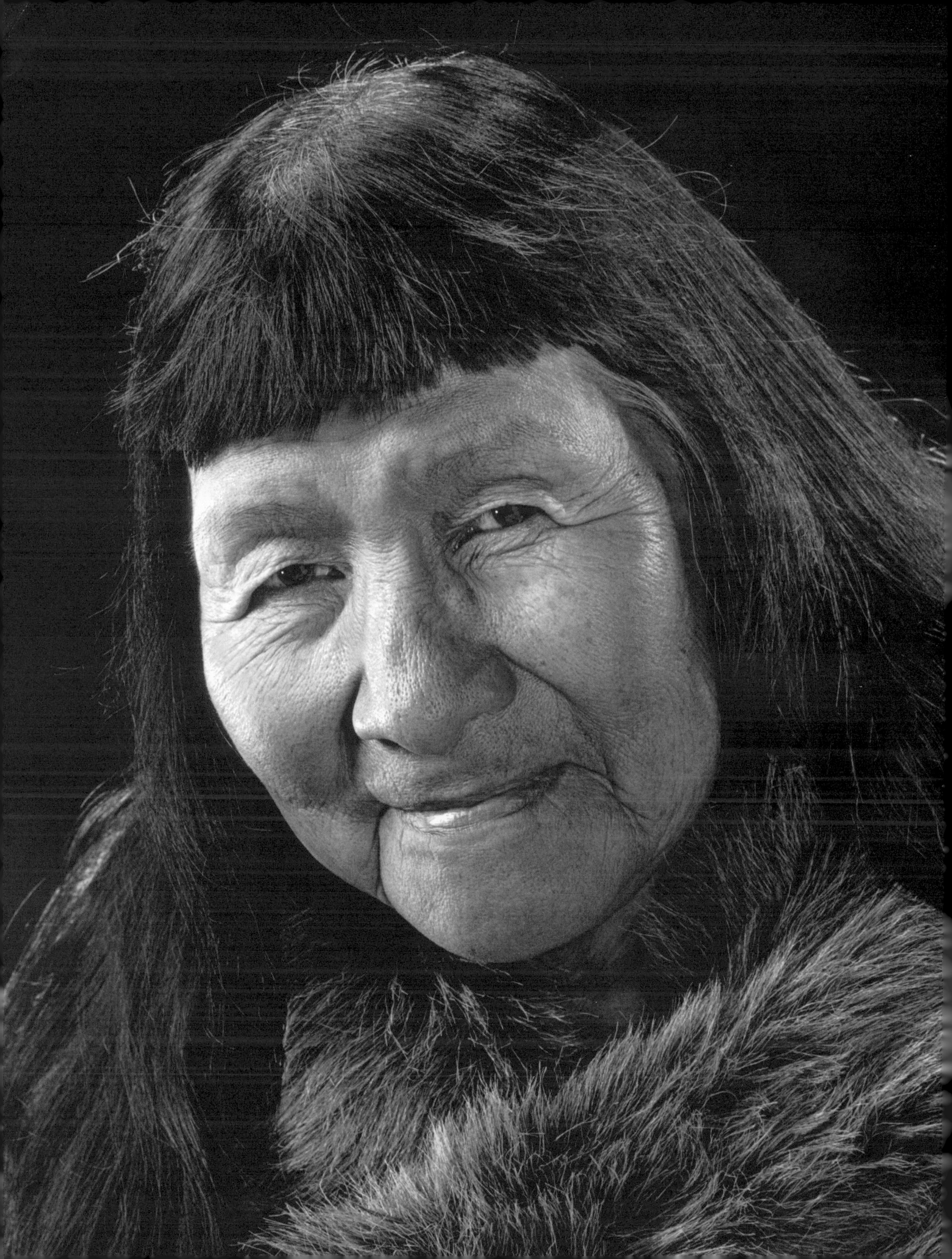

Model

This young man had been on the street a couple of years when I met him. I had seen him on several occasions and asked if he would be interested in letting me photograph him. He stood me up at my studio several times. Then one day he showed up unannounced. I cancelled my other appointments in order to shoot him.

I gave him a neutral tone shirt to wear in the photograph (since he came dressed in a light colored sweater). It was only when I went to shoot that I realized he had buttoned it wrong. I decided not to fix it; after all, what I want to show in these images is people as they are. Fortuitously, the mis-buttoned shirt also causes the collar to fall in a way that compliments the composition of the image.

Lighting

The main light placed to the right of the subject creates split lighting on his face. A hair light was placed above the subject, and a fill light was used next to the lens. A reflector was placed under the model's chin to minimize the shadow in this area. Skimmers were placed to either side of the model. These cause the specular highlights on his nose.

According to standard lighting rules, it's bad form to highlight a subject's nose. Although I'm certainly aware of rules like this, and know how to shoot that kind of photo if I want to, I find these rules can be too confining. Following the rules doesn't help you grow as a photographer, experimentation does.

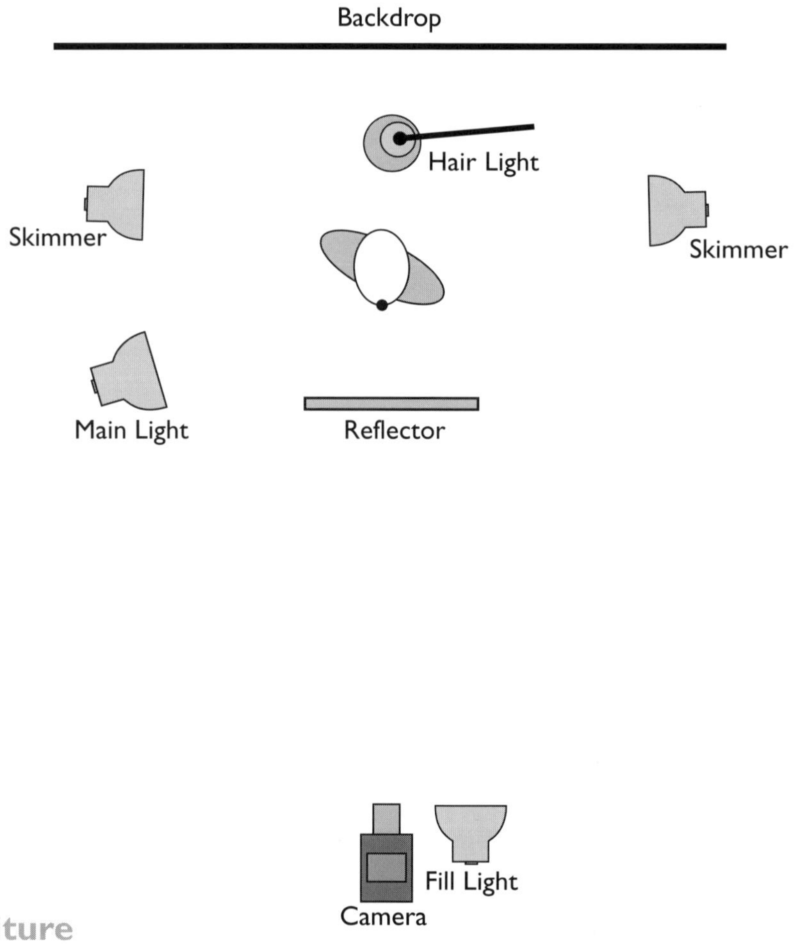

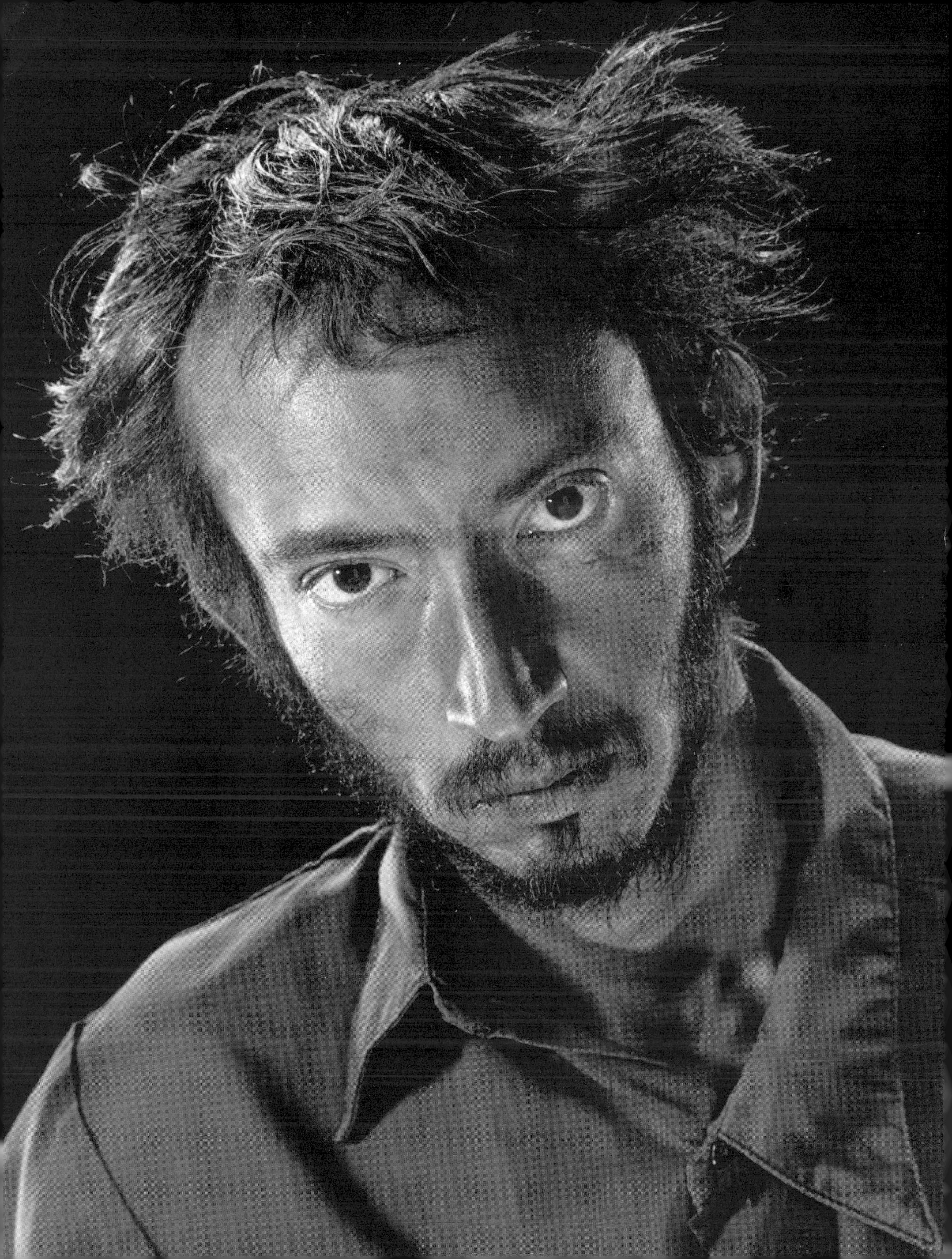

Model

This man is someone I met in my neighborhood. When I approached him, he agreed to let me photograph him and came to the studio. The resulting photograph is now part of the PPA Loan Collection.

Working with homeless people is something that stems purely from my love of photography. Although delivering product for a client pays the bills, images of that kind don't always show the truth. Photographing the homeless allows me to capture images that are completely true and real; people being who they are. On a technical note, working on these images gives me an opportunity to play with more technical lighting. I also love the chance to talk with these subjects, hear their experiences, and get to know people from all different walks of life.

Lighting

Three lights were used to illuminate the model. The main light was placed to his right to create a loop pattern with strong shadows that give the face excellent depth and texture. A fill light was placed near the camera lens, and a hair light was used overhead.

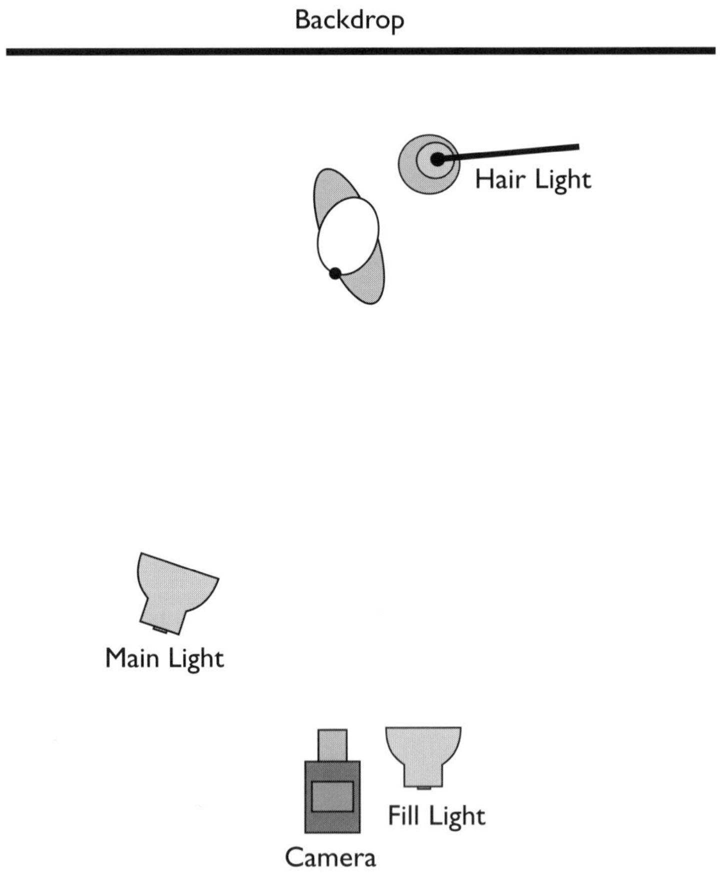

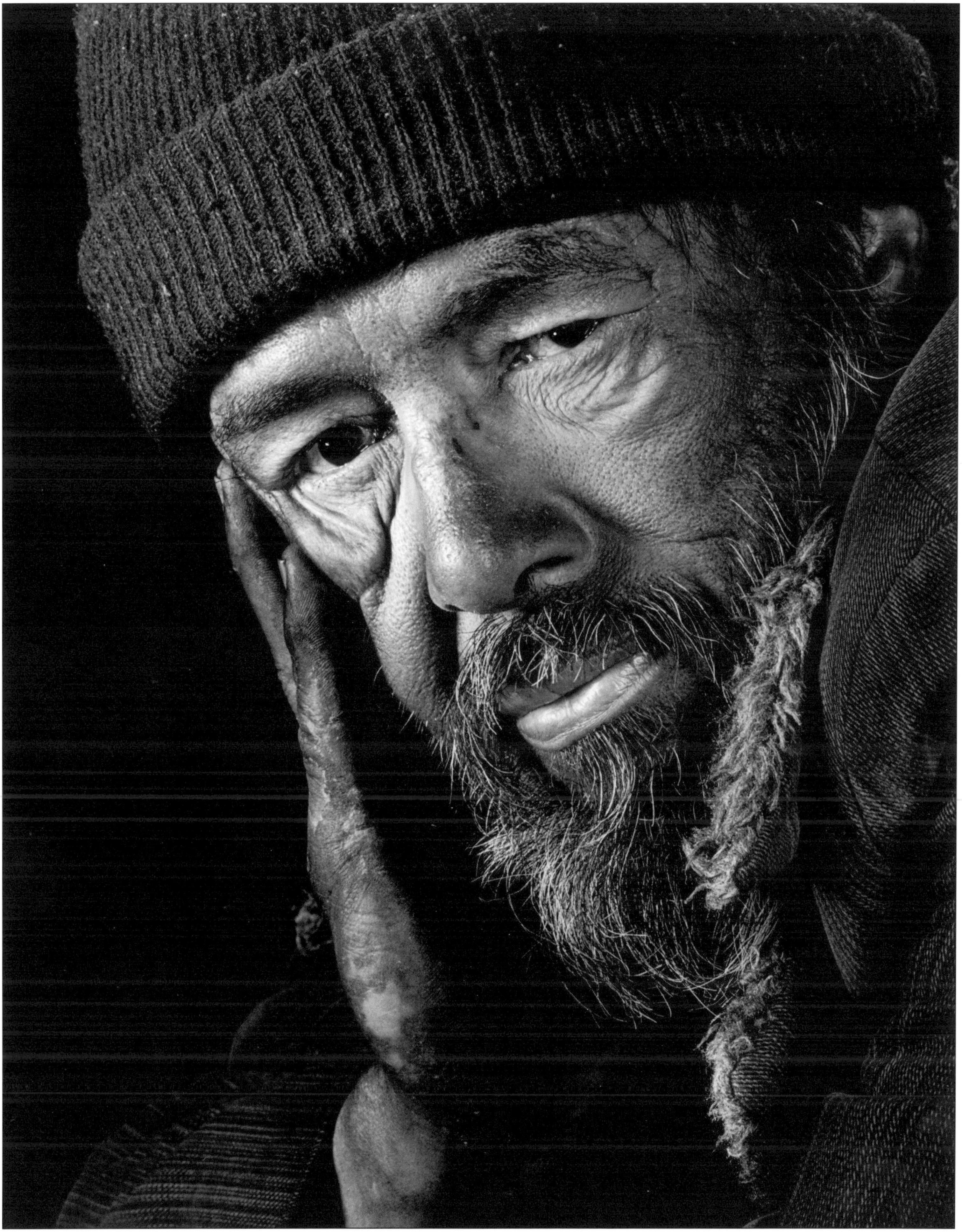

Model

I met this model when a friend of mine asked if he could sit in on a character study shoot. I agreed, and we went out and cruised around to find a subject. When we approached Jorge (the subject of this and the following image), he was on his way to the library. We gave him a ride there, then brought him back to the studio. As it turned out we had lots to talk about since he had been a photographer in the army!

Lighting

The main light was placed to the right of the model and rather low (to get under the brim of his hat). A fill light was used to the right of the camera. Skimmers were placed to either side of the model, and a top light comes in on his head from above.

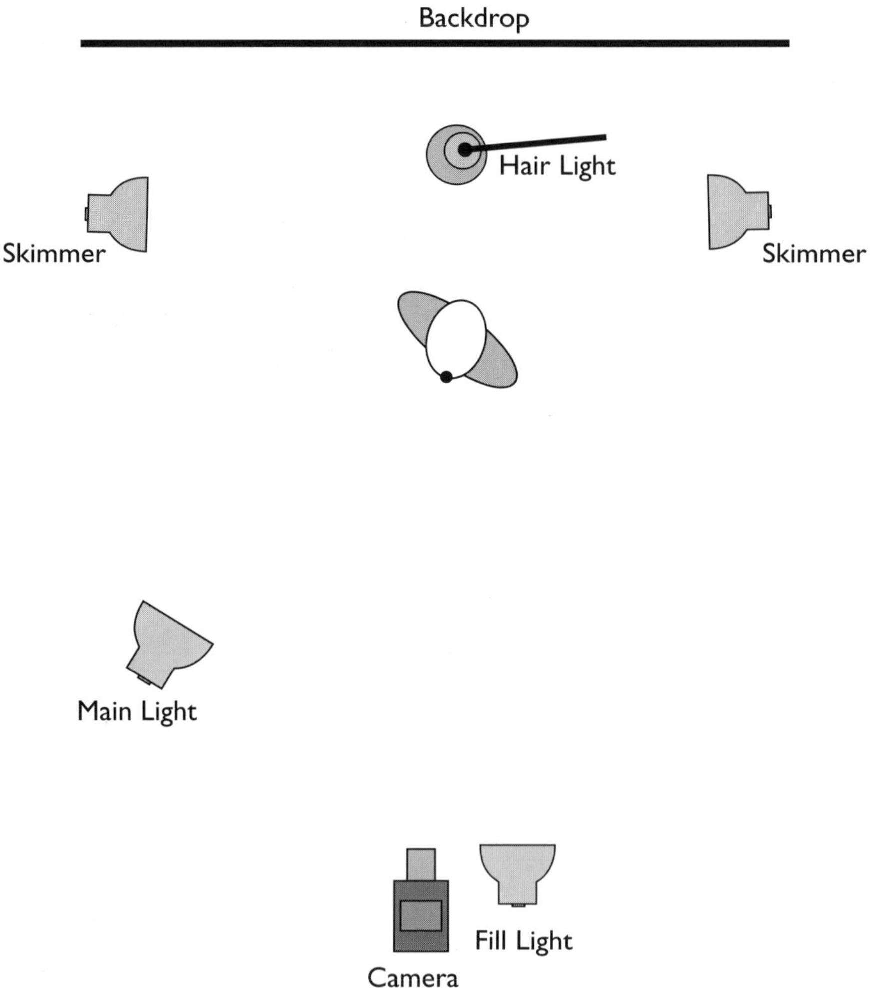

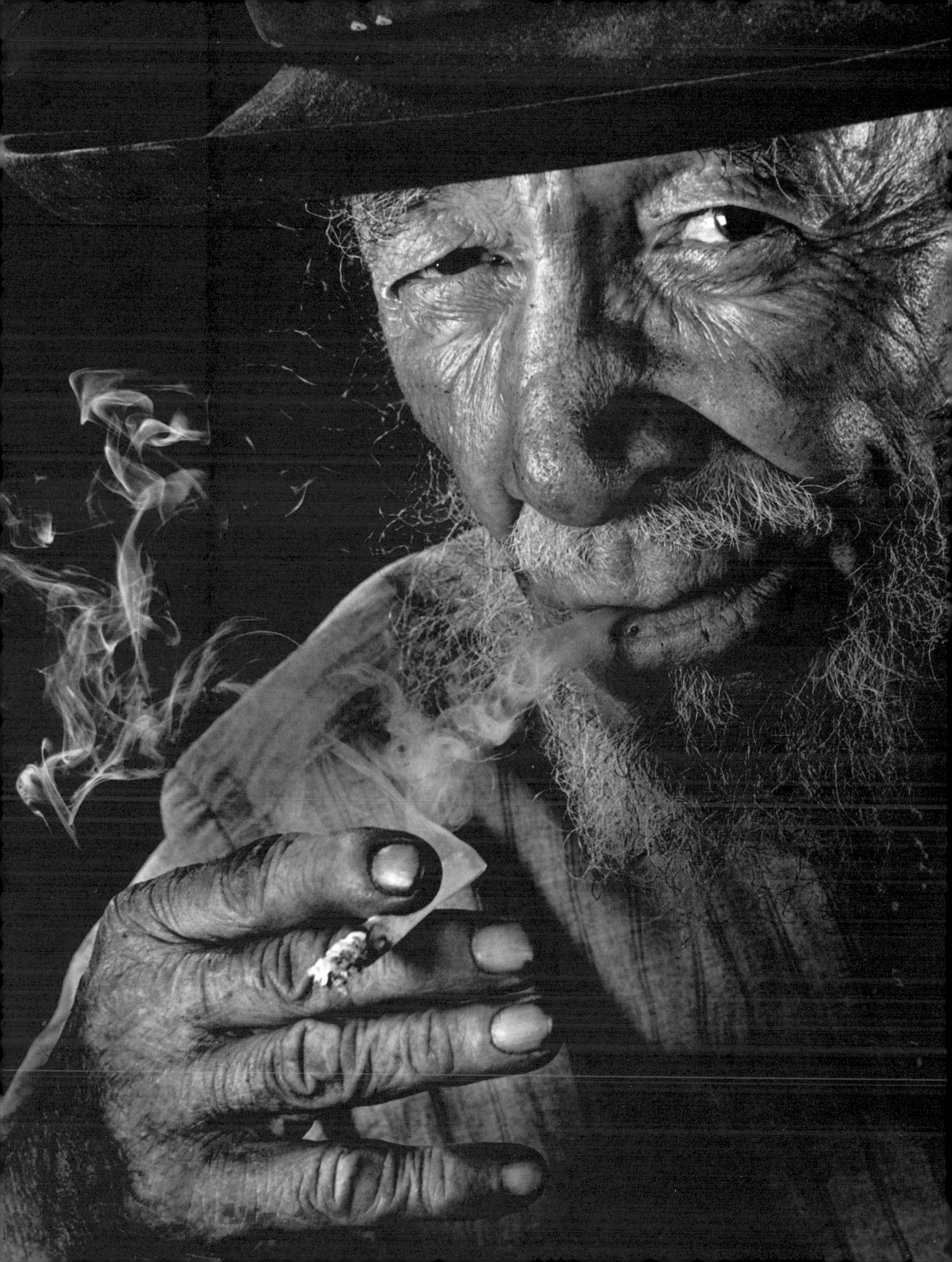

Lighting

With minor adjustment, the lighting set-up for this second image of Jorge is basically identical to the one used in the image on the previous page (a main light, skimmers, fill and hair light).

Posing

The previous image of Jorge is one that looks aggressive and outgoing. While Jorge was certainly very sharp, the image shown here captures more of what he was really like. The camera has pulled back to show him for the short and slender man he really is. The image also reveals a character that is much more mellow than in the previous image.

Payment

When shooting figure studies with other models, usually I exchange photography for a model release. With the homeless models I have worked with, since most have little use for photographs, I generally pay them a modeling fee.

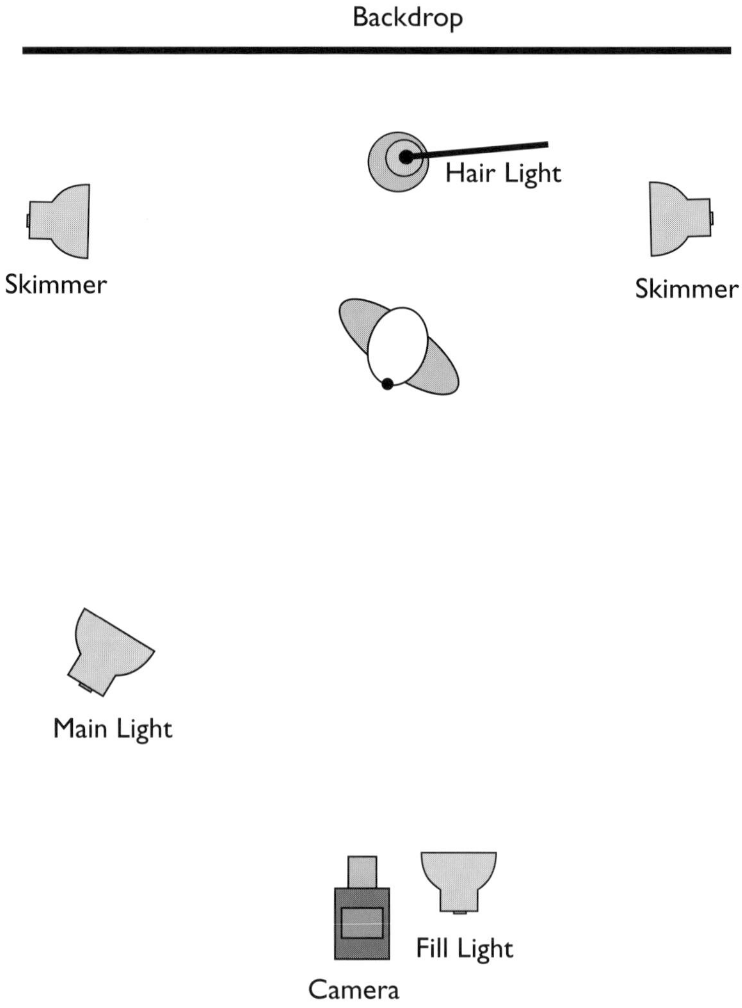

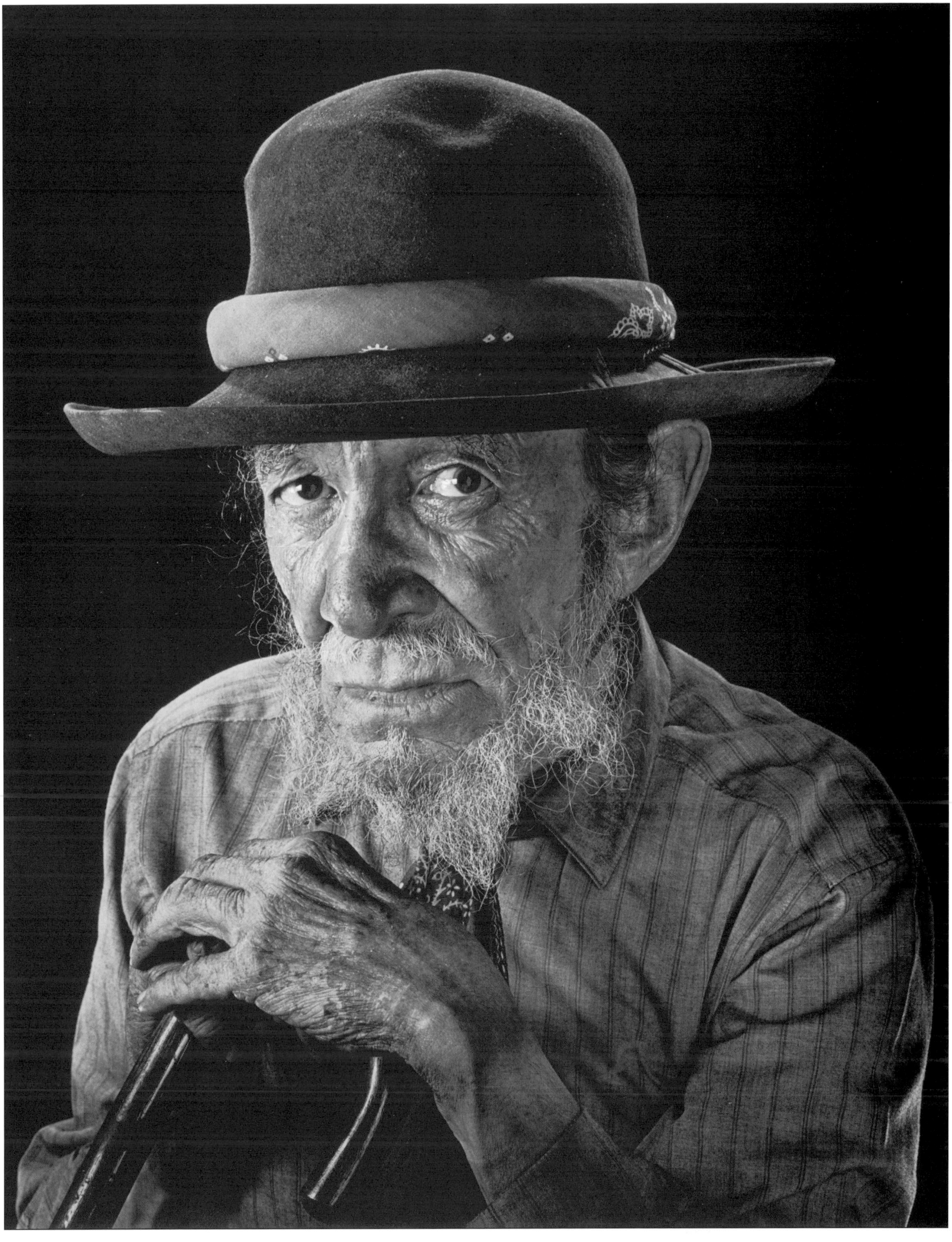

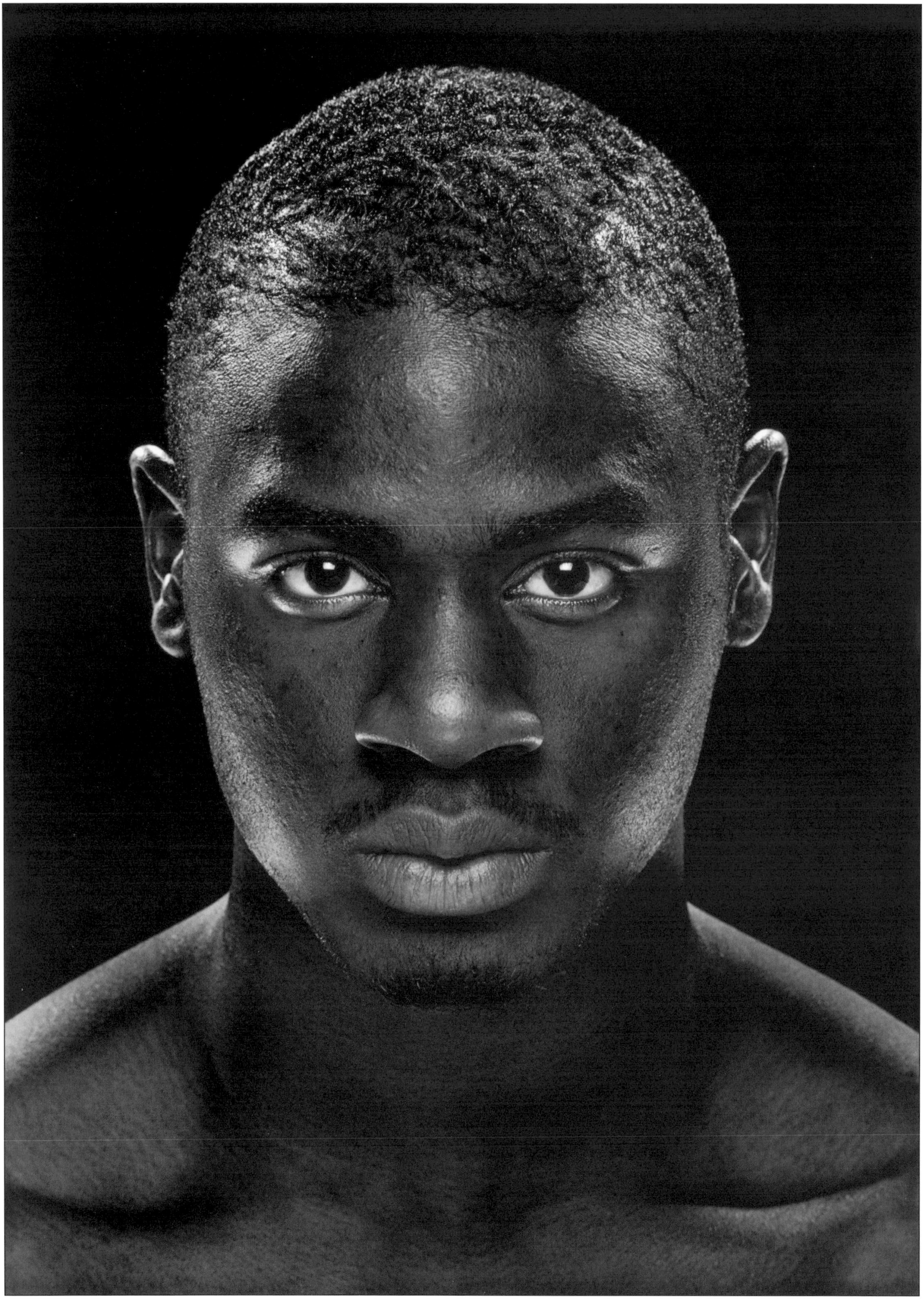

Coming of Age

Inspiration

A week before I took this photo I had gone to visit a Rodin collection. The dark bronzes with their great specular highlights really impressed me. Yet, I couldn't help thinking they would look even better if the highlights were in the right place, and not dependent on your angle of view. So I decided to do my own bust, based on his inspiration.

Model

The next step was to find a suitable model. This actor was recommended to me by a friend, and I brought him into the studio to talk. His highly symmetrical features were perfect, so we actually shot the image on the spot!

Posing

In terms of posing, this image breaks all the rules by putting the subject dead center, looking directly into the camera. (Of course, that hasn't kept it from winning numerous awards!)

Lighting

The main light was placed in front of and above the model, centered on his nose. In the butterfly position (shadow centered below the nose), a reflector reduces shadow under the subject's chin. A fill light was used below the lens, and skimmers were placed to either side of the model. Three hair lights were used to illuminate his dark hair. Light ratios were kept close together to help outline his dark skin.

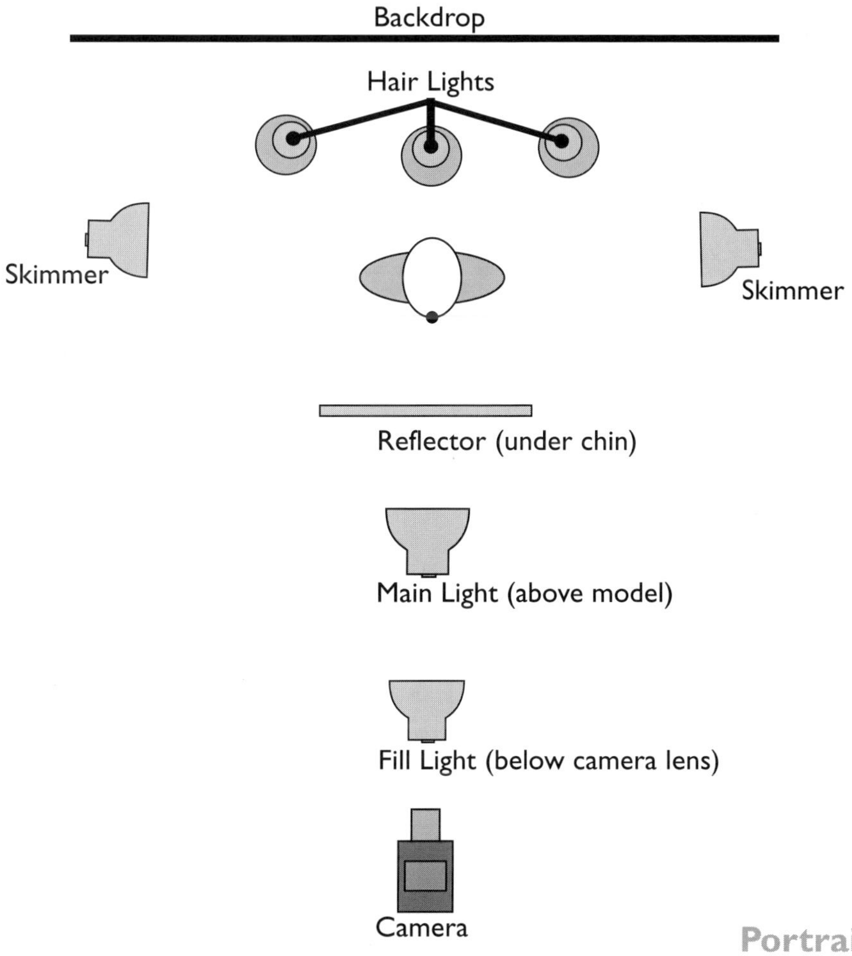

Model and Posing

This award-winning portrait was taken of a man who worked in my brother's shop. Posing the model with his eyes closed adds an air of mystery and emotion to the image.

Composition

This diagonal composition is one that appeals to me, even if I can't explain exactly why. To achieve it here, the camera was placed at an angle.

Lighting

Three lights were used to illuminate this portrait. The main light was positioned to the right of the model. A fill light was also used next to the camera lens. Finally a hair light was used overhead to illuminate the model's hat.

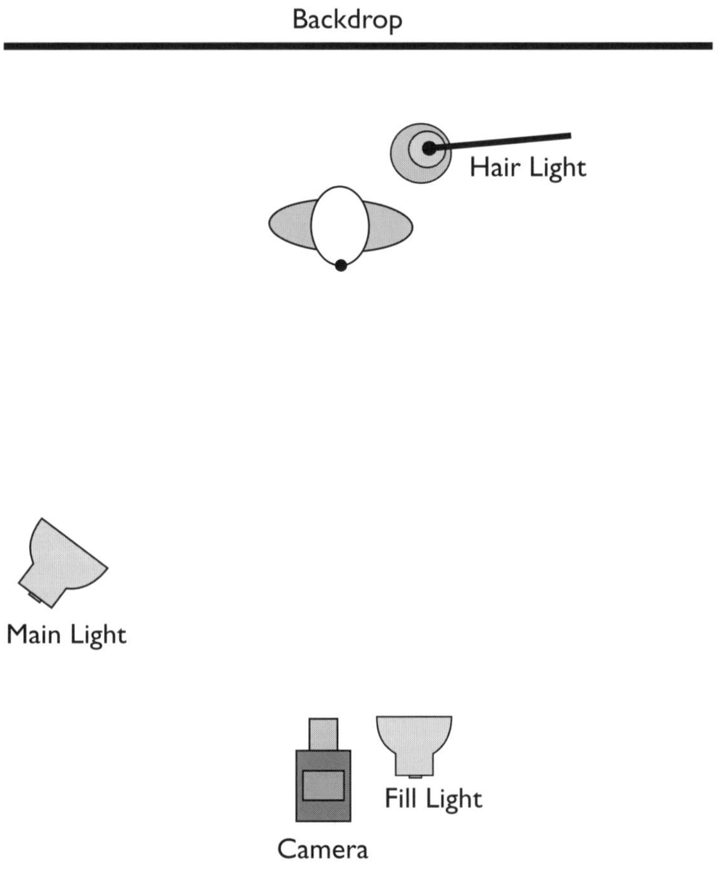

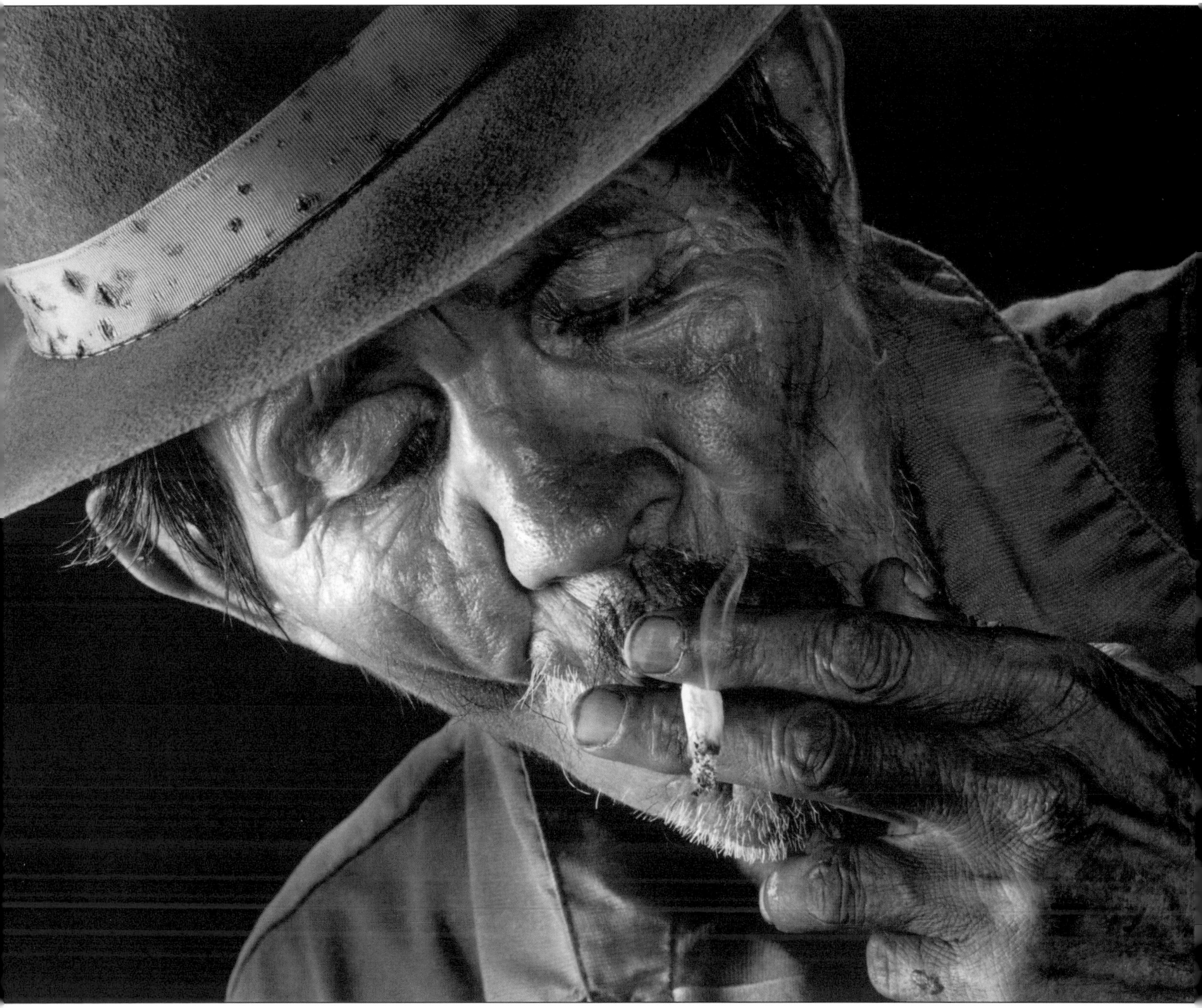

Goat Boy Holding Beard

Posing

While Goat Boy was in the studio, we took all sorts of pictures. Eventually, we added this hat, which happened to be in the studio. Since he had an interesting beard, I decided to work with it, and eventually ended up with this very symmetrical pose.

Although it is not conventional to photograph a subject with a hat over his eyes, conventional wasn't what I was interested in on this shoot, so I didn't care.

Lighting

The lighting here is somewhat unusual. Two main lights were used, one on each side of the model. This causes a shadow to form on the middle of his nose and creates dark eye pockets. A fill light was used close to the right of the camera lens. A hair light was added above.

Working with Models

Since we have a common cause (good photos) I find that most models pay close attention to my instructions and can be posed effectively with words and gestures. For more complicated poses, I may move them a little, but I'm careful about it and try to keep the whole mood very casual and fun on a shoot. Often, a break between shots is all that is needed to make posing work easily.

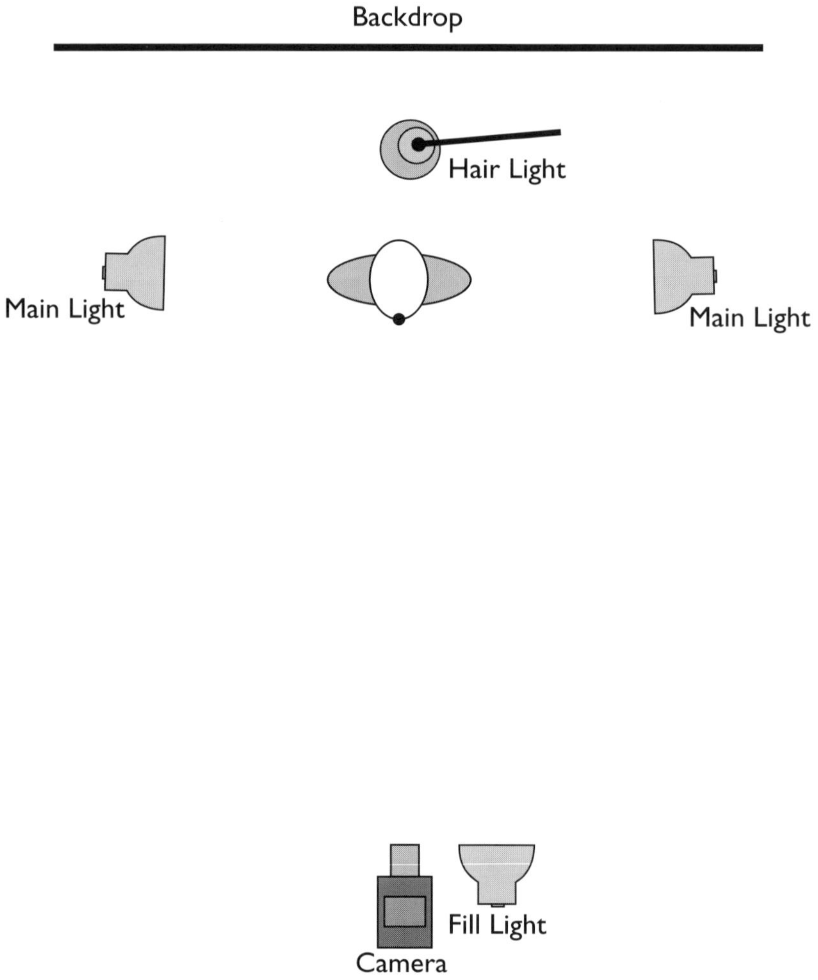

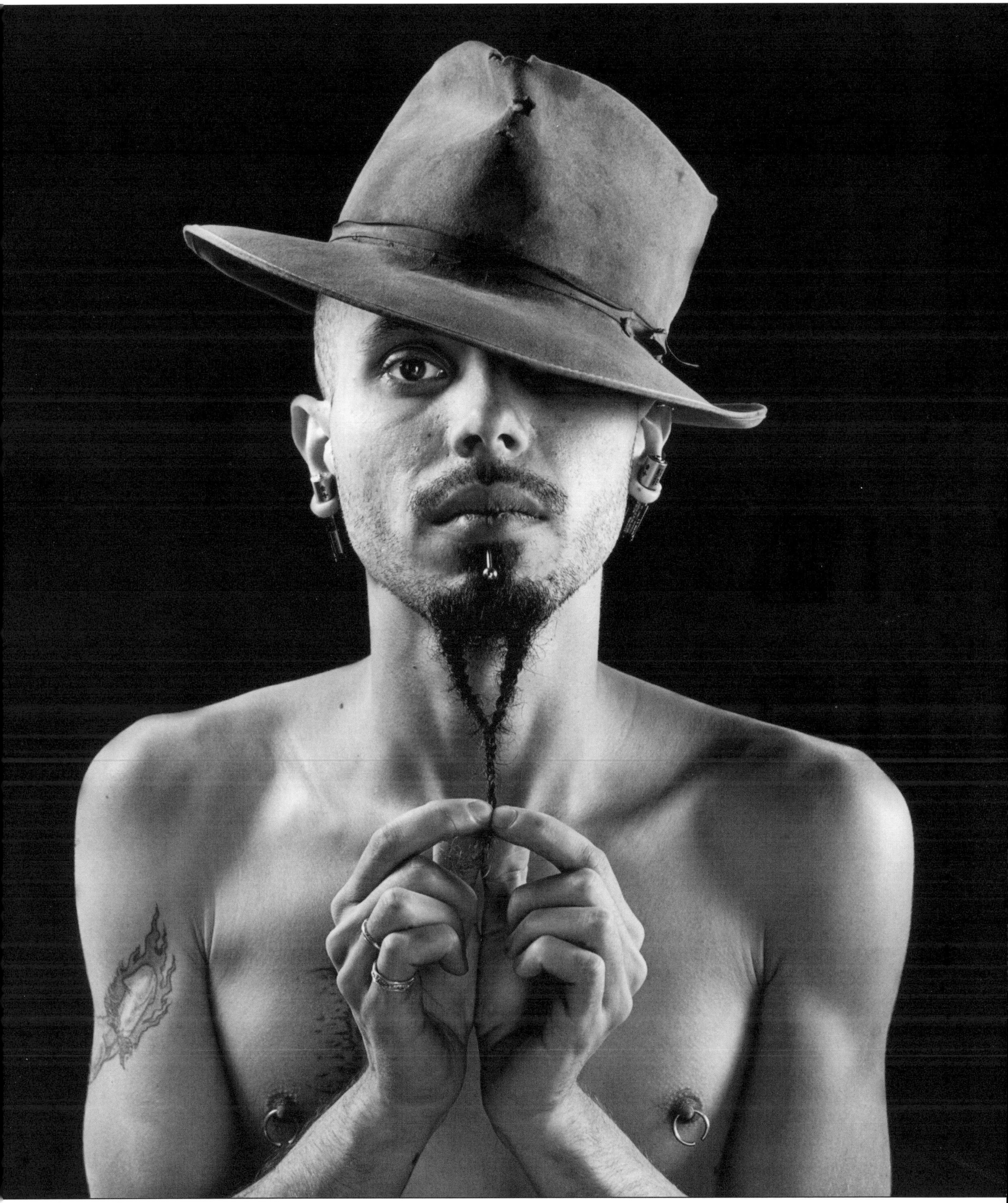

Power of Ages

Model

This model was someone my assistant knew. My assistant brought her to the studio when I decided that I wanted to photograph some more females for my character studies.

Posing

The pose was something that developed organically from the tired look on the old woman's face, and the interesting way her hair fell forward. I draped the woman in black up to her neck and had my assistant hold her head up from below. The camera was tilted to position the arm at the corner of the image.

Lighting

The main light was positioned a little to the right and above the subject. It does not catch a lot in the eye area but shows up on the protruding areas of her face. A fill light was positioned next to the lens. Skimmers were used to either side of the subject and a hair light was positioned overhead.

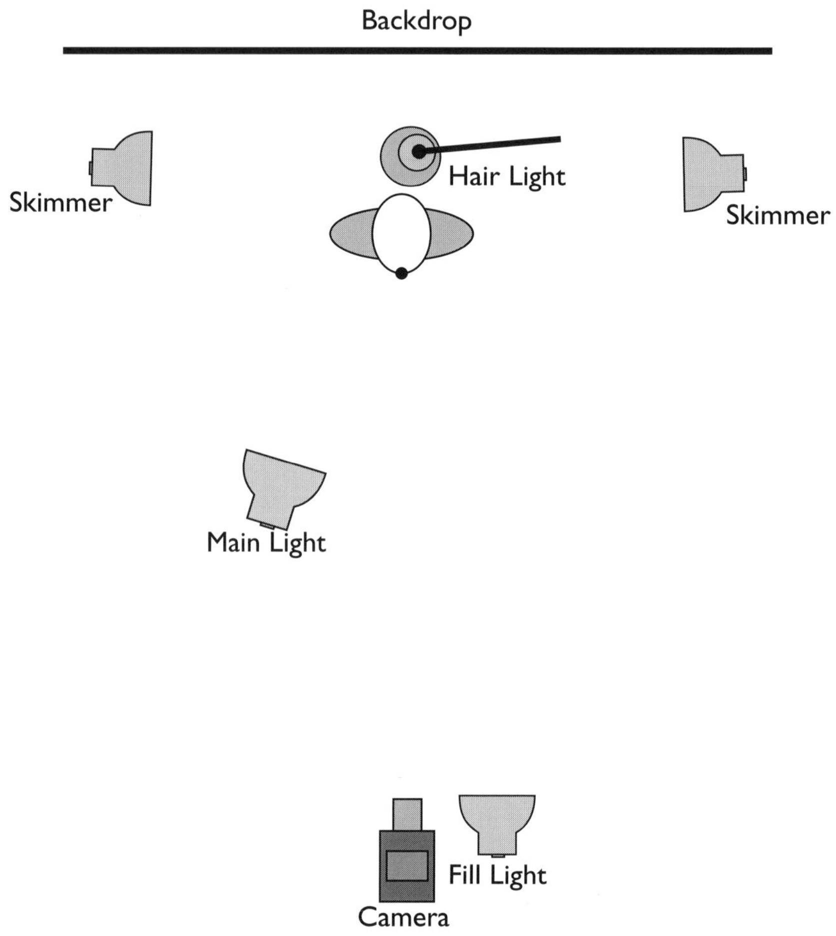

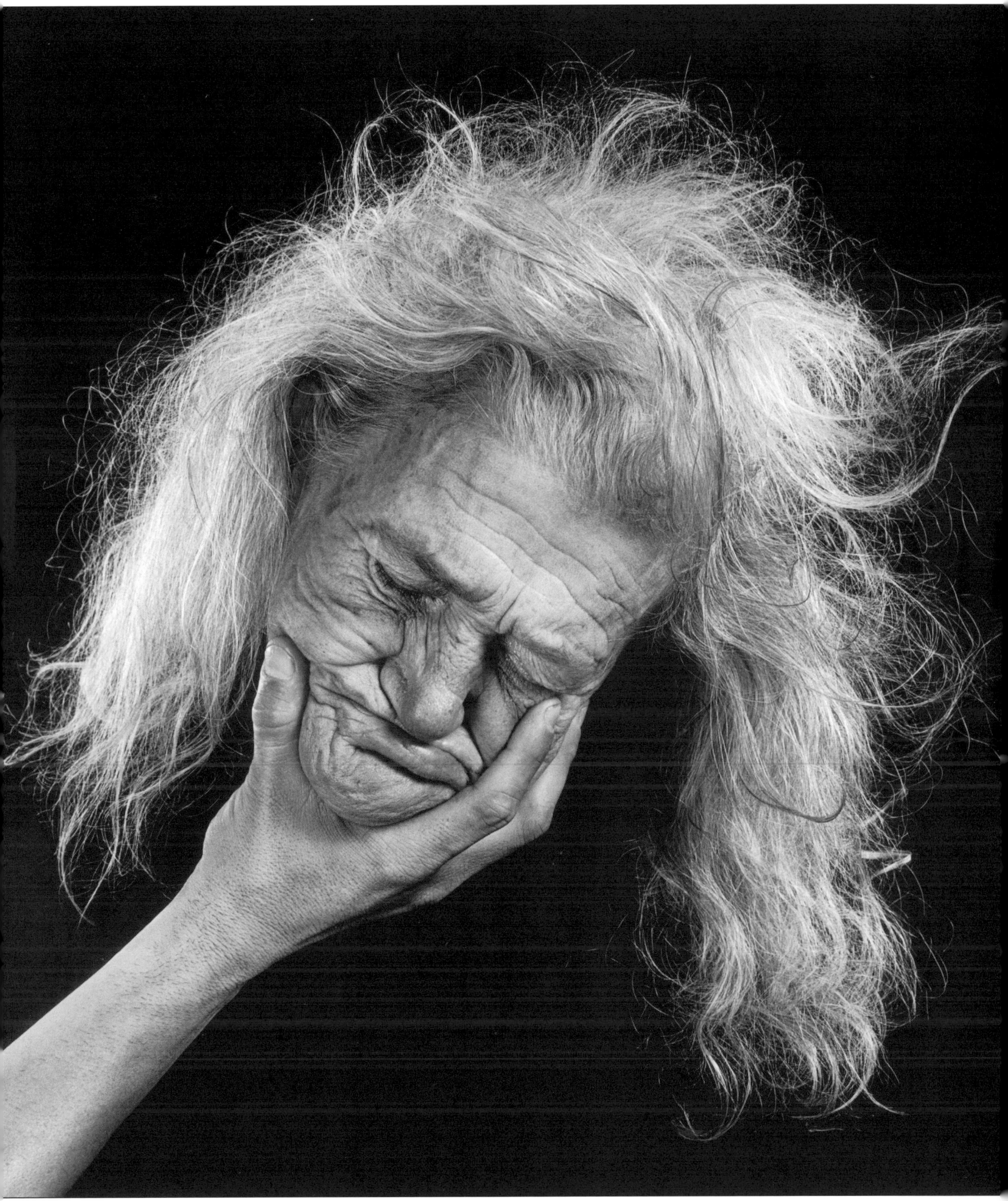

Model

The model for this image (Patricio Trujillo) is also my assistant, and an artist in his own right. He's been heard to say "Anything for art!" This photograph certainly put that to the test, since he had to shave his head and eyebrows to make it! Using my assistant as a model was wonderful, since he knows the work it takes to shoot a great photo, and was willing to sit patiently while I took my time with the lights.

Lighting

Since the fishing line in which the model was wrapped was pretty uncomfortable, I posed him first and adjusted the lights. Then I wrapped the line around his face in such a way as to compliment the lights that were set.

A total of eight lights were used. Three lights were placed above the subject to pick up all the different tonalities, even on the top of his head. Skimmers were placed to either side of him and a fill light was used next to the lens. The main light was placed to the subject's right. Finally, an accent light was placed on the floor in front of him to separate his neck from his chin.

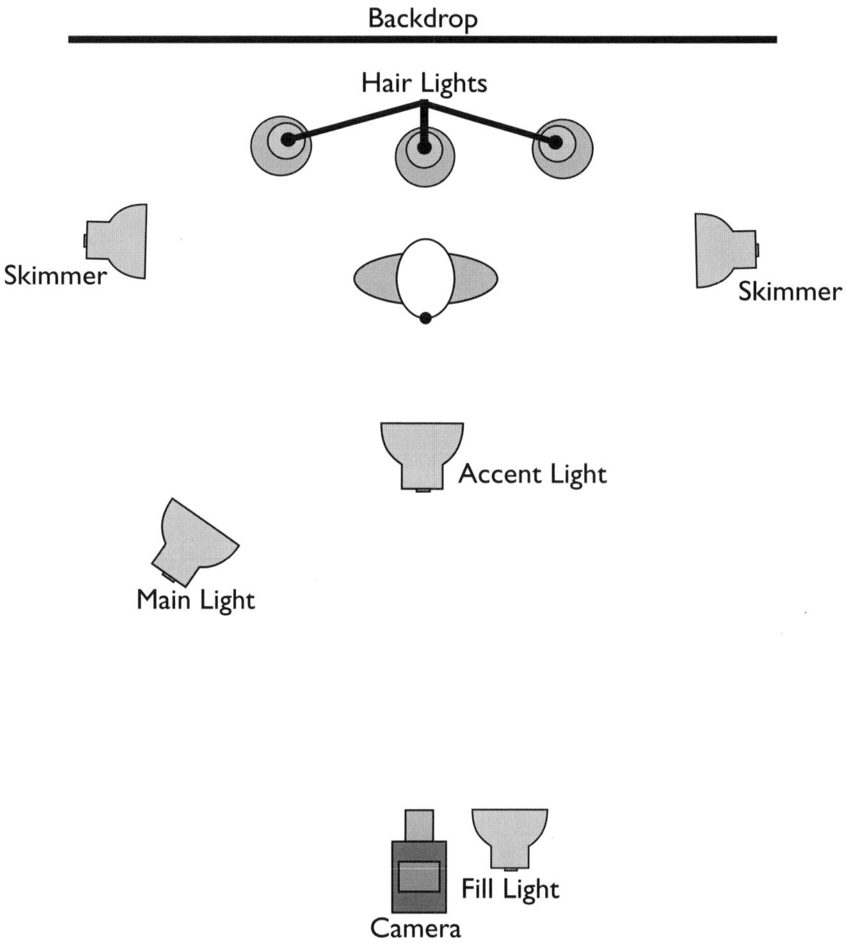

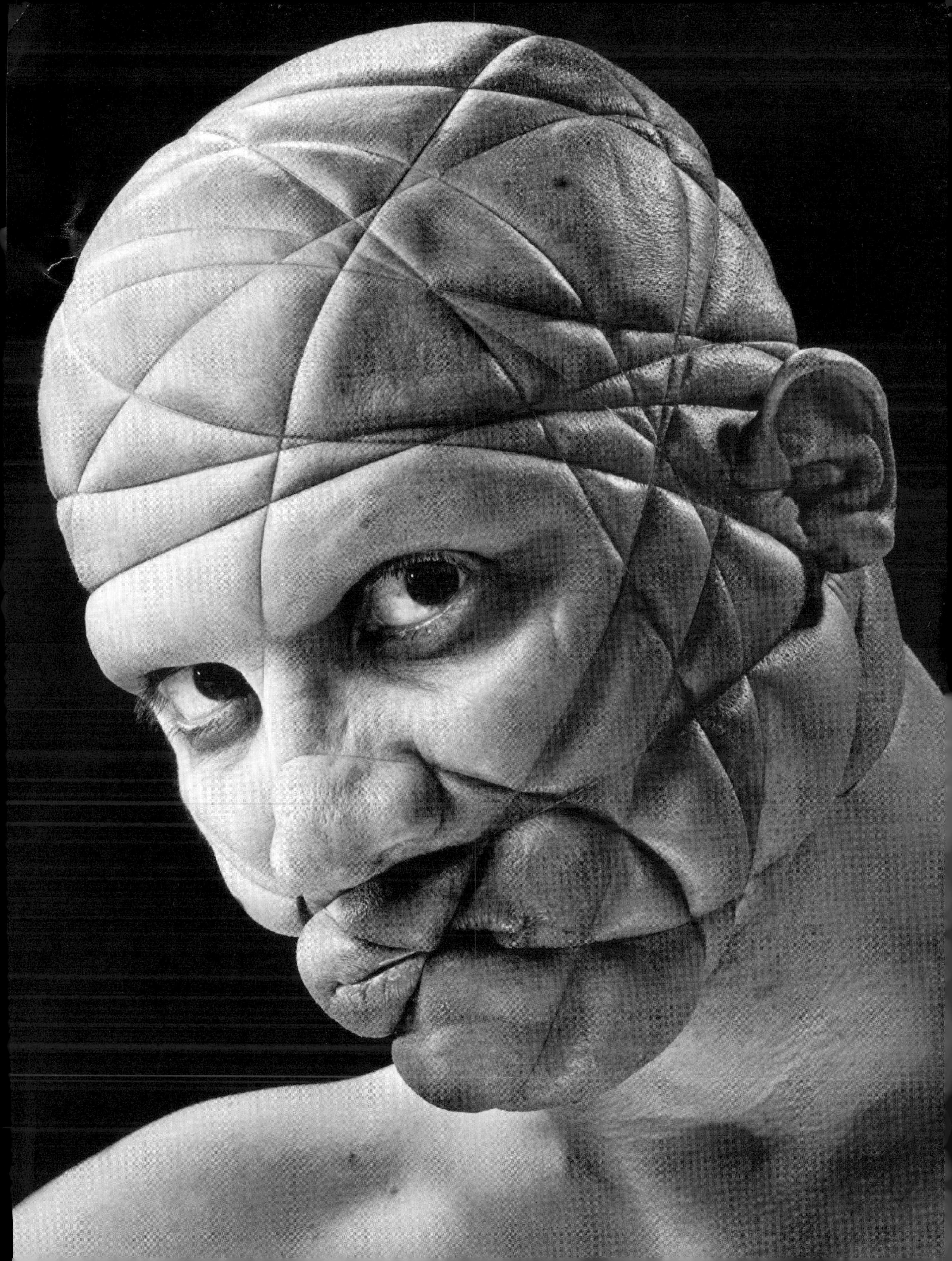

Index

Models

Other Books from Amherst Media, Inc.

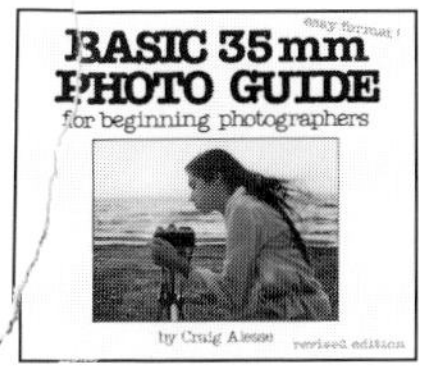

Basic 35mm Photo Guide

Craig Alesse

Great for beginning photographers! Designed to teach 35mm basics step-by-step — completely illustrated. Features the latest cameras. Includes: 35mm automatic and semi-automatic cameras, camera handling, *f*-stops, shutter speeds, and more! $12.95 list, 9x8, 112p, 178 photos, order no. 1051.

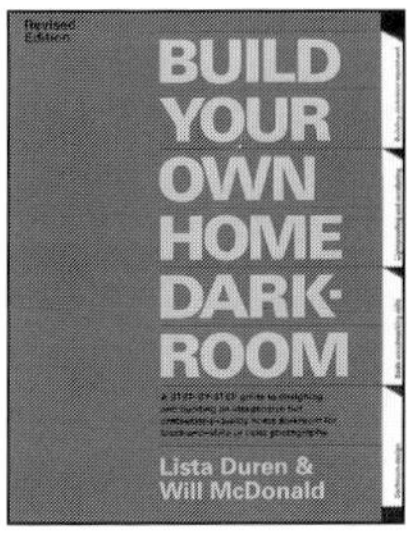

Build Your Own Home Darkroom

Lista Duren & Will McDonald

This classic book shows how to build a high quality, inexpensive darkroom in your basement, spare room, or almost anywhere. Information on: darkroom design, woodworking, tools, and more! $17.95 list, 8½x11, 160p, order no. 1092.

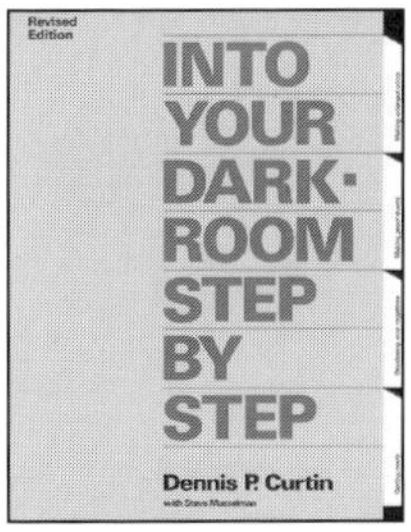

Into Your Darkroom Step-by-Step

Dennis P. Curtin

The ideal beginning darkroom guide. Easy to follow and fully illustrated each step of the way. Information on: equipment you'll need, set-up, making proof sheets and much more! $17.95 list, 8½x11, 90p, hundreds of photos, order no. 1093.

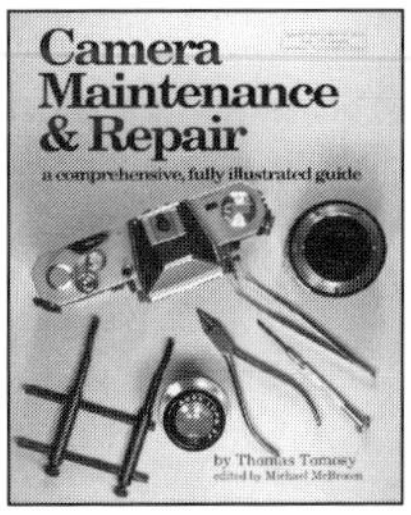

Camera Maintenance & Repair

Thomas Tomosy

A step-by-step, fully illustrated guide by a master camera repair technician. Sections include: testing camera functions, general maintenance, basic tools needed, basic repairs for accessories, camera electronics, plus "quick tips" for maintenance and more! $24.95 list, 8½x11, 176p, order no. 1158.

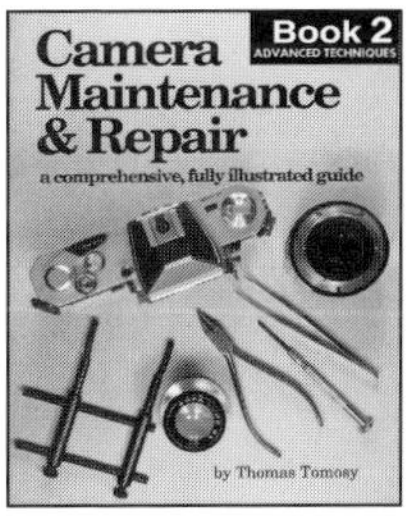

Camera Maintenance & Repair Book 2

Thomas Tomosy

Advanced troubleshooting and repair building on the basics covered in the first book. Includes; mechanical and electronic SLRs, zoom lenses, medium format, troubleshooting, repairing plastic and metal parts, and more. $29.95 list, 8½x11, 176p, 150+ photos, charts, tables, appendices, index, glossary, order no. 1558.

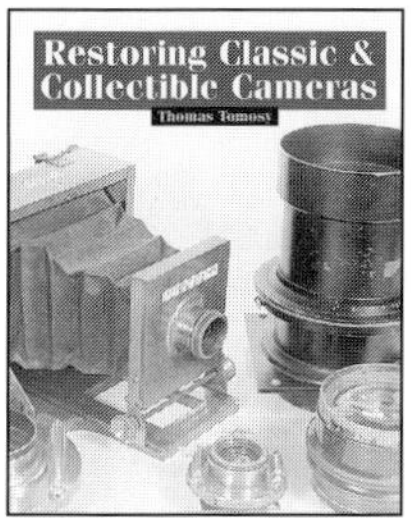

Restoring Classic & Collectible Cameras

Thomas Tomosy

A must for camera buffs and collectors! Clear, step-by-step instructions show how to restore a classic or vintage camera. Work on leather, brass and wood to restore your valuable collectibles. $34.95 list, 8½x11, 128p, b&w photos and illustrations, glossary, index, order no. 1613.

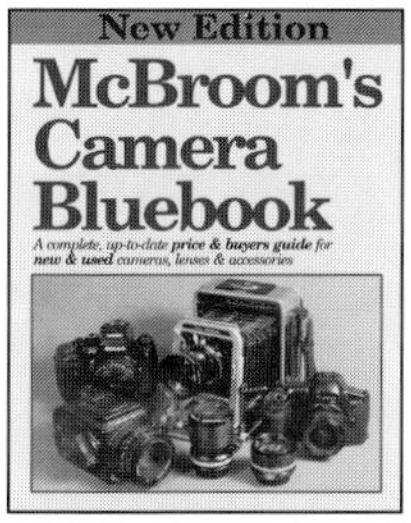

McBroom's Camera Bluebook

Mike McBroom

Comprehensive, fully illustrated, with price information on: 35mm cameras, medium & large format cameras, exposure meters, strobes and accessories. Pricing info based on equipment condition. A must for any camera buyer, dealer, or collector! $34.95 list, 8½x11, 224p, 75+ photos, order no. 1263.

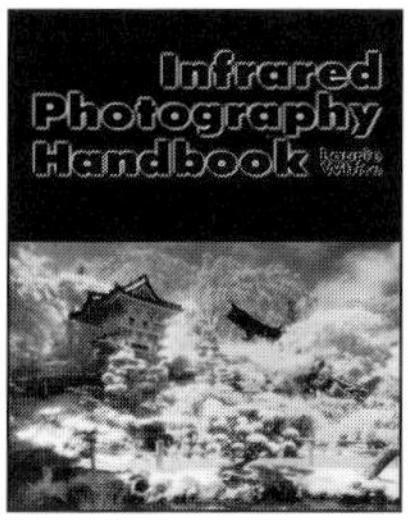

Infrared Photography Handbook

Laurie White

Covers black and white infrared photography: focus, lenses, film loading, film speed rating, heat sensitivity, batch testing, paper stocks, and filters. Black & white photos illustrate how IR film reacts in portrait, landscape, and architectural photography. $24.95 list, 8½x11, 104p, 50 b&w photos, charts & diagrams, order no. 1419.

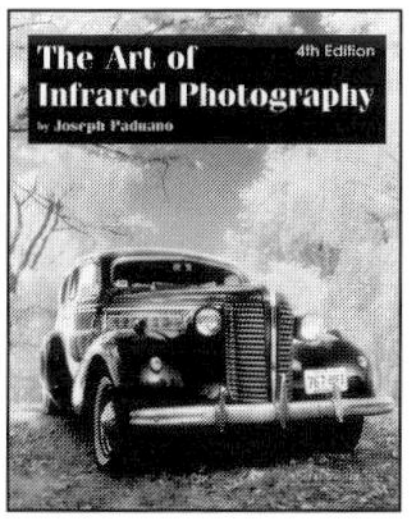

The Art of Infrared Photography / 4th Edition

Joe Paduano

A practical, comprehensive guide to the art of infrared photography. Tells what to expect and how to control results. Includes: anticipating effects, color infrared, digital infrared, using filters, focusing, developing, printing, handcoloring, toning, and more! $29.95 list, 8½x11, 112p, order no. 1052.

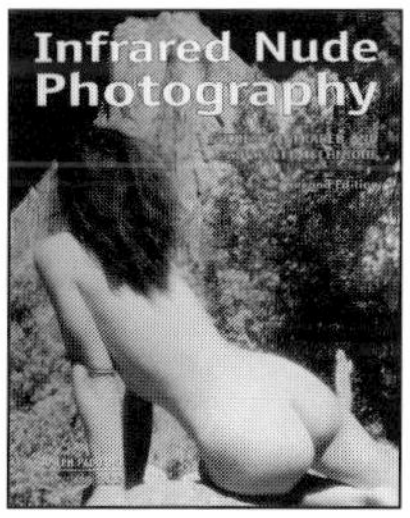

Infrared Nude Photography

Joseph Paduano

A stunning collection of images with informative how-to text. Over 50 infrared photos presented as a portfolio of classic nude work. Shot on location in natural settings, including the Grand Canyon, Bryce Canyon and the New Jersey Shore. $29.95 list, 8½x11, 96p, over 50 photos, order no. 1080.

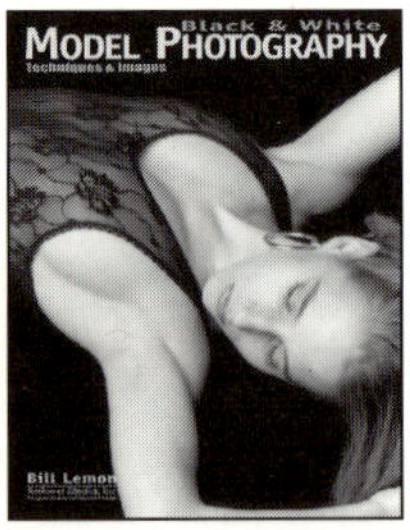

Black & White Model Photography

Bill Lemon

Create dramatic sensual images of models. Explore lighting, setting, equipment use, posing and composition with the author's discussion of 60 unique images. $29.95 list, 8½x11, 128p, 60 b&w photos and illustrations, index, order no. 1577.

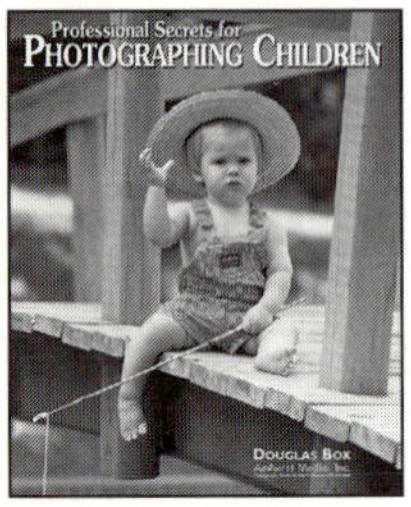

Professional Secrets for Photographing Children

Douglas Allen Box

Covers every aspect of photographing children on location and in the studio. Prepare children and parents for the shoot, capture a child's personality, and shoot story book themes. $29.95 list, 8½x11, 128p, 74 photos, index, order no. 1635.

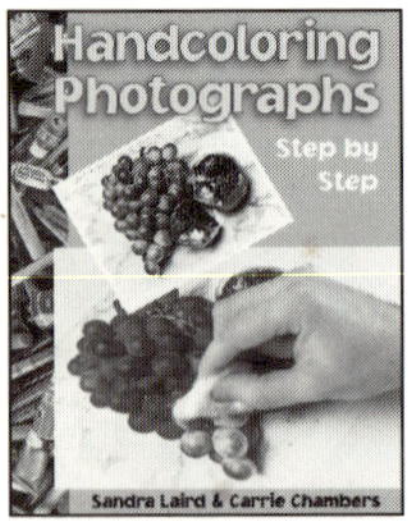

Handcoloring Photographs Step-by-Step

Sandra Laird & Carey Chambers

Learn to handcolor photographs step-by-step with the new standard handcoloring reference. Covers a variety of coloring media. Includes colorful photographic examples. $29.95 list, 8½x11, 112p, 100+ color and b&w photos, order no. 1543.

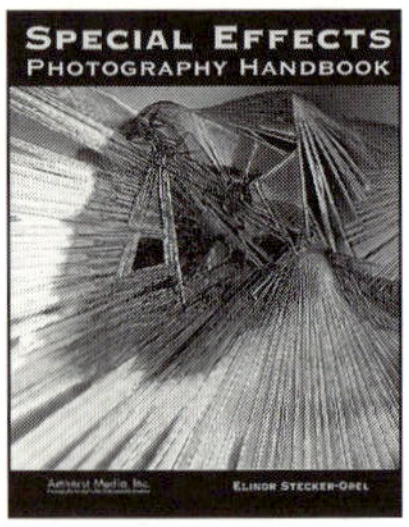

Special Effects Photography Handbook

Elinor Stecker Orel

Create magic on film with special effects! Little or no additional equipment required, use things you probably have around the house. Step-by-step instructions guide you through each effect. $29.95 list, 8½x11, 112p, 80+ color and b&w photos, index, glossary, order no. 1614.

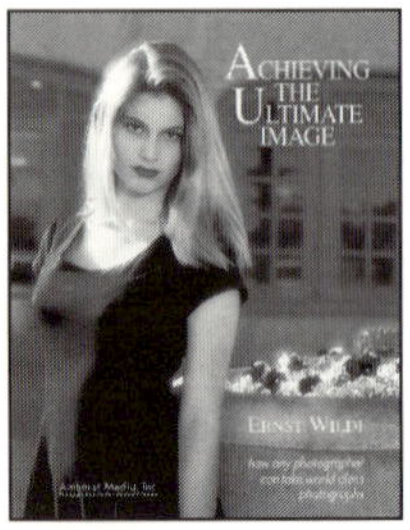

Achieving the Ultimate Image

Ernst Wildi

Ernst Wildi shows how any photographer can take world class photos and achieve the ultimate image. Features: exposure and metering, the Zone System, composition, evaluating an image, and much more! $29.95 list, 8½x11, 128p, 120 B&W and color photos, index, order no. 1628

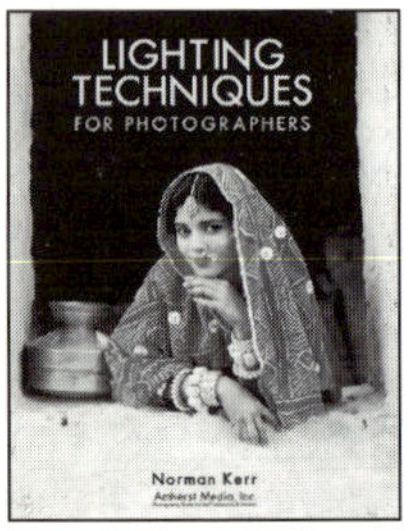

Lighting Techniques for Photographers

Norman Kerr

Learn to identify light qualities and control them to create dramatic images. Covers filters, choice of equipment, processing and composition for B&W and color images. $29.95 list, 8½x11, 120p, 100 B&W and color photos, index, order no. 1564.

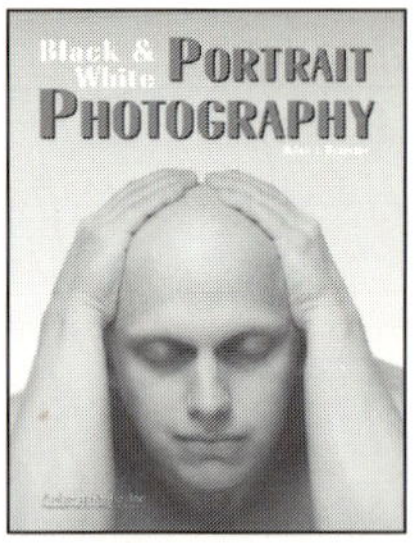

Black & White Portrait Photography

Helen Boursier

Make money with B&W portrait photography. Learn from top B&W shooters! Studio and location techniques, with tips on preparing your subjects, selecting settings and wardrobe, lab techniques, and more! $29.95 list, 8½x11, 128p, 130+ photos, index, order no. 1626.

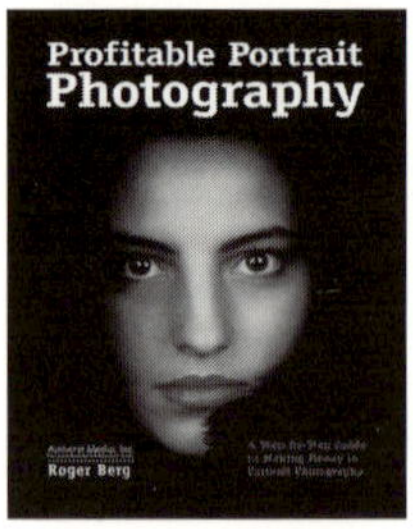

Profitable Portrait Photography

Roger Berg

Learn to profit in the portrait photography business! Improves studio methods, lighting techniques and posing, and tells how to get the best shot quickly. A step-by-step guide to making money. $29.95 list, 8½x11, 104p, 120+ B&W and color photos, index, order no. 1570.

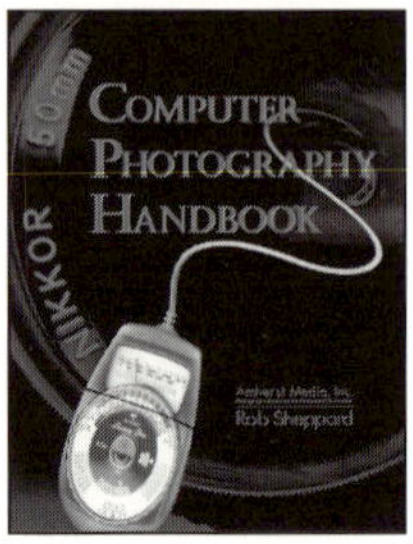

Computer Photography Handbook

Rob Sheppard

Learn to make the most of your photographs using computer technology! From creating images with digital cameras, to scanning prints and negatives, to manipulating images, you'll learn all the basics of digital imaging. $29.95 list, 8½x11, 128p, 150+ photos, index, order no. 1560.

More Photo Books Are Available!

Write or fax for a *FREE* catalog:

AMHERST MEDIA, INC.
PO Box 586
Amherst, NY 14226 USA

Fax: 716-874-4508

Ordering & Sales Information:

Individuals: If possible, purchase books from an Amherst Media retailer. Write to us for the dealer nearest you. To order direct, send a check or money order with a note listing the books you want and your shipping address. U.S. & overseas freight charges are $3.50 first book and $1.00 for each additional book. Visa and Master Card accepted. New York state residents add 8% sales tax.

Dealers, distributors & colleges: Write, call or fax to place orders. For price information, contact Amherst Media or an Amherst Media sales representative. Net 30 days.

All prices, publication dates, and specifications are subject to change without notice.

Prices are in U.S. dollars. Payment in U.S. funds only.